The Bathysphere Book

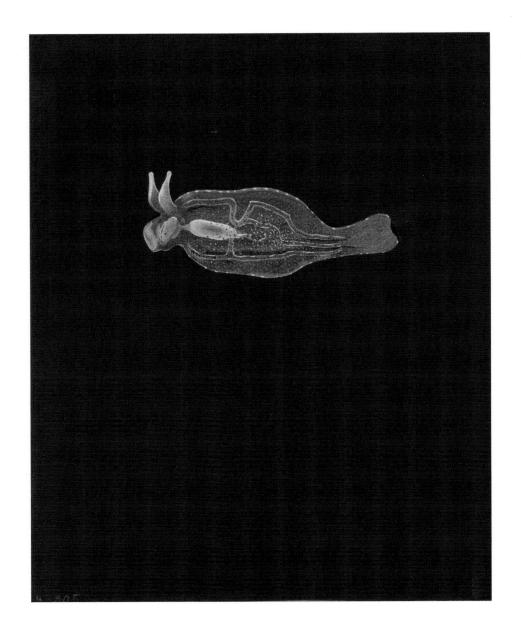

The Bathysphere Book

Effects of the Luminous Ocean Depths

Brad Fox

ASTRA HOUSE ⋀ NEW YORK

For information about permission to reproduce selections from this book, please contact permissions@astrahouse.com.

Astra House
A Division of Astra Publishing House
astrahouse.com
Printed in China

Library of Congress Cataloging-in-Publication Data

Names: Fox, Brad, (Bradley) author.
Title: The Bathysphere book : effects of the luminous ocean depths / Brad Fox.
Description: First edition. | New York : Astra House, [2023] | Includes bibliographical references and index. | Summary: "A gorgeous account of William Beebe's 1934 Bathysphere expedition, the first-ever deep-sea voyage to the otherworldly environment 3,024 feet below sea level"— Provided by publisher.
Identifiers: LCCN 2022041945 (print) | LCCN 2022041946 (ebook) | ISBN 9781662601903 (hardcover) | ISBN 9781662601910 (epub)
Subjects: LCSH: Bathysphere Expedition (1934) | Barton, Otis. | Beebe, William, 1877–1962. | Underwater exploration—History. | Deep-sea sounding. | Explorers—Biography.
Classification: LCC GC63.B38 F68 2023 (print) | LCC GC63.B38 (ebook) | DDC 551.4609—dc23/eng/20221118
LC record available at https://lccn.loc.gov/2022041945
LC ebook record available at https://lccn.loc.gov/2022041946

First edition
10 9 8 7 6 5 4 3 2 1

Design by Richard Oriolo
The text is set in Bulmer MT Std .
The titles are set in Baskerville Old Face.

Contents

The Bathysphere Book

1.

First Glimpse

Five Miles South of Nonsuch

Midmorning on June 11, 1930, a barge called the *Ready*, bearing the staff of the Department of Tropical Research, floated off the coast of the island of Nonsuch in the Bermuda Archipelago. Men in white sailor's caps and overalls gathered around a four-and-a-half-foot steel ball called the bathysphere as an enormous winch lifted it off the deck. The men stabilized the ball as it wheeled outward, dangling above the surface of the sea. It had three circular holes pressed tightly together like eyes. Suspended on the cable, it seemed to look down at the choppy water.

DTR scientist Gloria Hollister watched the winchmen lower the ball into the sea. When it splashed down and disappeared, she took a seat, picked up a canvas-bound notebook that served as the expedition log, and readied herself.

It happened to be her thirtieth birthday.

Photos show her with a focused expression, a telephone receiver shaped like an old hunting horn attached to her neck and a small speaker pressed to her right ear. She kept her chin slightly tucked as she listened and spoke and took preliminary notes. The wire from her receiver ran off the edge of the deck and submerged into the water, attached to the sinking bathysphere now lowering into the ocean depths.

Inside the ball, curled up and occupying themselves with various tasks, were two skinny men: Otis Barton and William Beebe. They had to be skinny because the opening to crawl through was less than two feet wide. Barton, who designed the ball and oversaw its production, monitored the water seal of the four-hundred-pound door, the functioning of the oxygen tanks that provided eight hours of breathable air, and cartons of soda lime to absorb the carbon dioxide exhaled by the occupants. He checked the telephone battery and the blower that circulated air.

He is irascible, jealous, and suffers from seasickness.

As they sank, the temperature inside cooled and water condensed on the ceiling of the ball, dripping down to form puddles at the bottom.

The ball was fitted with two three-inch quartz windows. There were supposed to be three, but one of the quartz panes was faulty so its opening had to be plugged with more steel.

Beebe, a bird scientist and protoecologist, curled up as close to the panes as possible. Entranced by the undersea world, he was highly aware of his status as witness to something no human had ever seen. An energetic man with infectious enthusiasm, he was already famous for his popular books describing trips around the world tracking pheasants, for an expedition up the Himalayas, and for risking his life to observe an erupting volcano on the Galápagos. He was fifty-two years old, bald and bony and almost knock-kneed, with a thin but stately voice pronouncing his observations as he descended. He'd been all over the world but still had the accent of his native New Jersey, so *worlds* and *birds* came out *woylds* and *boyds*.

The winchmen unwound the cable, and as the bathysphere descended further the light began to shift. The warm tones of the earth's surface were absorbed by the water. At one hundred feet, Beebe held up a red color plate and found it had gone completely black. Fish swam into view in the cool brightness of the greens and blues of the water outside. He called out what he saw to Hollister, who continued to jot down his statements in her expedition notebook:

100 ft	Red gone, color plates black.
	Linuche jellies.
200	Pilotfish around bait, 6 inches long,
	pure white with 8 jet black bands.
250	No red or yellow in sunlight. More
	jellies, tail of Pilotfish seen again.
300	Otis saw Pilotfish, fish many-colored
	at surface but looks white.

**LOG
BATHYSPHERE**
1932

Hollister

2100 feet — Tropic bird flying
overhead — Iguana
going splendidly —
Generator off —
2150 — Biggest fish yet in
distance — as in single
lights came + going
2150 pale cream —
2200 Temperature 70°
by — 4 big fish gay
hundreds going —
More jellies than ever
else Pteropods — Everything —
all light
lighted up — at least 6
see upper + lower
side of fish — Bean shaped
fish —

2100

400	Two strings of Salpa.
	Shrimps look pure white.
500	Transparent fish with only food visible.
550	Temperature 75 degrees. Large Leptocephalus.
	Many Cavolinia. Several Myctophids.
650	Flashes of light in distance.
800	Pretty dim. Meter wheel reading 237.
900	Several mists of little Shrimps.
	Large Serrivomer.
	Light off.

As they descended, this interplay continued: the shifting of the spectrum until the world outside the steel ball was blue, blue, and nothing else, slowly fading to black but still bright with a strange brightness Beebe could not put into words. Their spotlight cast a dismal yellow glow out the quartz windows, but now at a thousand feet it dimmed quickly.

The beam switched off, and the water outside filled with miniature explosions. Tiny shrimp. Beebe had seen them carried up in nets, lifeless. Now he could see them for the first time in their native habitat, lighting up the black depths with quick oxidations of a chemical produced in their bodies called *luciferase*.

When the explosions ceased, the strange brilliance returned, and it was like there had never been another color in the universe. He was sure he could read by it, but when Barton held up a page he couldn't make out a single word. Beebe turned back to the circular window, continued to observe and speak, and Hollister on the deck recorded it all in the lined pages of the log:

1050	Blacker than blackest midnight yet brilliant.
	Air splendid. 20 little fish might be Argyropelecus.
1100	Thick rat-tailed long pale white Macrourid-like fish
	with six lights went around bend of hose.

1150   Beam of light showing clearly—light on.

1200   Idiacanthus. Two Astronesthes.

1250   Fish 5-inch-long, shaped like Stomias

3-inch shrimps absolutely white.

Argyropelecus in light beam.

2 luminous pale white jellies.

1300   6 or 8 shrimps. 50 or 100 lights like fireflies.

Small squid in beam of light,

seems to have no lights, went down to bait.

Cyclothones. Two-inch shrimps.

1350   Light very pale.

Temp. 72. Meter wheel reading 403.

1400   Looking straight down very black.

Black as hell.

Then a huge flash of light. Like a strobe light illuminating something outside the window. What had caused it? He could see nothing now but shrimp and jellyfish, but a form was etched in his mind.

It had been a thick, eel-like creature, fanged. He'd seen a mouth wide open, small jagged teeth like nails through a board, but the mouth gaping. What kind of terror and hunger had he just seen? A slipped gear in the grind of reality, and he'd been thrust briefly into a nightmare of fluorescent tearing and gnashing. And then it was gone and he was back in the ball.

Outside were the familiar undulations of jellyfish.

A feeling came over him that he'd seen enough. He told Hollister to pass word to the crew that it was time to haul them up to the surface. When they reached 150 feet the crew could see the vessel underwater.

The winchmen dropped the bathysphere back on board and unscrewed the bolts to let the skinny men out into the afternoon sun. Beebe emerged into the now unfamiliar daylight. He unbent his knobby knees and stamped his feet on the deck of the boat. He looked off at the low hills of Bermuda in the distance and knew something in him had permanently changed. Later he would try to pin down what it was. Something to do with the light he had seen.

The yellow of the sun, he wrote, "can never hereafter be as wonderful as blue can be."

Transparent Bodies

Gloria Hollister began exploring the subaquatic world as a little girl, going under the Mahwah River with an oilcan helmet and an air hose.

She made her name by developing a new method of staining fish so that their skin and internal organs became transparent and their skeletons showed in vivid hues under ultraviolet light. It meant scientists could now view their osteological structures without dissection.

In 1926, a colleague at the zoo brought her by Beebe's office. She was in her midtwenties, intense and intelligent and physically strong—Otis Barton called her "a golden-haired scientist of Amazonian stature."

She was a privileged child of wealthy New Yorkers. When she joined Beebe's team at the Department of Tropical Research, the *New York Evening Journal* published a piece called "Girl Fleeing Gay White Way Finds It at Sea Bottom." A picture shows her fixed gaze as she clutches her little dog, Trumps. In the accompanying interview she described the colors of undersea life, the bioluminescent organisms, as brighter than Broadway.

The October 1930 issue of *Popular Mechanics* carried a feature on the bathysphere sandwiched between articles on needle sewing, a silent violin, and animal dentistry. An illustration shows Hollister taking notes in the logbook during a dive. She presses the earpiece to her head with her left hand and takes notes with her right. Her knees are held together to support the notebook, and her feet, in white tennis shoes and ankle-length socks, are angled together suggesting anxiety or focus.

Beebe kept extensive journals, but he didn't want the readers of the future to find out about his personal life. He wrote about his early romances, but later ripped out those pages. He also developed a substitution code—a monkey meant the letter *a*, a small insect was a *b*—so he could write things he hoped no one would understand. The biographer Carol Grant Gould broke the code only decades after his death, revealing the boyish thoughts of a middle-aged man:

"I kissed Gloria and she loves me."

Beebe and Hollister had already been working together four years by the time of the first bathysphere dive. Gould describes them hiding from tropical storms in caves on Nonsuch, then emerging to glory in rainbows that shone in the mist. They worked together during the day cataloging plants and animals, everything they found on the island and in the sea.

"They exchanged visits at night," Gould wrote. "But only with a caution that heightened the experience."

Hollister kept her own diaries, covering piles of plain white unbound paper in looping pencil marks. They don't mention kissing Beebe or hiding with him in Nonsuch caves. She is cryptic, introspective, struggling with ideas she'd had about her life, now starting to fall away.

She watched a scarlet sunset and marveled at the "crystal bright planets." The next day was so perfect, Beebe canceled work. He sent everyone to Castle Island except Hollister, who had been ill.

His coded writing the next day records that she was "well over her sickness."

In her own papers from that day is a copy of Howard Barnes's work on crustacea. Penciled faintly and upside down over the scientific findings, as if she might have flashed it at Beebe surreptitiously while they worked on opposite sides of a lab table, Hollister had written, "I am forever yours."

When her mother visited at Easter, they attended service together, the first time Hollister had been to church in many months. It took all her strength to maintain her composure, because she could feel a wave of powerful conflicting emotions swell up. She maintained her calm by focusing on what she imagined the first Christians had felt at Easter—"those who had caught the image—the vision."

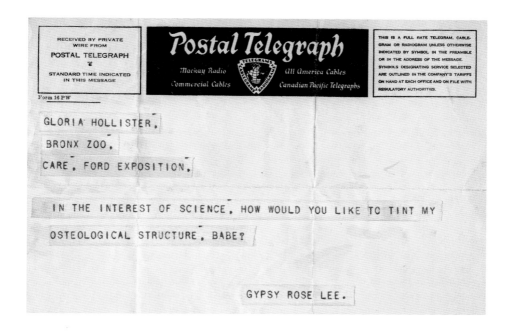

GLORIA HOLLISTER,

BRONX ZOO,

CARE, FORD EXPOSITION,

IN THE INTEREST OF SCIENCE, HOW WOULD YOU LIKE TO TINT MY

OSTEOLOGICAL STRUCTURE, BABE?

GYPSY ROSE LEE.

"Even in despair and depression," she thought, "it should carry some stimulation of the right attitude toward death."

Two weeks after Easter she lay sleepless when a strange sensation came over her about her relationship to her surroundings:

"It is difficult to write for my ideas are not thoroughly formulated yet. It came to me that my world is not at all one of matter. It is one of interpretation and thought. I see beyond cedar trees and breaking waves to a certain Deity of Beauty Deity of Right."

She went on:

"Christianity is formulated on a doctrine of *wrong*. What about a faith drawing strength and inspiration from the Beauty of Nature instead of a 'sinful' act of a human? A queer sense of strength surges over me and an understanding of surrounding forces."

Hollister lay awake at night stirred by thoughts of what she'd seen during her dives. What if the entire world is different when you wake up? What if your own body has transformed?

"What happens to the brain of a flounder during the migration of its eye?" she wondered. "Imagine going to sleep with eyes normal and waking up flat-faced!"

The creatures she came to know in her explorations of Nonsuch opened her to an entirely new world of possibilities.

That first summer, dredging in the deep waters, they brought up a fish shaped like a large tadpole called a melanostomiatid and managed to transport it to the lab alive. It was quiet, nearly motionless at first, but when Hollister reached in to transfer it to a shallow dish, it whipped around and sunk its fangs into her fingers. She jolted at first, but the bite was not painful. She held up her hand with the melanostomiatid dangling from her finger. Beebe watched her move it toward the other dish and shake it until it dropped.

She now carried the fish into the next room, submerged in darkness, and set the dish on a table.

She was about to turn away when the fish made a spasmodic movement. The fish leaped from the dish, and at the same time, two white lights flashed somewhere below its eyes. Hollister felt herself cry out as a row of lights along its belly lit up, casting a silhouette of the fish against the ceiling.

She stepped forward just as the fish dropped back into its dish. She stood over it, looking down as it idled, now drained of color.

Soon she was diving along a reef forty feet below a bare jut of stone called Gurnet's Rock.

Through her copper diving helmet she caught sight of a large fish and several sharks. She was not afraid of sharks—she was used to them. But allowing her gaze to follow, she lost her footing. Instinctively, she reached out to grab the ladder next to her but found it had disappeared.

She looked up, and there was the ladder being dragged out of sight over the top of the reef. She stopped for a moment to watch, even waved goodbye to it, before turning to assess her situation.

There all around her were the sharks with their uncanny glide. She felt a sense of perfect solitude sweep over her as she stood wondering what to do.

She remembered horseback riding classes, where she'd suited up to trot around on the fine beasts. But before any elegant work could be done, she had to internalize one basic rule. *Remain neutral at all cost*, her teacher had repeated. *A horse senses fear and can take the upper hand.*

These monster fish, she thought, might know she was in trouble. They attack their own when under stress.

She quieted herself to take stock of her options. There were only two ways to escape this lonely, unsympathetic world: either tear off her helmet and shoot to the surface, or climb up the air hose. She decided losing her helmet was a last resort. She'd try the hose. But would it support her weight?

When she pulled, yards of slack fell into her arms, then tangled in the rocks below her.

The boat must be past the reef by now, she thought. And another wave of desolation swept over her.

I will get back, she repeated to herself. I will get back.

When she penciled this story in her notebook later, she wanted to remember her determination, her iron will. But instead she remembered that the moment of crisis had opened her to another temptation: letting herself go.

She thought of all her depressed moods over the years, the many times she'd yearned for escape from the miseries of life. Here was a chance. All she had to do was allow it, and it would be done. Release was as close as the ladder had been a moment ago.

Perhaps she could stimulate the right attitude toward death.

But now, knowing a single misstep or wrong move would end her existence, she found she wanted to live:

"My whole soul wanted to go back to my earth world and carry on."

She pulled on the hose again, and again received an armload of slack. As she drifted closer to the reef, she thought she might be able to climb it in order to get closer to the ladder. Just then a current surged, threatening to carry her under the overhanging ledge. Hanging on, she saw the base of the ship heading toward the rock, as if whoever was on board was not paying attention to where they were headed.

They must be looking off the back, trying to spot her.

She made a last effort to climb. She kicked and grabbed and made her way up the side of the reef, and finally reached the lowest rung of the ladder. She hurried up until she reached the ship and climbed on board, just in time to see them careening toward the rock face of a cliff.

When she thought back on the day, she wrote:

"I hope the Gods of Excitement will invite me to the edge of the precipice again. I feel at home with them and a glance over the edge helps this strange, almost irresistible pull that haunts my soul."

That afternoon on the *Ready*, Beebe arranged for her to go down in the bathysphere with his assistant, John Tee-Van—a birthday surprise. She crawled into the small opening, listening over the phone to the rhythmic clanging as the ten big bolts were hammered into place.

As she sank she saw a ctenophore wafting so close she could make out its eight rows of cilia. A large ghost-pale umbrella jellyfish trailing four stinging tentacles appeared and disappeared into the bluish green beyond. At two hundred feet, blue lost its yellowness. Colorless shrimps and carangid-like fish butted savagely against the window. Psenes continued to dart around. A long, slender eel-like leptocephalus undulated into view, like a strip of tissue paper with a glistening eye.

The winchmen unrolled four hundred feet of cable before Beebe ordered them to stop. Unafraid for his own sake, he could not stand the possibility that something might happen to his two companions, one of whom had become his other pair of eyes. Hollister begged to stay longer and go deeper, but Beebe was stubborn.

Hollister peered out the bathysphere's windows into an infinite depth of dazzling purple-blue. This "awful color," she wrote, held her attention like an indescribable force, calling her to descend deeper and deeper, "down to the dark, to the utter dark, where the blind white sea-snakes are."

gloria

Nothing at All

After Hollister's birthday dive, Beebe and Barton sent down the bathysphere empty except for a film camera. Through a remote activation mechanism, they shot fifteen hundred feet of film. When it was processed, the film showed "nothing visible."

My Profession Is Ignorance

When Beebe was eleven, his mother took him down to Broadway to see a phrenologist, who found him quick and critical and a good judge of character, but said his body might betray him. Beebe believed this meant he would never be an intellectual because his head was too small.

As a teenager on the deck of a ferry to Nova Scotia, he first saw the spouting and breaching of whales. To him they were primeval and utterly free—he called them "masterless, rioting in the vast expanse."

It was the first time he understood the boundlessness of the ocean.

In 1903 he punched out the bottom of a bucket and replaced it with glass. He pushed it into the seawater off the coast of Florida and declared what he'd seen miraculous.

He kept a pair of binoculars at the field station, still a rarity at that time. When newcomers arrived, he instructed them to point the binoculars at the moon. Their reaction to the sight told him all he needed to know. Only inarticulate amazement signaled a worthwhile character. Anything less meant the visitor's life was but a pointless march toward death.

He played the ukulele and the banjo and liked to drink cocktails. To celebrate one colleague's birthday he shaved off his mustache, donned a frilly dress, and put on lipstick. He taught his friends that a scientist could be found leaned back at his desk, feet up, "chatting with a lady about the right costume for the Beaux Arts Ball."

He was the first scientist to describe birds at play.

In 1900 he took Mary Blair Rice to see the new musical revue *Florodora,* which tells the story of a hunt for a rare perfume on a Philippine island. A character named Tweedlepunch poses as a phrenologist and examines the bumps on the heads of all the young women, looking for the bump of love.

All the while, a chorus line of six high-kicking girls sings *Hey! Hey! Alack-a-day! Our loving hearts asunder.*

After they married, he and Blair, as she liked to be called, set off to travel the world chasing pheasants, but as soon as they got back to New York she ran off with a neighbor. Years later, she published a novel about white people exploring Harlem, with a thinly disguised version of Beebe as a dry and dedicated man of science.

He met Harriet Ricker, the twenty-six-year-old novelist who published as Elswyth Thane, as she was finishing up *Riders on the Wind.* It was the story of a young woman named Sandy who leaves a boring academic husband to follow the explorer Blaise Dorin, aka Dodo, on an adventure through the Pamir Mountains of Central Asia. Dodo is in search of a ritual robe of woven gold encrusted with topazes, which he's promised to a sketchy dealer in New Orleans. The pair of adventurers dodge bullets and outwit swordsmen. They make it through one close call only because Sandy impersonates the goddess Shir Shan. They have the robe in their hands, but lose it at the last second, barely escaping with their lives.

The *New York Times* predicted the book would be read "long after the social analyses and adult confessionals of the majority of our owlish young men have disappeared."

And while her heroine thought of marriage as "some pagan ritual," like "being shut up in a box," Thane married Beebe a year later. The wedding took place on an extravagant yacht called *The Warrior*, with Edith Roosevelt as honored guest.

But Thane, unlike her heroine, had little patience for continent-crossing adventures and preferred to live alone in New England. Later she moved to London to prepare the staging of her play "The Tudor Wench." Beebe went with her and introduced her to his English friends. He chose Nonsuch as the site for his field station, partly because he thought she would enjoy Bermuda. There was an octagonal house on Nonsuch meant to serve as her studio, and there was a bit of high life he thought might hold her attention. She sailed with him to the archipelago and spent a few days in the octagonal house, but quickly returned to New York. Island life was not for her.

Through their decades of marriage, Beebe and Thane rarely saw each other. Thane described their arrangement, approvingly, as *modern*. In 1939 she wrote a novel called *Tryst* about a woman in love with a ghost.

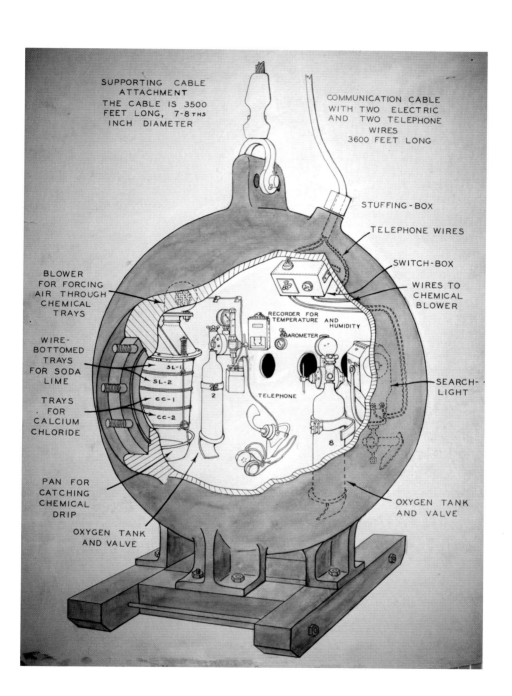

SUPPORTING CABLE
ATTACHMENT
THE CABLE IS 3500
FEET LONG, 7-8THS
INCH DIAMETER

COMMUNICATION CABLE
WITH TWO ELECTRIC
AND TWO TELEPHONE
WIRES
3600 FEET LONG

STUFFING-BOX

TELEPHONE WIRES

SWITCH-BOX

BLOWER
FOR FORCING
AIR THROUGH
CHEMICAL
TRAYS

WIRES TO
CHEMICAL
BLOWER

RECORDER FOR
TEMPERATURE AND
HUMIDITY

BAROMETER

WIRE-
BOTTOMED
TRAYS
FOR SODA
LIME

SL-1
SL-2
CC-1
CC-2

TRAYS
FOR
CALCIUM
CHLORIDE

SEARCH-
LIGHT

TELEPHONE

PAN FOR
CATCHING
CHEMICAL
DRIP

OXYGEN TANK
AND VALVE

OXYGEN TANK
AND VALVE

The Engineer

Otis Barton was an engineering postgraduate at Columbia University when he came across an article by Beebe describing a plan for a submersible to explore the deep ocean. Beebe had dreamed up the vessel with Theodore Roosevelt—a steel cylinder that could be lowered into the depths.

Barton's mind lit up. He'd had the same dream. It had first occurred to him watching pearl divers in Asia—how far down could we go? Back home, he built a makeshift submersible and explored the shallow depths off the coast of Massachusetts, at first hanging so much weight around himself he was nearly torn in half. He understood something critical about Beebe and Roosevelt's cylinder: under the huge pressures below the sea it would be crushed like a tin can underfoot.

Barton devised a simple sphere that would evenly distribute the pressure. It was elegant and ingenious. And Barton had money—he'd inherited a fortune from his father—that he was willing to sink into the project.

He wrote Beebe to propose a partnership. But Beebe received hundreds of crackpot proposals from amateur enthusiasts, and Barton's letter landed in the same pile. When Barton wrote again and offered to pay for the project himself, Beebe agreed.

In the design of the bathysphere, Beebe readily admitted, he could contribute only his enthusiasm. But Barton was envious of his fame and was known to murmur misgivings about his colleagues at the Department of Tropical Research—*Gloria the Amazon, Beebe the diva.*

The engineer was particularly flummoxed by the presence among the staff of what he thought of as *girl scientists.*

Perhaps amusing to look at, Barton thought, but suitable only for cataloging and organizing.

Was he expected to take them seriously?

Barton insisted he be inside the bathysphere for all its major dives. It was this condition that kept Beebe from taking Hollister, who could have verified what he saw, added to his insights, or made her own discoveries.

Barton was no life scientist, and busied himself checking battery and gas levels, fiddling with the blower, or making attempts at undersea photography. And as the bathysphere bobbed and swayed, he grew nauseous, often losing control and beginning to retch in the tiny, cramped space.

On one such occasion, Gloria Hollister heard Beebe's shouting voice through her receiver on the deck of the *Ready*:

"Oh God, Otis—Not now!"

And the staff repeated it, giggling with delight—*Oh God, Otis. Not now!*

Contour Dives

This time they were towed by the *Freedom*, a vessel that could support the bathysphere and still motor forward, so Beebe could track the descent of the shoreline and observe changes in marine flora and fauna at different depths. During these dives, which they called *contour dives*, the steel ball dangled, drifted, and swayed with the water and the movement of the ship above. As always, Barton checked instruments, levels, tried unsuccessfully to take photographs. Beebe called up to Hollister.

30 ft   Very large blotched Parrotfish, three feet long.
Oxygen gauge reading 500 pounds.
More Chaetodons, four bands, 12 inches.
Sounding 9 fathoms.

A six-foot Shark quite near. It swam
around a huge brain coral when it saw us.
Sounding 9 fathoms.

Several Yellowtails, three feet long.
Sounding 9 fathoms.

Bathysphere just missed a huge brain
coral on a pedestal.
Sounding 10 fathoms.

There is a big deep place with sand.
Small Shark swimming close to small
Guamacaia parrotfish.
Barton photographing.

Reading of oxygen tank gauge 300 pounds.
Always many Chromis and Clupeids.
3 or 4 species of Parrots.

Just missed a big crag.
Beautiful Clepticus parrae, two and
a half foot long.

Now over a neck of sand.
8 big Goatfish, they look like
reddish cows.

35   Enormous purple sea fans, 10 feet high.
Sounding 10 fathoms.

Passing over huge, deep canyons.
This looks like the end of things now.
I can look down forty feet.

It is raining Sardinellas.
When they become frightened they all
turn down like one fish and pour straight
down; an amazing sight.

Barton photographing.
The bottom is dropping off now into
dim vistas.

65   All the sea plumes have disappeared,
it looks absolutely dead
like surface of the moon.
Sounding 17 fathoms.

75   Absolutely barren, now passing over a ridge.
Not even old roots or stems of plumes. Few

pieces of old, dead coral in sight.
Cliff ahead.
Sounding 17 fathoms.

85   Clupeids and Chromis all mixed up.

100   Sloping down to a sandy place in distance
Looks like death.

About 400 two-foot Kyphosus
Nothing but sand in ridges and waves.
No Parrots, no vegetable-eaters present.

120   More pebbles. No growth except a
few spindly, dead plumes.
Not a fish in sight, yet back over
the last ridge there were scores.

140   We are 10 feet from the bottom.
Illumination is like brilliant
moon-light, purplish blue color.

2.

Spectral Visions

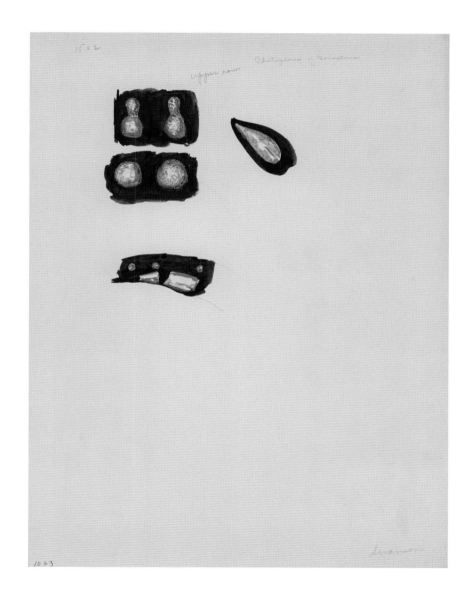

Linophryne arborifera

I saw a tremor run through the body—the fin waved two or three times, the tree-like growth of chin tentacles . . . a tangled snarl, then stretched wide to many times their contracted length, the mouth opened and partly closed, and the light went out of the great, staring eyes. What would I not have sacrificed to have been told what those eyes had seen in the black depths, what that great mouth had engulfed, what enemies had been avoided, what part might have the luminous head bulb played in courtship or in war, why the huge fangs should be luminous, why a great tree of hundreds of medusa-tentacles was necessary—why? why? why?

Instead of which there lay my lifeless little dragon, perfect in all his parts, with his secrets hidden.

Beebe on a scrap of white paper, undated.

Animal Light

On a dark night twenty-five hundred years ago, a young Greek philosopher was out rowing off the city of Milet, near the mouth of the Meander, when he noticed swirls of light set into motion as his oars stroked the sea. Anaximenes, as he was called, was a student of the philosopher Anaximander, who had taught him that everything in the universe was made of the same indefinite substrata. Anaximander called it *apeiron*, but his own teacher Thales had taught him it was regular water that was the origin of things. Considering the swirls of light within the water, Anaximenes suspected it might be air that was condensed into water and eventually stones and animals and clouds and everything else. How else could there be light in the water?

The writers of the Sanskrit Vedas and early Chinese odes described the luminous bodies of insects and worms, but such creatures were rarely mentioned in the Mediterranean. Pliny wrote of strange glowing creatures called *nyctegretos* or *nyctilops*, but it wasn't until the thirteenth century, when the Andalusian botanist Al-Bayṭār described an animal called *al-hubahib*—a winged insect that lights up at night—that fireflies appeared in the history of the West. Al-Bayṭār recommended collecting their shining bodies, grinding them in rose oil, and dropping them into the ear to stop pussing wounds.

Books of medieval science soon filled with glowing animals. The forests of Bohemia were reportedly full of waxwings whose red-tipped feathers shone like the sun. Fiery vapors gathered around temples and especially cemeteries.

Alchemists like Albertus Magnus and Paracelsus recommended burying the glowing abdomens of fireflies in manure and allowing the mixture to ferment. This produced what was called *liquor lucidus*, a glow-in-the-dark ink only visible at night or in pitch-black rooms.

The Swiss editor Conrad Gesner thought all glowing creatures were powered by the moon. He collected a thousand drawings of lunar animals before he died of the plague in 1555.

Twenty years later an English professor of divinities named Stephen Batman published an encyclopedic work on the natural world that contained an entry on the glowworm, a little beast that "shineth in darkness as a candle, and is foule and darke in full light." Batman believed all these strange glowings were works of the devil and wrote about them in his book *The Doome Warning All Men to Judgment*.

Luminous fish appeared in the *Margarita Philosophica* of George Reisch. Glowing lamb's flesh was reported in Padua. There were glowing eggs, glowing stones, and glowing clods of earth.

Francis Bacon saw light in the snap of a sugar cube, and Descartes believed cats could beam light from their eyes. The linens of honorable men, it was said, luminesced when removed in darkness.

Athanasius Kircher described sea creatures that could be rubbed on sticks so they glow like fire.

He had seen it himself in Marseilles and Sicily.

Thomas Bartholin claimed that humans, too, have been known to shine, especially when full of desire. His examples included Theodoric, King of the Goths; Carolus Gonzaga, Duke of Mantua; and an Athenian sex worker called Lampyris.

There were luminous minerals like the diamond, ruby, and carbuncle; there was the light emitted by dried cod. Light erupted when a woman combed her long hair in the dark. And all this was the result of fermentation. Sand on the beach was fermenting, cat's fur was fermenting. The sun was a giant fermentation pot, a model to meteors and the air around the high mists of ships.

But unlike the sun, this light gave off no heat. Cool light, like what shone from the mixture of sulfur and acid, was a matter of grave paradox. Light was an exhalation of effluvium mixed with air, the attrition of gems; light was a corpuscular material body. There was cold fire confined in ætherial globules, calcined belemnites, in the boring mollusk brought to Bologna by Marsigli.

That light was a kind of matter was proved by the electroluminescence of evacuated vessels or mercury shaken in a glass tube. There were pyrophores and there was phlogiston; there was the phosphorus of Kunkel in the Torricellian void. Light shone from borate of soda, sulphate of argil, tartrite of potash, and silicious stones.

Bronislaus Rodziszewski found that compounds containing the triphenyl gloxaline ring give off light when dissolved in alcohol and shaken with air.

In 1799, Alexander Von Humboldt stimulated a jellyfish.

Darwin contemplated the bright thoraxes of Elateridae and the shining abdomens of Lampyridae. He thought animal light served to attract mates and food and confuse predators. MacCulloch thought it was to see in the darkness of the deep ocean.

Afloat on a small boat near Haiti a few years before, Beebe had noticed phosphorescence in the water and sent for a shotgun. He fired straight down, then marveled at what looked like a comet of glowing shot, arced into the deep and swept by a "train of trembling paleness."

When he saw bioluminescent fish darting outside the bathysphere, they looked to him like "stars gone mad."

The Blue Light of the Sea

The incandescence of animal light thrilled Beebe, and the chance to see exploding shrimp and glowing tentacles alive and undulating in their liquid home was one of the great thrills of the dives. But it was the luminous blue water, its ceaseless frequency like a maddening hum, that transfigured his being. He had read that below two hundred feet, blue was gradually replaced by violet. Below four hundred feet, violet was said to be dominant. But when he arrived at that depth, he didn't see any violet. Instead, the blue deepened and became even more brilliant. He knew this was impossible, but he knew that's what he saw.

He read over an experiment where a scientist had shone ultraviolet light through a chunk of black glass. When light struck participants' eyes, most saw a violet haze and were unable to see anything else. But others did not see the haze. Instead, they saw clear blue. It sounded like what happened to Beebe at depth.

Was it an aberration? An ability or disability?

Beebe was not looking through a chunk of glass but the entire ocean. No laboratory could reproduce such conditions. It was up to him to form and measure a reality as they descended.

What actually happened to the light as they fell?

Beebe had the inside of the bathysphere painted black, and on the next dive, he resolved to pay close attention to changes in the spectrum of visible colors. He did this with the help of a spectroscope—a small telescope-like device with a prism, lens, and meter registering values—and by holding up color cards, trying to match what he saw with his eyes.

Hollister was back on deck to record Beebe's observations, which began as soon as the steel ball hit the water:

Surface red dimming

20 ft   Thin line of red, mostly orange
gone from 700 to 650 reading of
spectroscope. See hull plainly.

50 ft.   Red absolutely gone. Orange at 625. Other
bands as usual. 3 big Bonito-like fish about
15 inches long

100   Orange much narrowed at 600. Rest of spectrum normal
but dim.

200   No orange present, faint yellow; less green
than at the surface, less blue and more violet.

250   Violet and blue same as above.
Green dim but almost as wide.
Rest dirty yellow with brown edge.

300   Psenes silvery white with no blue at all.
Whole spectrum dim.
Yellow-green almost gone,
its dirty brown edge towards red end.
Violet narrower than at the surface.

350   Brown edge of green gone completely.
50% of spectrum blue-violet, 25% green,
25% colorless pale light.
Red all gone.

450   Still see #30 at lowest aperture faintly.
Blue all gone. Nothing but violet and faint faint green.
3 Eels. 4 Cyclothones in light, but
absolutely invisible without it.

500   Every color of spectrum has gone except violet.
If I didn't know there was green at the other end, I
could not have named it. On circular color chart

there is not any color that can possibly be named.

600   Two Pilot fishes.

Color still dim. No color.

700   Thermometer a little above 70 degrees

Light light glow where violet was.

Fading off on each side toward the blue.

No color whatever.

When Beebe read these notes later, he found them frustrating. They made no reference to the actual impression of the color. The bathysphere descended to 800 feet, where again he could register no color using the spectroscope. But when he looked outside he saw the deepest black-blue imaginable. He thought of it as something beyond language, requiring a whole new system of descriptors. It was "a solid, blue-black world, one which seemed born of a single vibration."

When people asked Beebe how low he hoped to go, he always told them something specific—a quarter mile, a half mile. But really, he admitted, what he wanted was to go deeper than the sun's rays. The horizon of his desire was a step beyond solar light.

On September 22, 1932, he and Barton sank lower than seventeen hundred feet, and when Beebe held the spectroscope, it showed no glimmering of light. Outside it was black with no hint of blue.

He set down the spectroscope and bathed in darkness. No waves at all. That's what he'd wanted.

Except for the dull and lessening power of the spotlight, the only visibility was provided by the animals themselves, oxidizations of luciferin and luciferase casting their glow of desire.

Facing away from Barton, whose fiddling and whose breath he could still hear, Beebe faced the encompassing blackness out the window. Memory of all other colors fell away and he lolled in the inarticulate shine. There was no explanation and it illuminated nothing.

The Science of Delusion

It was a venerable philosophical impulse, to seek color in darkness. There was a nexus that connected darkness, blueness, nearness, and truth.

The eleventh-century Iraqi scientist Ibn al-Haytham saw that if you fill a pitcher with colored liquid and shine a light through it, the shadow acquires the color of the liquid. Even objects and houses take on the color of what's around them. If you see a white wall in a green meadow, it will appear slightly green.

Nothing is really a single color, he concluded, and all colorful appearances are suspect.

Leonardo da Vinci learned to paint mountain bases in lighter colors than their peaks, while objects in the foreground needed to be darker than those in the background. Darkness increased with the thinness of the air at elevation, he observed, but also with proximity. This was paradoxical, unless darkness increased as objects and animals revealed the truth of themselves. Darkness was not absence of light, but the effect of veils falling away.

Blocking out the sunlight in a salon hung with black velvet, Leonardo burned a few leaves and extinguished the flame. When the room filled with smoke, he drew back the curtain a bit until a beam pierced the darkness. Lit up in front of the black velvet, the smoke shone blue.

The Language of Color

Beebe's predecessor Robert Ridgway had traveled the United States identifying birds in the late nineteenth century, increasingly bothered by an old conundrum: Is what you call red the same as what I call red? How could he know if a bird observed in Connecticut was the same as a bird observed in California, if the two birders couldn't agree on vocabulary? His response was to encourage everyone to use his now classic *Color Standards and Color Nomenclature*, first published in 1912.

Holding up one-square-inch swatches, his guide allowed birders to distinguish Alice blue from methyl blue, livid purple from light phlox purple, asphodel green from invisible green, deep Quaker drab from pale ecru drab, xanthine orange from mikado orange, and to situate hellebore red between dark diva violet and rose dorée.

It became the standard text naturalists used to identify colors of specimens, and Beebe used it regularly.

Beebe's own *Color Notes* lists sightings of bittersweet orange, metallic opaline green, orange rufous and orange chrome, calliste green, cinnamon rufous, claret brown, carrot red, bittersweet pink, and scarlet spots which were lost in darkness.

The Studio

Several miles off Gurnet's Rock, dressed in a bright red swimsuit, her cropped curls tinged with gray, Else Bostelmann swung a leg onto a metal ladder that dropped forty feet below the ocean's surface.

She had just returned to work a few years ago. She'd won prizes at art school in Weimar, but then had come to America, married a man named Monroe, and abandoned her career. Only when Monroe dropped dead eleven years later did she pick her brushes back up. She was skilled—she had a vivid and accurate style, adept at catching details of the natural world. A few small assignments attracted some attention before Beebe hired her for the Bermuda expedition.

With Barton's photographs useless, Beebe relied on staff artists to depict creatures he saw in the deep. This was scientific proof, evidence of new species. There was no room for inaccuracy.

He worked with Helen Damrosch Tee-Van, who married his assistant, John. But in Bostelmann he found a true collaborator. Like a police sketch artist, she had a talent for painting creatures she hadn't seen, based just off Beebe's words. While Beebe and Hollister completed specimen cards with detailed descriptions, Bostelmann rendered images, checking and altering until she got them right. Sea devils and angler fish, outlandish creatures that moments before she hadn't known existed.

The tentacle emerges here?

Now she scrambled down to the water and waited while Beebe placed a bulky copper diving helmet over her head so it rested on her shoulders. She grabbed onto the ladder with her right hand, and with her left clutched a zinc engraver's plate and steel pin.

Standing on the ladder, still at the side of the launch, she could feel the flow of fresh air into the helmet from the pump on board the launch. Breathing

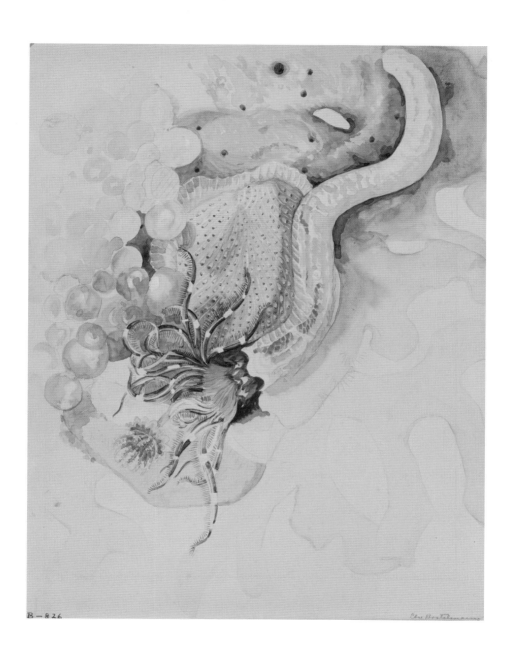

Chr. Bentelmann

naturally, she let herself down into the water, and as she sank, the sixty-pound helmet felt surprisingly light on her shoulders.

Looking down through the glass window of the helmet, a landscape of bright corals and multicolored underwater plant life emerged, more glorious than anything on land. She descended the iron rungs of the ladder thirty-six feet, then dropped onto the white sand of the sea floor, fine and soft as any sand she knew. Above her, sunbeams struck the ocean's surface and split into rays lighting up the water like dust in a dark room, brightly luminous but cool, all greens and splintered yellows and a blue that was somehow brighter than daylight. The brilliance around her faded quickly to darkness as she gazed into the near distance.

As if the water swallows the colors and the light, she thought.

There was constant movement within the complex architecture of the reef—squirrel fish and anemones and other creatures lurking and swimming and grabbing at food. The blunt yellow beaks of parrot fish appeared and disappeared from view, and jellyfish that reminded her of butterflies. She reached out to grab a piece of coral but came up empty-handed. The water obscured distance, so things were further away than they appeared. She took a step forward and reached out again only to draw back her hand quickly as the venomous coral burned her fingertips.

She stood still for a second trying to gain a sense of where she was, then jumped as she felt itches and stings everywhere. She turned her heavy-laden head as fast as she could and saw a cloud of tiny fish taking small sharp bites at her arms and legs. Reassured they were not dangerous, the bites became ticklish and hilarious.

She gained her bearing on the sea floor and once again looked up to see several objects looming above her: an iron music stand, as light as a feather underwater, and a shallow metal tub. She reached up to grab them as they fell and guided them to the white sand at her feet. A bundle of paintbrushes attached to the tub stood on end due to the buoyancy of their wooden handles.

Soon a stretched canvas appeared, and she affixed it with tacks to the music stand.

Now she just had to get into position. She took a step and it felt like she was moving through glue. She leaned forward as if into a headwind and dragged her gear several feet from the reef. Finally she got everything in place and was ready to get to work. She eyed the reef, mentally composing the canvas, then grabbed one of the upward-pointing brushes by its wooden handle and knelt to dab it with blue oil paint. But again misreading the distance, she stuck it into the green instead.

Oh well, she thought, and dabbed the green on the canvas to outline the form of the reef. But when she turned back to her tub full of paint it was gone.

Swinging around she saw it drifting away in the undersea current, its globs of color mixing into the landscape. She glanced back at her music stand, which she had weighted to the sea floor, then squatted awkwardly, moving on her hands and knees after the tub while struggling to keep her head up so the helmet wouldn't fall off.

In a few minutes she wrestled the tub back into place. The fresh air still filled her helmet, and she was able to catch her breath before grabbing a vertical brush and kneeling to dab it into the right color.

Next time I'll work with palette knives, she thought, not these bobbing wooden brushes. And I'll get a weighted palette and forget about this bathtub. She looked down at it, chained up and smeared with colored oil, and it reminded her of the wine cask where Diogenes slept after masturbating in the public square.

a.

Jan 16.
27, 827

b.

Jan. 19. 38
abajo - no numbe
A. Barker.

c.

28, 005

P. Barker
Z 163

Spectral Visions

Carnelian red . . . deep true purple . . . spectrum violet . . .
dark citrine strawberry pink . . . flame scarlet . . . grenadine red coral
pink . . . dark olivaceous . . . dark hermit brown.

Aristotle believed colors were sent by God from heaven through celestial rays of light. Colors emerged through a mixing of light and dark that related to the four elements—water, air, earth, and fire. Such beliefs were popular for two thousand years.

In the plague year 1665, twenty-three-year-old Isaac Newton was sheltering in his family home in Woolsthorpe. His father long dead and his mother off with another man, the solitary student roamed the salons of the house day after day. He stayed holed up in Woolsthorpe for two years, and in the isolation of those months he began all sorts of experiments.

He wondered if he could summon within his imagination the experience of staring directly into the sun. When he tested whether his image resembled reality, he almost blinded himself. Later he pushed a blunt needle into the back of his eyeball to see if it altered his vision.

Like Leonardo, he performed experiments in darkened rooms.

Just before noon on an August day, he drew the curtains tight, so only a single beam of light penetrated. The previous fall he'd bought a prism at Stourbridge Fair in Cambridge, which he now held up to the beam of daylight. The little chunk of glass refracted the sunbeam, casting a colorful smear of light on the opposite wall. Newton named this phenomenon *the spectrum* and spent the next seven years investigating it.

The scattering of light through water and glass had fascinated Aristotle and Leonardo, but they thought light was emitted by the eye and that glass altered and distorted it. Newton's prism proved white light was a heterogenous substance, and the glass merely separated it into constituent parts.

At the same time he began investigating color and optics, Newton was at work on a book called *Of Musick*, where he tried to understand how the human ear distinguishes between sounds that are sweet, harsh, or graceful.

Plato had suggested that the world soul is fundamentally musical, that the planets were tied to the sun by the seven strings of Apollo's lyre. But the sixteenth century saw the collapse in this belief—celestial structures, the human body, the function of certain medicines, and architecture could no longer be interpreted in terms of music.

That collapse became known as "the untuning of the sky."

Newton was obsessed with Biblical prophecy. He saw the world as unstable and tending toward corruption unless God continuously intervened to restore balance. But in his view, it was not colors that had been sent by God. It was Newton. He had been divinely appointed to unearth the hidden mechanisms through which changes in nature were wrought.

Both sound and light reached the soul by virtue of the same animal spirit in acoustic and optical nerves. Visual sensations were vibrations in the æther that passed from the eye to the sensorium through "pipes filld with a pure transparent liquor."

Color was an outward manifestation of esoteric mechanical structures, so three primary and three secondary colors were not enough. There must be a seventh color, Newton thought, because there were seven bodies in the heavens, seven days of the week, and seven deadly sins. More than that, he felt that sound and vision must be related—colors were like notes on a scale. So he bent the spectrum into a circle so that blue could flow into red through a violet octave. And he pried the circle open to introduce a seventh color: indigo.

Despite his obsession with the mystical number, after decades of studying alchemy and trying to decode the book of Revelation, Newton's final act was to refuse to accept the seventh sacrament: the last rites before the death of a believer.

With Napoleon at large in Germany, an unsettled Johann Wolfgang von Goethe began his own games with prisms. He angled the glass triangle so it bounced light against a white wall, where it cast no color at all. Then he moved it to a shaded part of the wall where the colors of the spectrum appeared in all their glory. Moving the prism back and forth across the line between the light and dark areas of the wall, Goethe concluded that Newton was wrong. There was nothing inherent in colors. They did not exist in the world the way a book or a house did. They were phantoms that appeared nowhere else but in the mind.

Like Hollister's world, Goethe's was not one of matter but of interpretation and thought. And perhaps his insight contained something that could illuminate Beebe's own consternation. Where Newton saw light as composed of colored particles passing through pure liquor, Goethe saw them as already existing within the soul. Light itself was invisible. How could it contain color? That was an absurdity repeated by the credulous for a century, in stark opposition to their senses.

Goethe saw colors as subjective phenomena that arise as mind, matter, and sense interact. They were emotional and aesthetic events, as everyone with a soul could verify.

Red was the highest color—graceful and dignified and attractive.

Yellow was calm but optimistic. At times it seemed to breathe on its own.

Orange was so high energy as to be intolerable.

Green was restful, a good choice for painting the walls of rooms.

Purple was as restless as Goethe himself, and laid across the floor it was as intolerable as orange.

Blue was remote, gloomy, and cold.

Combinations of colors had their own characters, too. Yellow next to red was serene and magnificent. Yellow next to green was cheerful but ordinary. Blue next to green was repulsive, a pattern fit only for fools.

Such were the colors around the *Ready* as it floated near Nonsuch.

The physics student Franz Boas came home to Prussia for summer vacation to learn his best friend had disappeared while out on the river. Boas spent four days wading through the water only to find his friend's body swollen and discolored from drowning.

He returned to university in Kiel hoping to write his dissertation on Gauss's law on the normal distribution of errors, but his advisor asked him to study the optical properties of seawater. He was compelled to bob in the Baltic, sinking zinc tubes and porcelain plates into the sea, then to sit in a lab gauging light as it passed through water-filled tubes.

Boas worked with sodium and lithium lamps, but it was impossible to generate light intense and homogenous enough for fine measurements. He resorted to an ordinary gas lamp held very close to his face, but found the weather, even a single cloud, affected results.

All his work and effort proved little more than the inadequacy of tools and the inaccuracy of measurements. Still, he demonstrated that water, while transparent in thin layers, acquires color with depth, and that these colors are different in different places, depending on the polarization and absorption of light.

The blue of the Aral Sea differs from the aquamarine of Nicaragua's Lake Yoyoa, he wrote. But how do we decide at what point to call a color aqua and not blue? Are we condemned, as Goethe suggested, to look for an answer in our soul?

He grew interested in *psychophysics*, the relationship between matter and measurement and perception, increasingly convinced that a materialistic worldview was untenable.

A head full of questions, he went to get drunk at a local bar. His table full of friends was approached by a well-known anti-Semite. Boas challenged the

Judenhetzer, as he called him, to a duel, slashing his opponent's face three times and earning a two-inch scar on his own cheek.

Why do people behave the way they do? Why do they believe what they believe?

He continued to chew on such questions as he stood at the edge of a steamer heading from Germany to Baffin Island in the Canadian Arctic. He dropped a framed white canvas tied to a line and watched it fall into the sea, attempting to describe any changes in its apparent color.

How could he make any objective statements about the water's transparency? What was that color called?

Far from physics and German universities, he spent the winter with an Inuit man named Ssigna, who taught him Inuktitut, told him stories of his life, and introduced him to methods of hunting and cooking. Lacking basic skills, his tongue tripping over a new language, Boas observed his companion handle a knife, a sled, complete his daily tasks. Boas felt self-conscious of his incompetence and became aware that he—the supposed observer—was himself being observed. Perplexed, he realized the people around him were possessed of a reality every bit as rich and complex as his own.

Despite all the zinc tubes and porcelain plates he'd dropped into the Baltic, he concluded nothing about the color of seawater.

Falling into darkness only to have luminosity increase, Beebe was confronted with such uncertain measures of transparency. Between absence and distance, the play of smoke and velvet, the brightness of the deep formed an inner clock by which he might reset what he knew. Orange and red were vivid and wonderful, but nothing could ever be as penetrating, as shocking, as overwhelming as the luminous blue of the deep. With that bath in the background—absence of color that might be violet or might be blue—he could try to communicate what he had seen.

3.

Sinking Lower

August 11, 1934

20 ft	Can see hull growth by looking up.
	Red almost gone in spectroscope,
	only orange left.
250	First Aurelia.
300	Barton sees Pteropod.
310	Beam on.
360	Beam off.
400	Beam on.
420	Beam off.
500	Water a luminous dark blue.
550	Barometer going down a little,
	lower than 77, just below this line.
600	Only gray visible in spectroscope.
640	One flash, now three more.
	Beam on.
	Copepods abundant.
	Sagitta, pale ones, and larval fish.
700	A mist of Copepods and other Plankton.
	Turquoise one-half the distal length of
	beam of light.
720	8-inch fish shot past.
760	String of Salpa or Siphonophores.
840	6 Cyclothones close together.
	Leptocephalus, 5 inches, with 2 black spots,
	swimming right into beam.
900	Beam out.

Apex

In 1910, Beebe and his first wife set off on their global pheasant-tracking excursion from London. They spent the last day at the National Portrait Gallery visiting Darwin and Huxley before they shipped out for Port Said.

On the Dover–Calais steamer, Blair sat next to a Catholic Sister of Charity, who had not been out of her convent in Sussex in fourteen years. She was on her way to Egypt to nurse her birth sister, who had contracted typhoid while acting as a companion to a Polish countess.

They trained from Calais to Brindisi. The fields of France were flooded.

Sailing south from Brindisi through the Adriatic, Beebe shot photographs of the Dinaric Alps to the east. He thought of them as home to unconquered Greeks called *Dalmatians.*

The pyramids were just as he imagined. The Egyptian countryside was straight out of the Bible.

Cairo was out of the *1001 Nights.*

They lunched with Capt. and Mrs. Flower, who ran the Giza Zoo. The Flowers had lived for years in Siam, which they advised the Beebes to avoid, as it was simply unhealthy.

By night in Giza, Beebe snuck past the guards and entered the great pyramid, walking up and down the cavernous, darkened stairways until he reached the central chamber, which he found occupied by bats.

Two thousand years ago, he mused, "Polaris blinked." And some twelve thousand years in the future, "the glow of Vega" would declare the day had turned.

Arriving in India, Beebe heard the faint *peemt!* of Night-jars.

Within a few months, he was high in the Himalayas—"the very summit of the world"—looking down at the treetops like "ghostly minarets," and watching the progress of Halley's comet.

A scientific mind in the high mountains, he turned to face the comet above the eastern horizon, contemplating its periodicity like the tunnel in Giza. When the comet last passed, he thought, Texas and California belonged to Mexico; there were no railroads, no telegraphs; Darwin was yet to write *The Origin of Species.*

Everything he took for granted, which he and so many of us rarely question, was erased with one sweep of these collapsible timelines, elastic histories. This was the only reason to know things, Beebe concluded. The point of facts was to reach "the clear heights of dynamic thought."

He would return to this memory in years to come, wondering how to understand his position. He, who would travel to the depths of the abyss, had once been in the highest mountains. What insight could he draw from that? Extending his mind back to the earliest moments, from heights to the depths, what could he see?

He had hiked up behind a guide named Hadzia, ridiculing him in his mind as a "pitiful bunch of rags." Now, with the comet wiping his mind clean, he wondered what Hadzia might be thinking. He wondered if Hadzia might be flushed with yearning and affection for the hills. He wondered if they might feel the same way about things.

Heading back to camp, he was overtaken by melancholy.

All of his expeditions, he felt, ended in sorrowful scenes. He met new people like Hadzia, at first alien and strange, then passed through many stages with them: suspicion, amusement, esteem, perhaps friendship. Their fates were tied together, they were united by common goals, they faced privation and danger together. But soon they went their separate ways and lived out the rest of their lives far away and in complete ignorance of each other.

What was it all worth?

Among the team that took him to Darjeeling was a man named Rassul Akhat, hired to travel ahead of the rest and prepare the site where they would camp. Akhat was elderly and, like Hadzia, dressed in rags. But he was tall, with a long gray beard, calm and gentle, with a commanding posture.

If he were dressed differently, Beebe thought, he might pass for "a holy-man, statesman or some great artist."

Instead of commanding the respect he might as a sadhu or great artist, though, he was treated with disdain. No one would sit with him at meals.

"Sometimes," Beebe thought, "he was the most to be envied of us all, for being unable to sink lower."

He was free to behave as he pleased—"for him there was no book of etiquette."

Perhaps brought on by these confused and ridiculous thoughts, when he descended to the town of Pungatong Beebe shut himself in a room in a cabin and was suddenly overtaken by inchoate anxieties. Now it was him who could not sink lower. If he tried to sleep, nightmares overtook him. He paced through the night, beset with fear. Nothing made sense except these voices of torment.

All his walks and excursions and investigations and specimens and struggles to understand and be understood, all this tracking and chasing—it was pointless.

"I hated pheasants, the jungle, and all its inmates."

He wanted to run back to America and never think about pheasants again: "to quit, and to quit at once was all."

Wandering confused around his bedroom, he opened a closet and found a pile of cheap books, all of them penny dreadfuls. He picked up a title at random and began reading. It was an adventure story that told of a strapping hero who "choked a baboon, shot a murderous native and rescued a beautiful maiden, carrying her off through an underground tunnel."

As they made their escape, the adventurer spotted paintings on the walls. Cave paintings created many thousands of years in the past. The pair stopped, awestruck, their attention inevitably drawn to these prehistoric depictions.

Among the various images, animals, and gods, they saw what first seemed absurd: depictions of themselves, the same strapping hero and beautiful maiden. In the image, they were escaping, just as they were at that moment.

They understood that they had met before, had been lovers in previous incarnations, that they were caught in a great loop of repetitions.

Beebe tossed the novel back in the closet and grabbed another one. He read more stories of far-flung affairs, more absurd twists and last-second escapes. He felt the stories begin to calm his anxiety. He began to feel numb to the inchoate fears that had tormented him. Finally, he could see that all these books were the same, as repetitive as the fate of the escaping lovers. He was reading and rereading a single book under different covers.

He might scream in terror at absurdity, or he might laugh. The madness of life, these unlikely adventures soaked through him until his fears quieted.

He shut the book he was reading, a last compact volume of infinite repetitions, closed the closet against the pile of pages, and got back to work. He would gather pheasants, study pheasants, learn all there was to know about pheasants.

Conversations with Roosevelt

Theodore Roosevelt, hunter, genocidaire, cofounder of the Boone and Crocket Club and the Bronx Zoo, invited Beebe and Blair to his house in 1908, impressed by the young naturalists' articles for *Harper's* and books on birds. After Blair ran off with the neighbor, Roosevelt became Beebe's rock. The president wrote his friend in 1915: "My dear Beebe, Can't you come down on Friday, December 3rd, and spend the night with me?"

Roosevelt visited Beebe in South America and did his best to get his friend a flying assignment during WWI.

While he was in the service, Beebe published stories in *The Atlantic* about bombing raids and visits to the trenches. He described the tact and humor of the French he met in the hell of artillery fire.

Digging graves together, one of his French colleagues jumped in, to see, he said, if the tomb would fit. When Beebe saw trenches bombed with phosphorous, the devastating effect on human bodies reminded him of Bosch. He thought he was witnessing the creation of the earth in reverse.

Beebe was zigzagging through trenches toward the front, pressing himself against the muddy walls from time to time so medics bearing wounded men on stretchers could get past. He picked up a human scent, approaching from behind, which he described as "neither white, Negro, nor Mongolian, nor the old familiar odor of crowded Calcutta bazaars." It turned out to be a group of indigenous Canadians, who he later identified as "Algonkins and Iroquois."

He realized that he'd imagined native Americans as "bowlegged, pot-bellied fellows, ne'er-do-wells, who at best sold blankets and cheap beadwork." He was surprised to find eight good-looking men: "rangy, tall, swift of motion, and graceful in their mud-matted khaki." One of the Canadians was carrying a piece of sausage. Another had tobacco and a bottle of wine. Beebe joined them as they made their way through the trenches, eating and drinking and smoking. Beebe realized his prejudices had been dashed. When he thought of Iroquois in the future, he concluded, he would imagine these men: "athletic, wiry, virile, the menace of the German line."

Roosevelt—who himself had once expressed the belief that nine out of ten native Americans ought to be killed—thought it was the most splendid thing anyone had written about the war. But he wanted Beebe to write more about himself, put himself at the center of the story.

"Make your reader know it is you who do these things; write of your bombing with the French in Germany, of your killing the snow leopard in the Himalayas."

Roosevelt imagined Beebe devising naturalist epics, nonfiction thrillers, scientific verse. He fantasized that Beebe could describe the evolution of the modern horse, from the Pleistocene to today, in the language of Wordsworth.

Edith Roosevelt also wrote Beebe. She described her husband entertaining a baby by roaring out the chorus of "Fifteen fathoms and a dead man's chest. Yo ho ho and a bottle of rum."

A year later, Roosevelt was ill, and Beebe brought a copy of the first volume of his book on pheasants to the hospital. The former president opened it on a table and flipped through in silence, inspecting a passage and a color plate here and there. Shutting the book, he stood up, grabbed Beebe and embraced him.

"When you and I are gone and the world says, 'Let's see what did America give the world in the past, that was worthwhile,'" he said, "this will at least be worthy of holding up as the work of a creative brain and a generous gentleman."

But, Roosevelt said, I never want you to do this again. Never a book on a single subject:

"I want you to begin to think and work in generalities, in big fields of ecology. That is your future! Take the bricks and mortar which ordinary scientists shape for you, and build out of them enduring structures, based on knowledge, wisdom, and truth."

A few days later Beebe woke up at 4 a.m. in a cold sweat. After stirring in bed for fifteen minutes, he got a call informing him of Roosevelt's death. Beebe felt it as an earthquake or a volcanic eruption, something that shook the roots of his existence.

"A diamond of the first water has many facets," Beebe wrote, "and from each is directed a single direct ray of purest, white light. Theodore Roosevelt had a hundred sides, a host of interests, and whichever one was at the moment presented, sent forth a searchlight of clear, incisive relationship, which demanded in return, the best one had in one's soul to give."

Animal Life at the Front

All the lice and fleas and flies and rats, the dogs and horses and pigeons.

But then:

A hawk perched on tank tread.

A skylark soaring above the trenches—"those inconspicuous frontiers of barbarism." Crash landing in Northern France, he heard a wolf's howl in a forest.

Funny, he thought, I heard the only wolves left were in Russia. Must be on the move, like so many, driven by hunger.

A fox creeping through fresh graves in an ad hoc cemetery. Disconsolate herons in miserable marshes and swamps.

Mudhens and ducks, cowering partridges, the soft calls of evening blackbirds through "the boom and kr-rump of distant guns."

The air full of flocks of rooks and crows.

Magpie nests in leafless poplars surrounding ruined villages, farmhouses still smoking. The swans at Ypres, as persistent artillery fire turned a chateau into an old sponge.

Lying in a trench, looking up as bullets zipped by just above, snipping sprigs of trees so it rained mistletoe. Amidst that madness: a titmouse, a woodpecker, a jay, and a pair of doves sleeping peacefully.

An English sparrow landed dizzy nearby. For a second he thought it was a grenade.

4.

Upside Down

Buffon in the Trees

Back from the war, Beebe set up his first field station in Guyana. He sent reports to New York and published books titled *Jungle Night*, *Jungle Peace*, and *Edge of the Jungle*. These books expound on frogs in moonlight, army ants and leaf-cutter ants, the philosophical advantages of hammocks, the mournful tone of prisoners Beebe hears singing in the distance as he sips his evening cocktail.

"Had I sat where I was for days and for nights, my chief danger would have been demise from sheer chagrin at my inability to grasp the deeper significance of life and its earthly activities."

Returning to his love of collapsible time, he contemplates a fallen etaballi tree. He imagines it taking root as Genghis Khan set out from Mongolia. The crusades reached their height as the tree joined the canopy overhead, its leaves stretching for light. He imagines the songs of the troubadours, the voyages of Columbus, still in the future.

It was in these early seasons in the jungle that he concluded "no action or organism is separate." That insight would drive his research throughout his career, his observations of animals and attempts to understand their motivations. In Bermuda, he would track the interlocking trajectories of wind, cedars, migrating birds, tectonic and volcanic forces. He would see, with sudden shifts in scale, how these relate to the human histories he was fascinated with.

He compares leaf-cutter ants to people he'd seen in the markets of South Asia at night or "in underground streets of Peking." He imagines the ants as workers in a labor union, satisfied with "a twenty-four-hour day, no pay, no rest." Beebe marvels at the collective spirit of the ants, their lack of individualism. They are not like wasps, who hunt alone. They are an aspect of a larger organism—"somatic cells of the body politic." He remembers a Buddhist priest describing *gashang*: "a state where plants and animals were crystal-like in growth and existence." He doesn't know how to name or conceptualize the leaf-cutters' ego. It might be *Vibration*, he suggests, or *Aura*, or "Spirit of the nest." Unable to enter into their mindset, he considers the ants clothed in ignorance. After spending a week with them, he professes, he longs for despots, "for kaisers and tsars, for selfishness and crime—anything as a relief from such terrible unthinking altruism."

More inscrutable than leaf-cutter ants were the three-toed sloths—so impassive as to boggle the mind. Beebe describes himself lifting a young sloth off its mother and placing it nearby, to see if the mother will find it once she hears the calls of her offspring. He describes firing a gun near a sloth to see if it will jump. He holds up flowers and carrion to see if the sloth will react to the scent. He shakes a sleeping sloth. He places a snake nearby, waves a red cloth like a toreador, and holds the sloth underwater.

"From our human point of view sloths are degenerate; from another angle they are among the most exquisitely adapted of living beings."

(Observing Beebe waterboarding a sloth, one wonders which of them would be considered degenerate.)

"They are either a mystery or are beyond belief simple and dull; which is perhaps another way of saying that I am not able to put myself in their position and get their point of view on life."

Beebe considered this awareness of his own ignorance a chief strength. And as compared with other scientists observing sloths, he congratulates himself for his generosity. He remembers that the French polymath Georges-Louis Leclerc, aka Le Comte de Buffon, described the sloth as a rare incidence of imperfection in nature.

"One more defect," the Frenchman concluded, "and they could not have existed."

For Beebe, this was true only if you imagined the sloth in Paris, if you picture the animal hanging from a tree in the Jardin de Luxembourg, its fur encrusted with the moss of the north. But Beebe here turns the tables: he imagines "Buffon clinging upside-down to a branch of a tree in the jungle," and concludes it would not be the sloth in Paris, but Buffon in the trees, who would first drop dead.

Morbid Flux of Exquisite Bodies

Beebe hired Isabel Cooper, who had been teaching science and art in New York public schools, to work as a sketch artist at his first field station. She described this work in a series of articles for *The Atlantic*.

Cooper lists her previous experience as "assisting at the legerdemain of interior decorators . . . degrading oriental perfections to the terms of a modern rug factory," and "filling in the cracks of time with painting lessons."

Now her assignment was to record as accurately as possible the colors of animals before they were killed and shipped back to New York.

She described Guyana as having "the look of a mirage or something seen in the bevel of a mirror." She worked in what she called "tiny flowery places," where she met dragonflies "like red velvet dirigibles" and fish "with cynical silver gills."

She spent hours studying the faces of snakes, which she concluded had three characteristic expressions: "a silly pious aspect when they roll their eyes upward, a nasty crafty look when they partially submerge them in their upper jaw, and a travesty of grim early-Victorian pomposity when they look down their nose."

Lizards' backs displayed "dim, glowing, fenestrated colors," the most brilliant lined up against the deepest and dullest "in splendid climaxes of chiaroscuro." She marveled at the way these patterns on lizards' bodies would be reproduced on their faces with greater complexity or be reprised in new variations. The periwinkle whose presence on a lizard's back was barely perceptible would be "developed into tiles of blue faïence on his sculptured cheeks." A color that appeared dull and rusty on the body would soften into "velvet-black" on the throat. Gazing through a jeweler's loupe at a lizard's head, Cooper found that what she'd taken for gray and blue also contained "keels of coral," which would "flower alarmingly into cabbages of sharp turquoise around the abalone pearl of his eardrum."

Lizards had black eyes "with cuneiform patterns traced over them; and level slits of pupils between great coronas of blazing color; and dull eyes flecked through the flakes of gold like the 'eau-de-vie de Danzig' we got once in Martinique."

She painted reptiles covered in "dusty plush; embossed suède; old stippled parchment; crumpled fruit-skins . . . mould-covered marbles, or the decaying skin of Camembert cheese."

She was fascinated, most of all, by the effect on color of death. Feathers and butterfly wings retained their brilliance, she noticed, but reptile scales faded; toad skin became grizzled when preserved in alcohol. Lizards, who in life are full of personality, "sink utterly, like a person prostrated in the depths of despair." In death, dullness envelopes them with the inexorable creep of a coming shadow.

The most significant changes were in the eyes, especially of snakes: "The instant they pass, a dreadful mildew creeps up over the sparkling black pupil and the decoration of the brilliant iris, until the eye looks like a mouldering moonstone."

Her challenge was to anesthetize the snakes so their color might linger. Or even better, keep the animals alive, in captivity, so she could study them. But even captivity affected animal colors. A lizard whose blazing green body flashed in the garden became ash colored in a cage. Only when enraged did its former color flare up. Cooper watched the waves of color emerge and recede, and when death came, she noted, all color drained "in one terrible ebbing."

If people living near the field station showed up with animals, living or dead, Beebe would buy them. This scheme ensured a steady stream of specimens. At times, Cooper would be presented with an animal that was dying right then, so she rushed to capture its color as it disappeared. She watched as a blue-gray sheen fell over a brilliant boa; orange turned to purple and black turned to blue "as if millions of rainbow prisms in the scales were giving off a fine fiery mist of spectrum colors." In a few moments, it was nothing but "a horrid faded shoestring."

Cooper studied "old mossback crickets, and gold-plated bees, and topaz wasps preying on Roman-striped caterpillars; membracids with Eiffel Towers and Crystal Palaces on their foreheads, and ghoulish, gleaming beetles."

But like the reptiles, these insects, with their "papier-mâché masks and queer gossamer costumes," collapsed to colorless husks when they died.

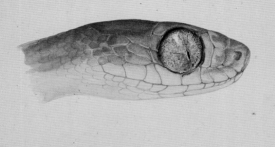

232

Imantodes cenchoa

I-ON-A-CO

The field station in Guyana had been donated by Gaylord Wilshire, a man whose faïence cheeks were framed by combed brown hair and large ears. He wore double-breasted suits and favored the bow tie. The *Los Angeles Record* described him as the possessor of "dark and lustrous French-pointed whiskers."

Born in Cincinnati to a banker invested in railroads and gas companies, Wilshire studied political economy at Harvard but dropped out after a year. In 1884 he moved to San Francisco where he worked for his brother selling scales and safes. In 1880, the brothers moved south and began buying up real estate in LA and Orange County, including the huge tract of land that would become Wilshire Boulevard.

For reasons he was never able to explain, Wilshire declared 1887 to be the year he became a socialist. He liked to play golf, he said, but preferred giving speeches.

He joined the Nationalist Club, partly to be near the club's voluptuous secretary, and ended up president of the branches in Anaheim and Fuller-ton. He even ran for Congress on the club's platform: limit the workday to eight hours, nationalize the railroads and telegraph, cut the military budget, and spend liberally on education. He believed that America's capitalists would bring about socialism by "crushing out their smaller rivals and concentrating wealth into fewer and fewer hands."

While the rich enjoyed "a wonderful conglomerate of beefsteaks, truffles, champagne, automobiles, private cars, steam yachts, golf balls, picture galleries, food and clothing for their servants, etc.," the contemporary worker— "eating tuberculous beef, drinking typhoid bacilli in his milk and fusel oil in his whiskey, and absorbing intellectual garbage through his yellow journal"— has reaped no benefits from new technology.

On the campaign trail Wilshire prophesied that unless drastic steps were taken, the economy would implode within five years. He offered to pay the Republican and Democratic candidates a dollar a minute to debate him, but neither took him up on the offer. He barely cleared a thousand votes.

He bemoaned that teaching socialist economics to the population at large was futile. Americans would never understand macroeconomics until they had no money for dinner.

The nation was adrift on the Niagara, he thought, with socialism waiting beyond the falls.

Dismally defeated after his first campaign, he vowed that the coming economic collapse would vindicate him, then married a wealthy Welshwoman and took off for the UK. When they moved back a few years later, his wife charged him with desertion and adultery. She said Wilshire "let her starve while he was reforming people."

Wilshire published a popular muckraking magazine called *Wilshire's Magazine*. He hung a large portrait of Marx above his desk. To attract readers, he held competitions where new subscribers could win gold watches or pianos. He also sold stock in gold mines in British Guiana and Colorado, promising thirty percent dividends. The Colorado mine was run by a German American who had translated *Das Kapital*. Wilshire, with the help of several prominent socialists, raised over a hundred thousand dollars with the sale of gold stock schemes.

When Beebe first traveled to Guyana in 1908, Wilshire connected him to British colonial government officials and helped him make his way into the Amazon via a network of mines and plantations run by US Americans and Europeans.

Beebe described Wilshire's socialism as "a sort of brotherly love idea, with every man earning just according to the real value of his work. No division of wealth or anything like that."

Wilshire's gold stocks failed in 1910, and a few years later he moved back to LA and bought a citrus farm. He published the last issue of his magazine in 1915. It was only four pages and he was the only writer. The great developer spent his last years trying to sell vacuum cleaners and a cure-all medical device called the I-ON-A-CO.

Looking Backward

Wilshire may have joined the Nationalist Club to be near its secretary, but his membership brought him in contact with the ideas of Edward Bellamy—the club was inspired by Bellamy's 1887 novel *Looking Backward*.

In the book, a Boston man named Julian West is interred in a stone vault in 1887 and wakes up in the year 2000 without having aged. West meets Dr. Leete, who shows him around the new world. He finds that in 2000 all businesses have been nationalized and life is enhanced by many new technologies: planes, submarines, radio, and television (showing that Bellamy, like Leonardo, had the power of prophecy—none of those technologies existed when the book was written).

Every citizen enters a national industrial army at twenty-one. Women remain at work after marriage, but leave when they have children, reentering the workforce whenever they feel like it up to age forty-five, which is the age at which everyone, male or female, enters retirement. There is no money. Everyone receives a generous yearly allowance managed by the state.

Dr. Leete explains the mystery of three generations of his family in the nineteenth century living off one grandfather's income, and there being more money in the bank every year. How did they do it?—"The art . . . of shifting the burden of one's support on the shoulders of others. The man who had accomplished this . . . was said to live on the income of his investments."

It was a clear critique of class divisions, of exploitative relations, but it was also a vision of communism without cataclysm, where the new order arrives through mechanization and monopoly, not by overthrowing anything.

Bellamy was his own first convert—he was not interested in socialism until he wrote the book. It was a massive bestseller. Through his vast readership, Bellamy could be said to have been more influential than Marx in popularizing socialist ideas.

Beebe liked to contemplate his own versions of *Looking Backward*. In his utopia, rather than retiring early or watching television, citizens of the future would be required to carry telescopes. Beebe imagined that every toothbrush would carry inside it a miniature telescope, and each citizen would have to gaze at the night sky as long as they brushed their teeth.

He imagined observatories atop every prison and church. He thought that if every king, president, congressperson, mayor, lawyer, soldier, merchant, farmer, and student would be required to spend five minutes every evening staring through an opera glass at the night sky, it "would bring the millennium as near as any of us want."

An Epic Tale, by William Beebe

"Once, in a tropical jungle, I had a mighty tree felled. Indians and convicts worked for many days before its downfall was accomplished, and after the cloud of branches, leaves, and dust had settled, a small, white moth fluttered up from the very heart of the wreckage."

How He Was

Beebe sat at his desk in the field station, and, looking around, saw a green leaf shooting out from the desk. The wood his desk was made from, he realized, was not dead and dry, but still living, and he, sitting there, was an element of its landscape. He bore this image in mind when he stepped outside to collect specimens.

The jungle was an effusion of forces so luxuriously interconnected, it was hard to know at times where one being stopped and another started. Everything was multiple, crawled on by multitudes. It was their density, their close association, that brought the world into being.

The mountains descended and the trees thickened. Vines intertwined, crept through piles of leaves, grasped trunks, dangled from branches, sprouted roots that were not only brown and green and sand colored, but lemon yellow and brick red. Roots that might have been vines reached downward into rushing streams. Mushrooms grew on lichens that grew on rising trunks that were themselves bundles of vines.

But hacking through the vines and underbrush, eventually the trees grew sparse and the air dried. The jungle gave way to desert, which soon sank under the sea. He could get up from his living desk, if he chose, and walk away. Which meant there were borders, after all, between one thing and another.

A bird nesting in a tree gripping a hunk of lava on an isolated ocean island, the songs of South Asians and descendants of enslaved Africans imprisoned in Guyana, and the scent of gin rising up from his glass as the sun sank beyond the canopy; it must represent not only a historical intersection, but a reality underwritten by the same natural forces. The jungle and the desert were aspects of the same embrace.

No action or organism is separate. The rule of brotherly love vies with a thirst for tsars and conquerors. The flush of life shines brightest in the shadow of death. These paradoxical forces ran through Beebe's belief in the emancipatory power of natural wonder. But reality could be opaque. It was easy to imagine the shift from jungle to desert was a shift between two realities. It was even easier to imagine an edge to oneself, which meant organisms and actions were separate after all.

Beebe was not ready to see the Parisian sloth, the dangling Buffon, and himself—the bridge between them—as panels in the tower of mirrors, distinct entranceways to an all-encompassing world, the only book ever written. Instead, he clung to, or he dangled upside down from, an image of himself as guide to the unknown, the one true source of awareness. He worked, he enjoyed, and he was celebrated, and as such he knew who he was. It was as deeply engrained as the march of ants.

Maybe what he didn't learn from the prisoners, from himself in the jungle, he might learn from other people of the past, from the lost, the seeking, and the hiding, the wanderers and explorers who sank beneath the horizon one after the other, like coins into a slot machine that always came up three Xs that were blanks and that were crossbones.

5.

Blunderbuss

New Species of Deep-Sea Fish

Melanonus unipennis
    the head is smaller
    the snout is longer
    the anal more numerous

Pseudoscopelus stellatus
    mouth pale, speckled with black and scarlet inside
    line is a deep groove
    overlapping fleshy flaps
    In life these meet
    the trough is open
    After death
    thick mucus
    Night green
    clear and intense
    densely speckled with black
    adumbrating the ocellus
    deep violet
    bluish-violet
    peacock blue
    emerald green and gold
    laid thinly over the black of the eyeball

The Hiss

Beebe added Ruth Rose to the field station staff in 1922. She spoke with the flat a's and elided r's of her hometown of Somerset, Massachusetts, but she'd sharpened her tongue acting on Broadway and surviving in New York, and she'd accustomed herself to circumstances further afield while driving official cars along the front lines of WWI. Beebe hired her to work as a household manager in Guyana, but when the utilities monopolist Harrison Williams put up cash for an expedition to the Galápagos on the steamship *Noma*, Beebe made sure Rose came along. She researched and planned, and as they steamed around the Pacific she improvised doggerel verses satirizing the crew. When Beebe organized his notes from the trip into an eventual book, Rose contributed key chapters.

She wrote not only tightly styled narratives of the ship's search for resources, a drama of coal versus water, but also took on the role of historical researcher. She read everything that had ever been written about the Galápagos. She read until the islands became a lookout point extending over continents and centuries, each story containing a shadow of a previous story, a rumor, a ghost.

Rose began her tale with the Incan king Tupac Yapanqui, who had turned his gaze from his vast Andean territories to face west, where the sun plummeted like a bird into the sea each night. Drawn by this vision, Yapanqui boarded an inflated sealskin and disappeared beyond the horizon, reappearing in the Incas' high-mountain capital a year later claiming to have visited the islands of the sun and moon. But his grandson was imprisoned, his empire destroyed by Pizarro, and nothing was heard of the islands until a crew of thirsty Spaniards washed up there by mistake, appalled by the islands' silence.

Legends circulated of a place of sea lions and flamingos, beaches covered in giant sea tortoises, but it wasn't easy to find. Often, navigators assumed the islands must be mobile, evading subsequent visitors by sinking into the sea to hide.

Rose devoured testimonies of the "irruption of filibusters" when Caribbean piracy entered the Pacific, accounts by the likes of Bartholomew Sharp, Lionel Wafer, Basil Ringrose, and John Coxon. She tells of the ship *Batchelor's Delight*, captained by John Cook and "on slaughter and rapine bent." Among their booty, Rose notes, were recorded "eight tons of quince marmalade" and "a stately mule." Captain Cook fell ill on the way back from their excursion into the central Pacific, and died, as is customary for sick seafarers, once the continent was in sight.

Among these pirates was an early botanist of the Galápagos, William Dampier, who Rose describes as a man whose life, full of hardship and misadventure and very little success, was spent "in the pursuit of pure knowledge."

The botanist described the Galápagos as almost completely devoid of flora. There were no herbs or grass at all; just a few "dildo trees," which, he explained, is a leafless and spiny shrub some ten feet high, as thick as a thigh, and "fit for no use, not so much as to burn."

Dampier served as navigator on a ship called the *Duke*, from which in 1708 he spotted a fire on a deserted island. Coming ashore, the crew found a man clothed in goatskin, speaking halting English. They learned he was a Scot who'd been shipwrecked for four long years. In that time, he'd gone through some kind of transfiguration—hardship and isolation had refined his being.

He'd eaten only when hunger overcame him, and slept only when exhaustion overpowered him. He'd learned to run across the rocks with such swiftness, he said, that he'd been cleared of "all gross Humours."

Eventually he conquered melancholy and carved his name—Alexander Selkirk—into the bark of a tree.

Dampier guided the *Duke* back to England three years later, with this castaway on board. Upon arrival, Dampier, after forty years at sea, dropped dead, though Rose could find no information about his remains.

Selkirk, meanwhile, hungry and penniless and seeking to sell his story, knocked at the door of a young writer named Daniel Defoe, handing him a stack of pages containing an account of his experience. Defoe, Rose tells us, looked over the manuscript and handed it back, unimpressed, "and discouraged Selkirk from further effort."

Not long after, Defoe published *Robinson Crusoe*, which became an instant bestseller, read and taught around the world to this day, while Selkirk died broke.

Rose delights in stories of buried treasure: pirate booty and Incan gold, the precursors, she explains, of recent rumors of oil on the islands. She is horrified by the notion of "oil derricks on the beaches where pirate ships once went through the unspeakably picturesque process known as careening."

The first human establishment on the Galápagos, Rose reports, was an ad hoc post office for whalers in a bay on Charles's Island still called Post Office Bay. It consisted of an anchored barrel where sailors could place letters home, and returning whaling vessels would pick them up and deliver them. These same whalers would capture Galápagos tortoises and keep them aboard, where they would stay alive for months without food and water, serving eventually to feed the crew.

"No wonder that in 1923," Rose writes, "the *Noma* expedition found but one solitary tortoise which, for all that we can assert to the contrary, may have been the last of a great race."

Rose is particularly struck by the tale of the first long-term resident of the Galápagos, which she discovered in "Captain Porter's *Journal of a Cruise.*"

It seems an Irishman named Patrick Watkins had fled an English ship to Charles Island and built for himself a squalid hut. Watkins managed to raise potatoes and pumpkins, which he exchanged with passing sailors for rum or cash. Contemporaries described him as ragged, lousy, sunburnt, and ill-natured, interested only in keeping himself drunk.

An American ship landed and deployed a sailor to procure some vegetables from Watkins, but he found the Irishman with a musket, commanding the sailor to come with him. Watkins informed the sailor, who was Black, that he would be his slave. But the American caught Watkins off guard, disarmed and bound him, threw him over his shoulder and dragged him down to his ship.

However, an English smuggling vessel sailed into the harbor at the same moment.

The English smugglers knew Watkins, were already sick of him, and seeing him bound, took him from the American and beat him, asking where he kept his cash. The Irishman led them back into the interior of the island, but gave them the slip along the way, managing to evade the English and American sailors until they left.

Watkins filed the shackles off his wrists and planned revenge. He went back to selling potatoes for rum, but now and then offered to split the rum with the visiting sailors, getting them so drunk they passed out, at which point he hid them from their crews until their ships left. Watkins forced these abandoned sailors into servitude and, in such a way, raised a crew of five men. This scraggly band managed to ambush the next batch of visiting sailors and make off with their ship.

Watkins apparently arrived in Guayaquil alone, having perhaps killed his crew of captives. There he romanced a young woman with stories of enchanted islands, and was about to set off with her back to sea when he was captured and locked up in Payta gaol, where, according to Captain Porter, "he now remains."

Rose recounts subsequent historical tales spanning the Napoleonic Wars to the taking of New Orleans, tales of sailors on desperate searches for water, sailors cooking *pastel de nopal*, and (as Beebe and Rose would later) witnessing volcanic explosions when mid-ocean mountains burned through the night, the surface of the sea littered with pumice.

After independence from Spain, one of the first acts of independent Ecuador was to colonize the islands, which had belonged to no one. Three years later the *Beagle* arrived bearing Charles Darwin, who spent five weeks in the area. The island population then was about three hundred, and it swelled and shrunk over the decades.

Through Darwin, the Galápagos spawned the theory of natural selection. Through Selkirk and Crusoe, the islands gave rise to the English novel. Rose points out references to the islands in Poe and suggests elements in the horror stories seem to be endemic to the islands. Melville described them in a story called "The Encantadas." Rose claims it's the best description of the islands ever written:

"The jackal should den in the wastes of weedy Babylon; but the Encantadas refuse to harbour even the outcasts of beasts. . . . No voice, no low, no howl is heard; the chief sound of life here is a hiss."

Fumaroles

On Easter, 1925, Beebe noticed a glow on the horizon over the largest of the Galápagos islands. He ordered the vessel to be directed that way, and soon he was crawling with difficulty over sharp stones, covering his mouth with a handkerchief, unable to stop to rest for the heat. But finally he reached the volcanic vents and was able to gaze down at the boiling lava. Retreating to the safety of the ship, Beebe and the crew moved away from shore and watched the spectacle through the night.

The next day he tried to describe what he'd seen.

Smoke gushed from a hundred holes and eventually masses of glowing lava broke through the mountain ridges. As the sun disappeared over the horizon the entire sky grew pink, then dimmed into "fiery gorgeousness." The clouds above them were the deep, felty scarlet of certain roses. And everywhere the land was "dotted and smeared with red hot lava." They thought of a great city, a fire, a battle, but then brought their minds back to what they were watching. In comparison to the sight, these similes fell away. Description, he concluded, was useless. Soon they headed back toward Panama to refuel.

The Lay of the Noma

BY RUTH ROSE, CURATOR OF RECORDS,
CATALOGUES AND LIVE ANIMALS

Two hundred miles from Panama
Cried Curtis with a whine,
And leaping into the ice Machine
Sank down into the brine.

Eighty miles from Panama
Isabel screamed, It's a hunch,
For I've stood me up, and I've lain me down
But I'm always losing my lunch.

Sixty miles from Panama
Bob Mickie roared at a stoker,
I may have to shuffle along the deck
But I always hold the joker.

Fifty miles from Panama
Sees Gilbert prepare for death.
His cigarettes are wet all through,
So he commits harikari.

Forty miles from Panama
and Ruth like a Captain's daughter
Will not be dry, when she does die,
For she sleeps under water.

Thirty miles from Panama
And Frobisher (ever a cynic)
Leaps off the stern and becomes an intern
In the mermaid's dental clinic.

Ten little miles from Panama
With Beebe scanning the blue,
He slips from the mast, falls into the funnel,
And promptly dies of the flu.

There's Harrison and the Captain left,
Two aged, tottering tars,
But they've lost their way, for they cannot tell
The sun and moon from the stars.

So ends my verse and I might do worse
Than to warn you off a yacht,
Don't go to sea, where e'er you be
But die in a vacant lot.

A Ride with the Shipwrecked Sailor

A year after the expedition, Beebe was cabbing through New York City and began chatting with the driver. He was a Norwegian immigrant to East Harlem named Red Christensen, who said he used to be a sailor. Beebe mentioned his trip to the Galápagos, and Christensen said he too had been to those isolated islands.

Twenty years ago, he said, he was on a Norwegian ship called the *Alexandria* en route from New South Wales to Panama, when six hundred miles out in the Pacific they hit an idle spot and stayed still "as a painted ship upon a painted ocean."

They strayed and attempted to get back on course for three months, running completely out of food and water. The twenty-man crew divided in two and climbed into a pair of lifeboats and began to row. The lifeboats were soon separated. Christensen remembered watching the other disappear from view, never to be seen again. Christensen and his mates rowed for seventeen days, and finally found land on the Galápagos.

The men killed a few giant tortoises, drank their blood, and ate their meat. But one of Christensen's mates, a man named Fred Jeffs, began to fade. Christensen knelt by him and moistened his lips with seawater.

Jeffs said: "Red, I'm done for. If you get out of this, see my family knows."

Christensen vowed to do so, and survived—they were found after three months by a Chilean vessel sent to search for them—but he'd been unable to fulfill his promise, as he had no information about Jeffs's family.

Beebe suggested Christensen broadcast his story on the radio, and on a Tuesday night he went to the studio at WEAF and told his tale on the air.

It so happened that Jeffs's sister, now going by the name of Mrs. Henry T. Claridge, was listening from her home in Queens Village, Long Island, and she phoned in to the studio and spoke to Christensen, who promised to come visit his shipmate's relation at her home.

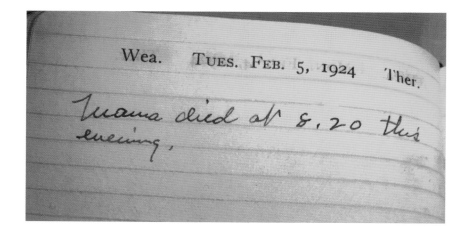

Thomson, Keating, Fitzgerald, and Flower

Beebe's next sea adventure was aboard a yacht called the *Arcturus*. Again they would sail around the Pacific. Beebe brought along a documentary filmmaker, Ernest Shoedsack, aka Shorty, who had just completed a film about a Pacific island and was anxious for more experience. Ruth Rose took a liking to Shorty Shoedsack, and Beebe was crestfallen. He wrote in coded messages in his journal that he would have to stop flirting with Rose. Before she and Shoedsack went off together, Rose wrote an article for the *New York Times* about her final expedition with Beebe.

The article tells the story of Cocos, a tiny and remote Pacific island that over the centuries had appeared on maps, disappeared, then appeared again. Strong crosscurrents made the island difficult to approach, so it was still hardly surveyed and not easy to locate precisely. But it was mired in legend— mostly surrounding treasure that had been hidden away there by sailors rioting in the vast expanse of the Pacific.

Again the legend begins in Peru. During the war of independence, wealthy citizens gathered their valuables to the port of Lima, hoping to hide them in an English ship called the *Mary Dear*. The ship was loaded with jewelry and money as well as the stash of gold held by the Catholic Church. But the English crew of the *Mary Dear* promptly beat the well-off Limeños with clubs and hauled up anchor, setting out to sea. The legend held that they made their way to the Cocos, where they hid treasure worth some twelve million pounds. Soon, though, a Peruvian vessel caught up with them and shot every Englishman on board except two, who were ordered to act as guides back to the treasure. Before the Peruvians could escort their captives back to Cocos, the two captives escaped and swam to a nearby whaling ship whose crew stowed them in barrels below deck.

One of the two stowaways deserted the whaling ship in Hawaii and dropped out of the story. But the other, called Thomson, eventually resurfaced as a member of the crew of the great pirate Benito Bonito, who also used the isolated Cocos as a safe. When Bonito's ship was captured in the late 1830s, the captain killed himself and the crew were executed—except Thomson, who once again managed to escape. He reappeared in the Caribbean in 1844 and told his story to a sailor from Newfoundland named Keating, then promptly disappeared.

Following instructions from Thomson, Keating put together an expedition and sailed around South America into the Pacific to locate the island. He found the treasure, but his crew wanted a larger share of it and attempted mutiny. He plied them with rum and snuck off into the night with another associate to carry as much booty as they could by themselves. Keating claimed his associate drowned at sea, while he somehow made it back to Newfoundland with gold ingots worth thirteen hundred pounds. On his deathbed Keating shared his story with a Canadian named Fitzgerald, remembering landmarks on the island—*walk a hundred paces north from the cove and you'll find a large flat stone on the face of a cliff. Push the stone and it will revolve, opening an entrance to the cave where the treasure lies.*

Fitzgerald never made it to Cocos as far as we know, but a young friend of Keating finally made the trip herself many years later. She too was unsuccessful. Only a sailor named Bob Flower managed to get his hands on something, when he lost his footing, fell into a ravine, and found himself clutching a gold crucifix.

Rose, Beebe, and the *Arcturus* crew spent ten days on Cocos. They found it enveloped in rain clouds, lush with hibiscus and tree ferns, and surrounded by leaping dolphins. They made no efforts to locate any buried treasure, preferring to helmet dive in the clear water of the bay or identify the birds and butterflies of the jungle. Scrambling back to the coast after one such excursion they slipped and fell into a freshly dug hole, most likely the work of someone still on the hunt.

The Pirate's Den

Also on board the *Arcturus* was a New York restaurateur and cartoonist named Don Dickerman. An old friend of Beebe's, Dickerman was hired as a deck hand but began sketching specimens found over the course of the expedition and was later promoted to staff artist.

As a youth Dickerman had worked as a "manmangling human gorilla" at county fairs in Maine. He showed up at art school in the Village wearing knee boots and an old buccaneer's hat and never abandoned the style.

After his voyage on the *Arcturus*, he opened a bar on Sheridan Square called the Pirate's Den.

Theodore Seuss Geisel, who would go on to write *Cat in the Hat* and *Horton Hears a Hoo*, had just sold his first cartoon to the *Saturday Evening Post*. He used the money to rent a place upstairs from the Pirate's Den, where he described playing polo with rats in the kitchen.

Inside the Pirate's Den the walls were hung with cutlasses, blunderbusses, and ships' bells. A coffin hung outside served as a signboard. Customers entered down a gangplank to find Dickerman—standing six foot six and dressed in his buccaneer's hat and boots—with a live macaw he claimed was a hundred years old, who continuously shouted "Hello!"

The waiters were also dressed like swashbuckling pirates, with eye-patches and earrings.

Occasionally they acted out sword fights and scenes from *Treasure Island*, reciting dialogue rife with pirate slang.

During Prohibition Dickerman employed a rum runner named Pickle Puss Armstrong, who also swept up the broken glass after bottle throwing competitions.

One visitor described the mostly male crowd as "fearsome looking except for their mild eyes and blameless mouths."

6.

Falling

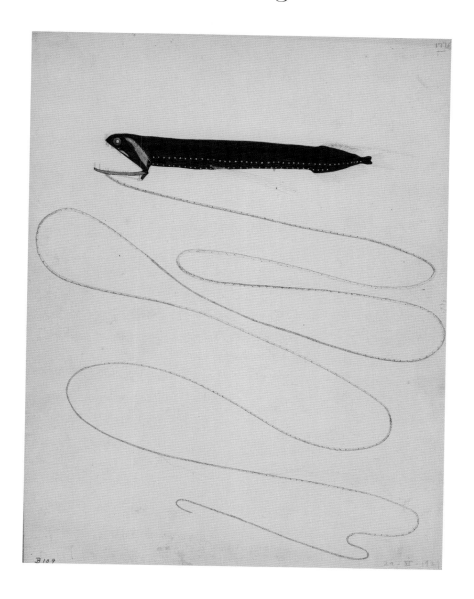

New Species of Deep-Sea Fish

Parabrotula dentiens
    no apparent division
    except the anus
    well developed, long and slant

Chaenophryne crossotus
    Snout
    and blunt
    peduncle
    on each ramus
    pairs of vomerine
    half of the lower lip
    rises up the deep trough
    a brown inner core
    quickly into the oval
    arises a pair of black spheres
    notch and flaring
    from which springs a tuft of seven tender, thread-like white tentacles

The Pond Bureau

In 1856, eighteen-year-old James B. Pond ran away from home on the Wisconsin prairie to join John Brown's band in Bleeding Kansas. After Brown was hanged in Virginia, Pond went looking for gold in Colorado, but he was back in Kansas during the Civil War. In Lawrence and Baxter Springs, he fought Quantrill's Raiders, including the young Jesse James, barely escaping with his life.

After the war he drifted again, heading west.

In Salt Lake City he met Anna Eliza Young, nineteenth wife of Brigham, and when she bolted from the family, Pond arranged speaking engagements for her in New York and Boston and took a cut. This matter of booking speakers turned out to be good business, and he started the Pond Bureau to arrange tours for writers and entertainers and explorers, traveling with Mark Twain and Booker T. Washington and Henry Ward Beecher.

Two days after Christmas, 1930, the Bureau (now run by Pond Jr.) held its annual gala at the Hotel Astor. Guests included Arctic explorer Captain Robert A. Bartlett; Sailendra Nath Ghose, "Leader of the Movement in the United States for the National Independence of India;" Carola Goya, whose "charming Spanish dances have captivated New York;" De Wolf Hopper, of whom "there is no need to explain;" Gene Lamb, "Explorer of Tibet and personal friend of the living Buddha;" contralto Gloria La Vey; Irish poet George A. Russel; Margaret Sanger, "International champion of birth control;" prison doctor Amos O. Squire; and the "mastermind of magic" Harlan Tarbell.

Also among the guests were Dr. William Beebe, "who has recently abandoned the depths of the jungle for the depths of the ocean," and Gloria Hollister, "one of America's leading women scientists."

Between Expeditions

Beebe and Hollister went to Nonsuch together to set up the field station, scout locations, and perform a series of helmet dives. Later, they took a month to sail around the Caribbean, identifying fish, assessing bays and reefs, idling in the ports of Barbuda, Martinique, St. Kitts.

On San Salvador island they got dressed up in evening clothes and climbed down the ladder to port to go dancing. They stayed out all night, and when the naval officer came to invite them for lunch the next day, they were too hungover to get out of bed.

That night, Hollister wrote, the rain fell like shiny new dimes.

Hollister smoked Lucky Strikes and was happy to find some in Havana, where she and Beebe went to see "Be Mine, Tonight," which Beebe called "a good singing movie." Never having encountered subtitles before, he was scandalized to see "Spanish explanatory captions" printed *on* the film.

After the movie they went to the Club Madrid. Waiting around for the cabaret number to start, an American woman approached Beebe and told him she'd seen him lecture in San Francisco.

Beebe had drunk many daiquiris already and was in the mood to chat. They sat at a table at the edge of the dance floor. Finally the band took their positions, picked up their instruments, and began to play the intro to a mambo, nice and slow. The dance floor was empty, and the crowd waited for the music to heat up.

A shout of fright from across the hall distracted Beebe from his talk with the San Franciscan.

Something began moving on the floorboards. A large tarantula was making its way across the dance floor toward one of the tables.

Amid more screams, those seated nearby stood up and moved away.

With Beebe still seated next to his American admirer, Hollister rose calmly from her chair, grabbed a napkin, and picked up the spider.

A waiter followed her outside, where she carried the enwrapped tarantula. She set it down and let it crawl off into the night. The waiter said there were hundreds of tarantulas, just like that one, living in the holes in the ground surrounding the club.

Hollister went back inside and grabbed Beebe, and they danced until 3 a.m.

They anchored in Chatham Bay, a glassy shelter on the coast of a rock jutting from the sea near Grenada. The map identified it as Medusa Island.

There was a village on the back of the hill, but mostly they had the bay to themselves. After a few days swimming and inspecting shells, they went ashore to have a look around. At the top of highest point of the island they came across some old masonry and a cannon. They sat to scan the horizon, wondering what could be seen from this lookout point, when an islander approached, accompanied by his young daughter.

"Go on, Priscilla, make friends with the lady."

Hollister reached out and shook the girl's hand. Her father introduced himself as Immanuel Stewart.

Beebe asked about the cannon, and Stewart said it had been built by Queen Victoria to defend against American slave raiders after the English outlawed slavery. The Americans used to abduct fishermen like himself and sell them into bondage in Alabama. Many had disappeared beyond the horizon.

Beebe and Hollister listened to this story and bought a dozen loggerhead turtle eggs from Stewart and his daughter. After eating the eggs, the two American scientists were alone up the hill from the bay:

"The night closed down and the half-moon shone and the Southern Cross hung on the hillside and our last evening in Chatham Bay was a perfect one," Beebe wrote, while Hollister's mind was full of ideas about Black Caribbeans. The mix of African and European, she thought, created "a superior race."

Slave raiders, distant powers jostling for advantage as Black Caribbeans disappear beyond the horizon—the story impressed itself on the imaginations of Beebe and Hollister, who both wrote about it at length in their diaries.

Afterward, in the years to come, Immanuel Stewart and his daughter Priscilla would reappear in the two naturalists' memories of that season—a basket of turtle eggs under a half moon and the Southern Cross, the perfect beauty of the bay, so peaceful except for the lone cannon, that record of abductions punctuating the silhouette of Medusa Island.

William Beebe Esq.
Tropical Research Station
of the
New York Zoological Society
Kartabo
British Guiana

South America

DUNSANY CASTLE.
Co. MEATH.

P.O. & TELEGRAPH.
DUNSANY.

STATION DRUMREE.
MEATH RY.

Feb: 19th 1928

My dear Beebe
        I am shortly going
to look in at the New York
Natural History Museum
to see if matrimony
and fame and eight
years have changed
you.   I sail on March 7th

Falling

Before the deepest dives, Beebe returned to the UK.

He visited A. A. Milne, who had tea brought to the garden where they sat between sculptures of Pooh and Eeyore. He corresponded with Kipling, who accurately predicted a future where submersible drones would beam images of the deep to our living rooms, and he received fan mail from Arthur Conan Doyle, who wondered if Beebe had found evidence of Atlantis. But of all these rarified writers, the one he corresponded with most regularly was an Irish aristocrat named Edward John Moreton Drax Plunkett.

Lord Dunsany, as he was known, was embraced by Yeats early in his career, but later disowned. From his twelfth-century castle in County Meath, he dashed off stories of centaurs and jewel thieves in the lands of Ag and Snood, of spider-idols, the temple of Moung-ga-ling, of endangered daughters who escape great dangers only to have platitudes worsted on their tea cozies. Dunsany wrote tributes to the idol Chu-bu, once a god in a temple but now on a mantel somewhere, whose miracles are reduced to helping his possessor at bridge; and to the merchant Thomas Shap, who dreamed himself King of Larkar, drifting slowly across imagination's threshold until he forgot the train, and his shop, and London, and remained in bed:

"Even as the firm found fault with him his fancy watched the yaks."

Dunsany hosted Beebe in his castle in Ireland, and Beebe took Dunsany to the Natural History Museum when he visited New York. On seeing a photograph of a four-thousand-year-old redwood, the fantasist imagined being "big enough to eat it like asparagus . . . to pluck it up, put some sauce on it, dip it in a geyser and eat the foliage."

While on hunting trips to North Africa, Dunsany enjoyed pulling out a quill pen and writing to Beebe, covering small cream-colored sheets with elaborate and oversized script:

What wonders
have you brought to
light from the
annals of tiny peoples
that gnaw the stems
of flowers?

Dunsany wrote about hunting gryphon, marking his return address as simply *The Sahara*. He described chasing a rare antelope called the monflor, with "his goat's beard, his stag's body, his monstrous horns, his winged ways." He concluded with a flourish:

The back valleys are full of
images that the red rocks have
made by themselves, statues of
demons and idols waiting for
ages to be worshipped
      Yours ever
      Dunsany

Not to be outdone, Beebe assured that his exploits could take place only beyond the imagination, for they "pale before ink and sicken under attempted chronicle." He wrote of workdays lasting from dawn to midnight, of discovering Dutch hatchets on an uninhabited island, the remains of a sunken ship. Dunsany delighted in these scenes and suggested the two of them travel together and collaborate. Beebe would write "on the wonders of the world that is," while Dunsany would describe "the world that isn't":

Of course
you would have to be
scientifically accurate in

everything you said,

as you would otherwise be trespassing on my

shore of the entertainment.

Both were, in their way, children who remained grafted to their early dreams. Like Shap eschewing humdrum London for the wonders of Larkar, Beebe and Dunsany shared a disdain for a mundane world that both, by luck, by birth, by tricks of fate, had largely avoided. Dunsany, author of *The Book of Wonder*, aged into a reactionary ranter, a great hater of table salt and furniture polish. While Beebe, before he left Guyana, wrote that the only creatures whose dignity he admired were the black buzzards flying high overhead. As for the humans, the colonial governor had so impressed him with his "slobbered shirt" and "banalities in cockney" that the scientist longed "to go to the slaughterhouse and feed on offal."

Dunsany's stories lacked a truly prophetic quality—they were mere games and trifles. One exception, perhaps, is the story of the master thief Slith, who stole a box of the greatest poems in the universe and, to evade capture, leapt off the world and began to fall, the box of poems still in his grasp. He continued to fall through all points in time, so that wherever we are, his falling accompanies us.

Songs of shipwrecked sailors, world-making epics, enchanted gossip from the back of the market, mind-melting verses of subtle insight—we will never know what's in that box, and its distance from us is a gauge of our present.

Slith is falling and falling still, Dunsany writes, "through the unreverberate blackness of the abyss."

7.

The Deepest Dives

1930

The first bathysphere dives occurred as the shocks of the Great Depression swept the United States. Thousands of banks closed and Hooverville shanties sprang up, quickly infected with TB. A terrible drought baked the Great Plains. The soil grew so dry that it cracked and the dust blew around in vast dark clouds.

Back in New York, the shiny top of the Chrysler building was finally complete. The Empire State and the George Washington Bridge were underway.

Mickey Mouse debuted in January, Betty Boop in August.

It was the year that Haile Selassie was crowned Emperor of Ethiopia, Constantinople was renamed Istanbul, and Stalin began collectivizing farms in the Soviet Union. Gandhi began the Salt March from Sabarmati to Dandi, his first act in the campaign of disobedience that drove the English from India. By the end of the year revolution erupted in Spain.

In March a novice astronomer discovered Pluto. And in August a huge meteor crashed deep in the Amazon—an explosion thousands of times larger than the mushroom clouds that would bloom over Japan.

Nonsuch Days and Nights

They sailed to Bermuda with one hundred and ninety-six large cases of freight and a mountain of cabin luggage and were taken to Nonsuch in two small boats. After arriving back to the island, Hollister wrote that she felt born again. She and Beebe revisited the caves on the north side of Nonsuch and walked through "the wild sweet alyssum grains as tall as the dead, storm-battered trees."

In the evenings, she threw on scarlet and blue pajamas and went to dinner on a visiting yacht, whose owner had spent seventeen years designing it for perfect comfort. After dinner, they caught squid with a lantern.

Invitations requesting their presence arrived from Vice Admiral Sir Cyril and Lady Fuller, from His Excellency the Governor and Lady Bols, even from His Royal Highness Prince George.

Hollister and Beebe donned formalwear and headed into Hamilton to dance.

Other nights they stayed together at the field station and Beebe read to her from his books of Yeats and Kipling.

They explored in a boat called the *Skink*, and made lists of deep-sea fish. The wind rose and cut the telephone lines, and they were incommunicado on the island for days. A howling gale brought downpours of rain.

Beebe wrote in code: *G was with me last night and tonight.*

Hollister noted she had worked all day in the lab.

When the winds calmed, they were back on the *Skink*. Hollister donned the diving helmet and lowered herself into the ocean. She climbed down the chain ladder and stared into the blue-black emptiness below her. The only light came from a drifting moon-jellyfish. The momentum of the boat caused the ladder to angle, and Hollister struggled to keep her body straight. Then, from out of the "blackness without form" emerged an island—not an island but an almost-island, a submerged peak covered in brain coral and sea ferns and enormous fish. With one foot hanging off the bottom rung of the ladder, she stretched as far as she could, hoping to touch the coral with her toe.

New Species of Deep-Sea Fish

Chirostomias lucidimanus
    its small understudy companion
    blue-black, elongate, and somewhat compressed
    an ever-thinning mass of scattered spots and dots
    a single muscle at the tip of the bulb

Omosudis lowi
    on top of the brain
    in front of the anal
    iris is solid silver
    not a particle of bone
    except for a faint trace
    narrowing as they extend
    needle tips actually touch
    flaring, winglike, superior

Saccopharynx harrisoni
    this is sharp and the profile
    slender and curves up
    undoubted vision
    specialized, luminous
    pink, deepening to blood
    by rounded, raised rims
    separated by a septum
    exterior bounding
    a bluish white luminous substance

a single pink tentacle

an elongate spindle with a tiny bead

opening and closing

large, half-digested

faint, colorless glow

I drew out

being wrinkle

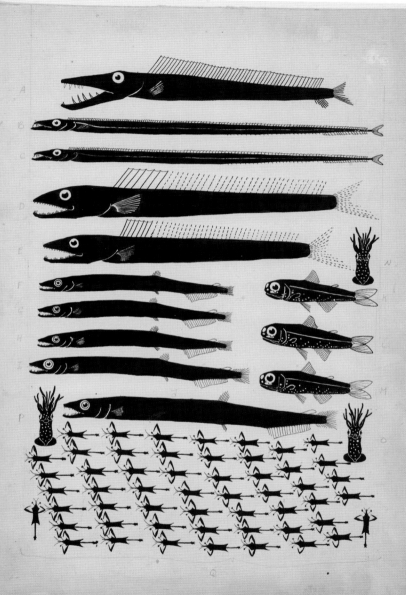

Across the Looking Glass

Beebe begins his book about the bathysphere dives, *Half Mile Down*, by describing several shallow dives over the course of delightful days and afternoons, wandering a few fathoms below the surface.

Seawater is our original home, he says. We can feel it in the lightness and grace when we move through it, effortlessly letting go. But to enter the sea now is not a return to an eternal past. The sea has a history just as we do, measured in part by its saltiness. The oceans were once fresh, and become saltier as minerals from shorelines and living creatures dissolve. So, even though constantly sweetened by rain and rivers, Beebe says, "today the ocean is very slightly saltier than it was yesterday."

While sea creatures' systems are open, freely exchanging with the environment as water flows through them, ours are not. Sea water is now three times as salty as our bodies. So we're not returning to our ancestral home, but to a new place, where things have moved on without us. It requires all our ingenuity to sink back in.

But unlike on land, Beebe points out, nothing that moves fears us. So "we are made to feel at home."

Crossing the reflective surface everything is different. What you saw above—a flat surface like the moon—becomes a living organism of brilliant colors and delicate shapes, unimaginable from the other side.

At first he was content to submerge himself a few feet, then a few fathoms, stretching his toe like Hollister for the almost island. But even these brief submersions changed the world and his place in it.

"I knew that I had added thousands upon thousands of wonderful miles to my possible joy of earthly life."

Once he rids himself of fears—of sharks and octopuses and barracudas, all the things conjured to terrify children—he is free. Tellingly, he calls this new habitat "a newly conquered realm"—conquest being nothing more than a perch from which to observe in relative comfort. But "after you have made a dozen descents," he says, "you will wish to do something more than stand amazed."

And here he composes a litany of bourgeois delights that can be enjoyed undersea: write on waterproof paper, shoot film, paint with oils while politely brushing aside little fish, or "shoot what particular fish you wish with barbed arrows of brass wire."

Though, he, an old hand, now prefers dynamite.

The denizen of the "kingdom of the helmet" may also engage in gardening: "choose some beautiful slope or reef grotto and with a hatchet chop and pry off coral boulders and waving purple sea-plumes and golden sea-fans and great parti-colored anemones."

These dispatches to his readers were as exotic as life with robots and flying saucers, and his familiarity with them was the mark of his achievement. It was one thing to get there, it was another to be no longer struck by it.

He knows he is accustomed to the subaquatic world, he says, when he no longer thinks of water as *wet*.

He had been in such a state some years ago, floating in his helmet in a bay in Haiti, comfortably gazing at the reef and the coral and countless colorful creatures, when he came to the edge of a drop-off. His luxury slipped away as he looked into the deep water, felt the darkness pulling him in, and realized his destiny was down.

Dive 30

Weather fair, light southerly breeze, and long low swell.

Left Nonsuch 6.45 a.m.

Arrived at *Ready* at Darrel and Meyer Wharf at 7 a.m.

7.30 a.m.	Left St. George's with tug *Powerful* towing; motorboat *Gregory* aft.
7.50	Out through Town Cut.
	Gadgets fitted inside of bathysphere in preparation for dive.
9.15	Door and wing-bolt prepared, cleaned, sand-papered, and white lead put on door threads.
9.20	Small generator started. Chemicals put in.
9.22	Position calculated to be 32° 14′ 40″ N. Lat.; 64° 35′ 40″ W. Long., 6 1/2 miles
	South-by-East of Nonsuch Island.
9.25	Beebe and Barton in bathysphere, Beebe with ear-phones and mouth-piece.
9.29	Door in position and nuts screwed on.
	(1700 lbs on oxygen left tank. Door in position)
9.32	Blower turned on. Hammering nuts home.
9.37	Wing-bolt going on. Oxygen turned on and set at 1 liter per minute.
9.40	Watching swells, ready to lift bathysphere during a calm.

The Bohemian Club

Beebe began as a birder, listing and classifying birds. He crept and peered and shot, collected birds in bags, wrote books and articles about birds. After his Himalayan waylay in the tunnel of absurdity, he produced *Pheasants: Their Lives and Homes.* Later there was *Ontogeny of the White Ibis, Home Life of the Bat Falcon,* and simply, *The Bird.*

For an early article on birdwatching in Brazil, he set himself up in a reclined chair with his notebook and gun at hand, "a *de-luxe* position," as he called it, from which to observe the birds that gathered in a wild cinnamon tree above him. He counted and named specimens—tinamous, toucans, yellow-rumped caciques—while knocking them dead with lead pellets. Later he dug up a bit of earth from beneath the chair and cataloged everything in it.

It was then, while killing and counting, that he had his early thoughts on vision. It was not the number of species that mattered, but how they all fit together, and to sense that, you had to feel around at the edges of things, above and below things, into the immaterial meaning of things. He surmised that insights did not spring from what you looked straight at, but what you half-sensed at the periphery. He called this *the oblique glance.* He cultivated such dispersed attention and sought connections rather than analysis: *no action or organism is separate.* This was what led to dynamic thought, not statistics. He could imagine nothing worse than to be consigned to inspect the world for purely quantifiable ends.

Beebe opens *Half Mile Down* with a vision of heaven and hell. In one direction lay utopian dreams of a republic driven by toothbrush-telescopes, of priests and prisoners united in mind-opening night views of starry skies and gaseous nebulae, the march of days and years charmed by the cyclical crossing of comets. In the other direction lay the reductive thinking of science.

Beebe quotes his friend William Morton Wheeler, who imagines dying and crossing the Styx to find himself, like all professional biologists, "condemned to keep on trying to solve problems."

Pluto, Wheeler thought, or whoever he found ruling the underworld, would no doubt sentence him to spend eternity identifying specimens, while amateurs, "who have not been damned professors," roam and explore, frolicking among "fragrant asphodels of the Elysian meadows, netting gorgeous, ghostly butterflies until the end of time."

Beebe then meditates on a statue he'd seen at the Bohemian Club in San Francisco—"The First Wonderer"—depicting a hairy early human squatting and, one supposes, wondering. He imagines this wonderer as the first of us free of blind need and terror. Having eaten and slept and checked for predators, stepping out of the cave simply to explore, this fortunate individual gets swept up in bare astonishment at the planet, basking in the color and texture of its multiplicity, all its changes and densities and pulsations. One imagines the sun erasing the cave's gloom as it had blanked out Beebe's mind when he emerged from his first deep dive in the bathysphere.

A birder and biologist, accustomed to the entanglements of the jungle, now turns his attention to the sea and is restored to this wonderer's condition.

Once encountered, he says, the vividness and strangeness of the subaquatic world can never be forgotten. The shock of it drives him from the realm of the strict naturalist. He can never again be a melancholy classifier and damned professor.

Water, after all, is what draws the borders of life. It returns us to our own transience and mortality. As long as there is a zone of the planet where water is neither boiling nor freezing, he says, we can find our way through the eighty or so years allotted to us, we can experience all the vicissitudes of life, the exaltations and disappointments, the daily grind of eat-breathe-sleep.

See the sun: a burning ball of metallic vapor; and the moon: cold, dead, airless, and waterless. It's as if we're gazing at our own planet in the heat of youth and quietude of old age. Our lives, those tangled balls of pettiness driven by egotism, dissolve over cool plains of stone.

"Like the monk's coffin in his cell," he says, "the ghastly cold of the poles foreshadows an ultimate doom."

Already on the other side of transformation, even with his visions of coffins and moribund planets, he is in a better place. He's been delivered from counting grubs in hell by immersion in bittersweet pinks and carnelian reds, at play among mucousy fangs and glowing tentacles. But for all his words, his crossing renders him inarticulate. What he's seen is untransferable. Beebe knows that much of what he describes and records will be entered into the history of science, but the true impact of the experience will follow him into the oblivion from which it came.

5"

150 fm Sel.

B-860   Else Bostelmann

Dropping

surface	Same puckered ceiling. 2 inch Flyingfish.
	Red sponges on side of *Ready*.
	Can see shell and regular reef growth on hull.
20 ft	Rays of light
	like those coming through cathedral
	windows. Looking up, can see last of the hull
	of *Ready*.
100	2 little fry, 2 inches long near lower edge of glass.
170	Many tiny Copepods, look like little
	silver motes.
260	Getting bluish-green rapidly.
300	Humidity 54%; Temperature 90°;
	Barometer 77, same as at surface.
320	Perfect string of Siphonophores.
360	Silver fry 1 inch long going past; several roundish
	fish, Psenes.
400	Silvery brown Squid went past, 2 inches long.
440	Another silvery Squid same size as before.
500	A dark fish went past swimming up. Think
	there will be no twist in telephone cable.
	I will risk it. Let us go down.

Of Submersion and Submersibles

Beebe imagines a time before the sea was explored, when it was a bottomless, unknown realm populated by *vengeful incomprehensible powers* and *insatiable Things.*

His history of sea exploration begins with Necho II, who ruled Egypt around 600 BCE. Necho sent a fleet of Phoenicians down the Red Sea. They stopped here and there to sow and harvest wheat before going on. Three years later they reappeared from the west, having passed through the pillars of Hercules at the mouth of the Mediterranean. No one, as far as he knows, repeated this trip until the sixteenth century. He lists Carthaginian mariners and other early sailors, before switching axes and plunging beneath the water's surface:

"The study of life under sea holds, at present, the heart of my mental interest, and the physical means of getting at my subject has taxed everything of ingenuity I could bring to bear."

Here begins Beebe's history of diving, with a contemplation of animals like frogs, penguins, and dolphins that are able to dive without apparatus. Then he considers the ingenuity of whirligig beetles and the larvae of the drone fly:

"When I have descended the diving ladder in a helmet and clamber about several fathoms down with the air coming to me through the hollow rubber hose, I am only a poor imitation of a rat-tailed maggot."

He describes a kind of spider that builds homes in bubbles of air beneath the surface, expelling waste in tinier bubbles pushed out through an opening that the spider sews shut. The spider brings a mate into its home and soon hangs fertilized eggs from the ceiling "like strings of onions and peppers from a peasant hut."

He attributes the earliest concerted human dives to pearl divers, and also wonders at their capacious lungs. He scolds Ibn Battuta for claiming to have been underwater for more than two hours. Though he prefers not to doubt Thucydides' account of the military dives during the battle of Syracuse, when the Athenians sawed through cords beneath huge vessels, by attributing to the Greeks the use of diving helmets.

He tells stories of Mark Antony sending a squad of divers to place fish on hooks in order to impress Cleopatra, and he spends several pages telling the stories of Alexander of Macedonia, that great submarine adventurer, who witnessed a creature so huge it took three days to pass by.

In a chapter on "Proto-Bathyspheres," Beebe describes the history of diving technology: from leather helmets cut with eyeholes and a breathing tube to an enormous upturned sixteenth-century lead-lipped pot from Spain that rested on planks set with candles. A seventeenth-century "aquatic corselet" was superseded by a thirty-foot rawhide construction supported on iron tubes. An Italian named Lorini devised a diving bell from a square wooden box, with a window tied to the diver with ropes made of hemp. Such contraptions were used to scavenge for sunken treasure or to smuggle—one was intended to rescue Napoleon from Sta. Helena.

A Dutch engineer devised a submarine called the Thunderbolt of the Sea, intended to reach the East Indies in six weeks. But it ended its brief career as a carnival attraction, "as though it were a bearded lady or a two-headed calf." The fate of the bathysphere would be similar.

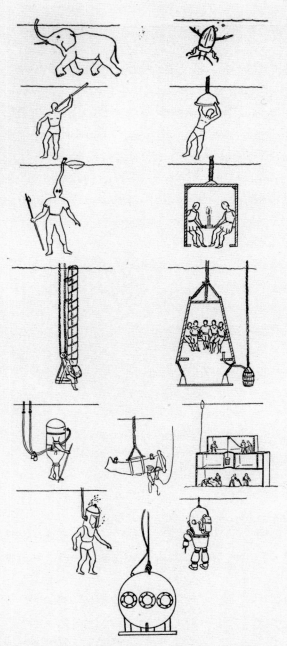

Fig. 20. The Evolution of Human Diving. The left column shows the various attempts at drawing air down from above to the diver, from the elephant's trunk to the modern helmet and hose. The right column illustrates the gradual attainment of success in actually conveying a supply of air beneath the surface. The water beetle does this, and points the way, from the inverted vase of Aristotle to the self-contained bathysphere.

Going Down

587 ft   Beam on, fan running slowly.

Many little Copepods.

Water filled with tiny creatures, like a dust cloud.

Beam off.

600   Atmosphere fine, no need of handkerchief

on mouth.

650   Water dark, rich blue.

670   First little flashes, much lower than usual.

720   Walls very cold. Humidity 45%.

740   Several sparks, close together, from some creature.

800   Barometer reading 76.

Big single light.

Beam turned on.

Thousands of tiny creatures as we descend,

chiefly Copepods.

20 Pteropods, long tubular kind. Creseis.

Larval fish.

Jellyfish one inch across.

Beam turns into pale turquoise where it

disappears at farthest end.

Many strings of salpa-like animals.

1 Leptocephalus, 3 inch, not very deep,

1 larval fish, one-inch.

2 big Coryphaena.

Beam off.

900   1400 lbs pressure in number one oxygen tank.

920   4-inch fish with 6 bluish-white lights along side.

950	Worms—no, they are Round-mouths. Light colored ones.
	Water blackish-blue, a dull color.
1000	Pteropods. Then a brilliant flash appears and goes out.
1050	12 flashes going on and off.
	Large dark body passing.
	Squid or fish?
1100	3 fishes went past, appeared out of darkness.

3 full-sized Argyropelecus swimming

upright and together.

Larval fish.

Whole string of luminescence spread out like

net work.

Many Copepods and Sagitta, all very active in beam.

Nothing very large. Jellyfish very luminous from food.

First eel, lighted up from beam. Serrivomer?

8 inches long, did not go into beam.

Something large up close to edge of light,

a very deep fish.

4-inch Leptocephalus, not deep, swimming

obliquely upward.

Small Siphonophore and Pyrosoma, 1 foot long with

no light.

Beam turned out.

The Wastes

When Beebe was a boy in 1880s New Jersey, he went out kite-flying. The wind rose, the kite went up, and as it flew higher Beebe could feel the pull of the wind. Watching the colored paper in the sky, a sudden fear came over him. He saw the kite sailing all alone through the vastness of space. He shivered when he felt the pull of the kite string now. He imagined he might be lifted off the ground and float away, speeding into the sky, never to return. He would float alone in the vacuum, a denizen of the great emptiness.

Before submerging in the bathysphere, he pictured the deep sea as only sparsely inhabited. The DTR staff had dredged and trawled and brought up creatures from the deep, but the changes in pressure caused most of them to explode. Often they pulled up nothing but shards of delicate tissue and a few dead fish. It was dark down there, and very cold.

Now they were to descend further than the reach of the sun, deep into the blue-black world he had tasted on earlier dives. He was about to see the culmination of his childhood fantasy: to enter a hostile desert of water, remote as deep space.

The bathysphere dropped, and Beebe looked up at the surface as the keel of the boat disappeared from view. It was their last visible link to the world above. In his four-foot ball with a seasick Barton, he drifted down into the void. Only Gloria Hollister's voice through the wire connected them to the world they knew. Beebe listened as she reported their depth, the weather conditions beyond the looking glass they'd now lost sight of. Beebe relished the thought of her there in the open air, listening. He had coached her to ask him questions continuously, knowing his mind tended to drift, become overwhelmed and inarticulate.

There were pockets where nothing could be seen. They passed further down into the dark ocean, only at a turn to be surrounded by spectacular displays of multicolored life, far more life than anyone had expected at these depths. Beebe realized the animals were more skilled than expected at avoiding nets, and that in their own habitat—accustomed to the pressure here, their bodies were outlandish in form but their movements were effortless and elegant. As foreign to him as they were, they were an essential node in the society of the planet.

These species, he thought, these other citizens of earth, are our only companions. Otherwise we are minuscule particles floating through "an infinite and unsympathetic waste of electrons, planets, nebulae, and suns."

How many suns could there be? He wanted to know.

With the discovery of new life his fear turned to joyful fascination. He had traveled to another planet with its own rules and games, its own gravity. He spoke excitedly into the phone, telling Hollister what he saw, then suddenly her customary responses, her questions and verifications, halted.

"My God!" Barton exclaimed. "The phone is broken."

Beebe tried to listen harder, as if the sound had only grown dim, but understood it was true—the line was dead. With Barton fiddling with the wire and connection behind him, Beebe looked back out the quartz windows.

All these companionable species, but no way to communicate what he saw. As limited as was this new vista, he was alone with it. The isolation made the ball shrink. The silence of the small orb began to condense and harden. He spoke to Barton in a whisper, as if the silence would not allow him to raise his voice. The green-blue outside the window, so luscious and alive a moment before, now appeared cold and inhospitable.

Beebe sat in silence remembering his trip to the Galápagos where he had watched molten lava gush from deep within the earth. He remembered being high in the Himalayas with Hadzia, watching Halley's comet cross the horizon. Here, in the silence of the bathysphere, cut off from everyone above, he felt an awful isolation unlike any of that.

The ocean depths blackened outside the window and he imagined himself and Barton as embryos, as clusters of cells waiting to gestate and be born, but it was like clawing out from Pre-Cambrian time, so far were they from the vicissitudes of human history, the politics of the day, the cocktail party the night before, the stifled laughter of Hollister when he crept into her room. This night was other, endless, and would swallow them completely.

Animal Life

Beebe heard Barton fiddling behind him to regain the phone connection. The bathysphere was still.

His mind had floated out through the three-inch quartz panes and fused with the darkening water. He saw clouds of small vibrating motes. He could not understand what they were.

He saw flying snails within delicate shells, as if made of tissue or wet parchment, with flaps of flesh wafting in space, pushing them forward.

He saw lanternfish lit up with iridescent flesh, as if the shining were a kind of armor.

In the silence of the ball, he heard the engineer's frustrated breath. It was awkward and cold and muggy.

He saw a pair of pilot fish outside, but they were so faint it was as if they were ghosts. Beyond them, in the distance, some dark forms hovered but did not approach.

He saw big silvery-bronze eels, some crustacea with flattened bodies. The phone reconnected with a click and a brief eruption of static.

Hello?

Beebe heard Hollister's voice again and reassured her. All was well. Yes. It couldn't have been more than a minute or two.

The bathysphere began to lower further, and he began talking again, listing and describing what he saw in as much detail as he could, as he'd trained himself to do. But it was as if his mind had stayed outside the vessel, afloat with the darkening forms as they disappeared and reappeared at lower depths.

How to talk to Hollister if he was as dispersed as the darkness?

He called up the names of flying snails and squids, a big leptocephalus, a golden-tailed serpent dragon, a kind of eel-like form, probably an idiacanthus.

He watched a beautiful, dime-sized light approach, until, without the slightest warning, it seemed to explode. The flash was so bright he jerked his head back from the window.

They passed through fifty feet of terrible emptiness, until, out of nowhere, a creature he could not name appeared.

He could hardly call it a body. It was like filaments, a network of luminosity, delicate, with large meshes, all aglow and in motion, waving slowly as it drifted.

Though this was not the only time he saw this nameless vision, he could never say what it was, or define it as a single creature, or even really be sure he had seen it.

They sank another fifty feet, and there he saw a series of lights flashing, like the electric grid of a city seen from the sky. He saw layer upon layer emerge and fade in the darkness but could not see or envision what was happening. Some kind of invertebrate lifeform, he guessed, so delicate and evanescent that there would be no sign of it if he brought one up in a net.

As they sank further, the beam weakened. Its light quickly absorbed by the dense water. There at the edge of its reach, he saw a large form. He'd seen it before but wasn't sure if he should even mention it. Perhaps it had been a trick of the imagination. But there it was again—a significant form appearing in silhouette. He guessed it was not really black, but a shade that appeared black among the blacknesses. Hardly visible, the slightest trace of a silhouette, a suggestion of color. It was swimming, or appeared to be swimming. Whether it was a fish or squid or some other organism, he could not say.

On Darkness

Beebe liked to contemplate varieties of darkness. The balance between day and night changed through the seasons, and through latitudes, but even if punctuated by fire or more and more by electric lights, it always kept accounts. Along the equator it was essentially one to one.

Beebe had learned that the root of the English word *night* was the old Gothic *hneiwan* or Anglo-Saxon *hnigan*, which meant "descend." So what he was doing in the bathysphere could be considered *nightening*.

In the jungle, night came with the sounds of animals that kept the mind alert. As darkness fell, other senses sharpened. Now in the deep ocean, the descent of night blossomed into a new kind of eternity that had no balance like the days and nights of the surface. There was no hearing and smelling in the deep beyond the unfortunate sounds or smells of Barton.

In the bathysphere, the nighttime alertness of the jungle mind gave way to awe in the face of the vulnerability of the human body. Crushed in the depths in a fraction of a second. Again and again, Beebe contemplated the quickness with which it might happen, how soon it could be over.

In a city at night, you might see even down a dark alley. At the edge of town, you might grab a flashlight. When the flashlight batteries go dead, you're left to feel your way forward with your hands or grab a stick and walk like the blind. Eventually, you might learn to walk like that perfectly well.

Beebe remembered a naturalist's assistant he once heard about, who followed his boss through the jungle. The naturalist went forward flipping stones, looking for ants, and the assistant went behind, in his path, carefully placing every upturned stone back in place.

Night was like that.

In the Beam

1140 ft	Beam on.
1180	Ctenophores with no light.
1190	Beam out.
1200	Sparks in all directions—dozens of them— died out.
	Large creature back again, out in distance, maybe longer than I thought.
	Pteropods, shield-shaped, shining by reflected light. Clio.
	Big glow in the distance, 6 to 8 inches across, light going up.
	Pediculate, 3 inches long, very deep, a pale lemon-yellow colored light on illicium.
	Now it is close to window. Same fish went past again. Between me and illumined front of this fish swam another 3-inch fish which was faintly lighted all over with a silvery luminescence.
1250	Same fish back again, with small tail and no lights of its own.
	Copepods brilliantly lighted in beam.
1290	Another flash, a pale rose-red.
1300	Pediculate around window, 4 inches, very near glass, dull luminous teeth, Melanocetus-type.
	Beam on.
	As many organisms as ever. Bathysphere rolling up and down very gently.

Big Leptocephalus, 8-inches by 1-inch deep, rapidly
vibrating.

Few Worms and a Siphonophore.

Beam fading off into rich turquoise.

Melanostomiatid-like fish, 1 inch long.

Smallest fish with double, lateral lights ever seen.

1320   Beam off.

1390   A lavender light right up to window, cheek light.

Slim, slender fish like a male Idiacanthus,

but seems much longer,

with a yellow cheek light.

Now a Siphonophore, or jellyfish, with luminous tentacles.

1450   Same large fish again.

Plankton abundant.

Beam on.

1500   Argyropelecus, four of them spinning

around beam, their lights glowing

downward.

4 of the slimmest fish I have ever seen.

They streak through light, about 15

inches long. Long slender jaws, yet quite

different from known eels.

Barometer reading 77.

Pale flesh-colored fish around 2 feet

long, no lights. It is a pale pasty whitish-buff

and very high melanostomiatic fins. Grand clear

view, memorized details.

Humidity 60%, temperature 80.

Beam out.

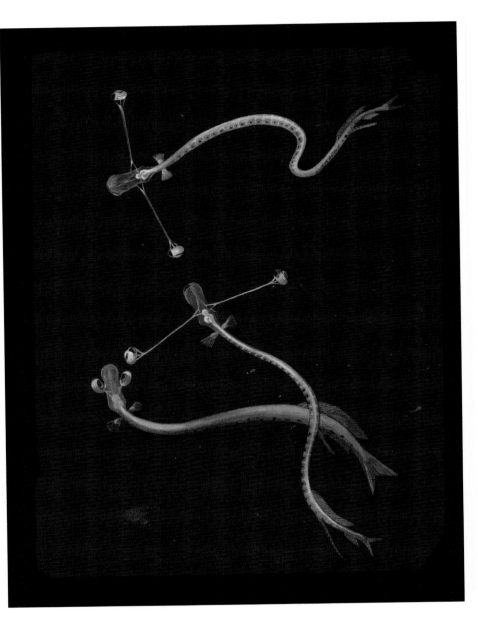

The Pressure

The bathysphere was squeezed at a rate equivalent to six tons per square inch—meaning the whole vessel was resisting the crushing weight of over five thousand tons. If it were to crack, if one of the quartz panes were to loosen, Beebe and Barton would not drown but would be ripped to shreds by drops of water shooting at them as fast as bullets.

Beebe found this impossible to conceptualize. How to understand the reality of such pressure? A physical fact on which their life depended, but he couldn't process it with the senses at all. It was like saying earthrise instead of sunset. He knew from some perspective it was true, but his bones did not recognize its reality.

Meanwhile, outside the window, he saw multitudes of delicate, fragile, beautiful creatures.

Something within them, in their graceful bodies that moved through the dense water, allowed them to withstand this inconceivable pressure. They swam and undulated, hunted and chased mates, glowed elegantly in the blackness, with a half-ton of weight bearing down on every square-inch of their bodies.

The greater the pressure, the softer the tissue must be, Beebe knew. Hard tissue cannot survive at these depths. No wonder his bones shrunk at the realization.

Crouched awkwardly in his ball, Beebe again felt like a blind man feeling his way through a huge city. He saw himself from the point of view of a distant God, for whom the bathysphere, human history, the planet itself, could be crushed and discarded in the blink of an eye.

The cracking of the bathysphere, their bodies torn to shreds, their own delicate flesh unable to exist in this world, like the exploded siphonophores he'd pulled up to the surface in nets.

Was there a difference between the exploding siphonophores of the surface and the crushing of a person at these depths? What did it tell you about the nature of their spirit? What kind of creatures were they? Only a fragile homeostasis allowed humans to walk on land without bursting into flames or being shredded by the atmosphere.

It was sinful, he felt, to be bored and self-absorbed. We have so little time, and the universe is so endlessly diverse and fascinating. The origins of the planet encoded within the dust beneath our feet, where we step anticipating the night to come.

Unknown Fish

"I have one hundred and fifty-four separate and distinct notes on Unknown Fish, and two hundred and thirty-five notes on Unknown Animals. To list these would most excellently reveal my abyssal ignorance of the majority of sparks, lights, half outlines, and glimpses of heads, tails, or eyes."

To the Threshhold

1530 ft   Lovely, bright, solid, pale
          blue light close to glass.
          Probably, oh, I don't know.

1600   Beam on. Walls of bathysphere very cold.
          Beam off.

1700   Beam on. Trying to catch sight of what makes the
          larger flashes.
          3 Melanostomiatids, 6 inches long, black, with
          pale yellow lights.
          Several fish swimming around beam of light.

1730   20 lights in sight at once, all swimming
          like mad, now and then an organism that swims
          steadily, a pale bluish.

1800   Ptax-like, 6 inches, glistening silvery, lighted
          by reflection, silvery all over.
          Beam on. Water in beam all getting turquoise.
          Again a school of 3 to 4 inch fish around beam.
          Shield-shaped Pteropods going through beam.
          Another Melanostomiatid-like fish with light
          organ in head which lights up own eye,
          its body lighted brightly and irregularly.
          Beam out.
          Maze of lights, saw fish, another Siphonophore.

1900   Beam on.
          Something went out of light when it was
          put on, a body of indefinite size, dashed
          out of sight.

Never have seen things so abundant. Barton sees
a baby Squid. Later a Stylophthalmus a foot away in beam.
I missed it.
Beam out.

Monsters in Eternal Night

Beebe referred to these never-before-seen creatures as monsters, as devils and dragons. But he thought of their bodies as philosophies, traditions of thought, as *schools of dragonism*. A college drop-out, he wondered what was to be learned at their great university:

An astronesthes with batteries of hells-eye lights on its cheeks, a looped string of twenty lavender glowing beads suspended from its hyoid dewlap. Graceful, but somehow heavy.

A thick, dark mahogany helix embedded in what looked like glass.

A squid that looked *chaste*, with its mouth molded in fine Chinese porcelain and decorated with moonstones. But from that delicate mouth rose a jack-in-the-box Punch-and-Judy head wearing a cap made of waving tentacles— long and thick and painted with stripes and blotches of red.

A face which is no face.

An infant hatchet fish, its hyaline eyes polished to the highest silver. Its mouth as if pouting and its body finely articulated, muscle fibers glistening, gathering around the backbone, just forming while its tail is already large and efficient.

An argyropelecus with eyes fixed on the upper part of its head, trained above toward the surface, while all the lights on its body point down.

A source of brilliant light in this deep blackness, he thought, destined never to witness its own glory.

Almost everything Beebe saw at this depth was either black or scarlet. So that he came to see scarlet as a shade of black. No matter how unworldly their shapes, whether they had derived from fish or snails or shrimp, they were united by this calling: to live in the cold and dark under enormous pressure.

The greater the pressure the softer the tissue.

A female angler fish some two feet in length, a tentacle emerging from her forehead, culminating in a glowing ball at the tip. At the base of her body was a two-inch growth—the male. Beebe imagined him with his enlarged nostrils, feeling his way through the ocean by smell until he encountered a female, then attaching to the female's belly. Over time his nostrils were absorbed into her body. He lost his eyes, eventually his stomach and his brains. An independent creature reduced to a parasite.

The only deep-sea fish, he thought, who ever finds a resting place here was a black swallower.

It looked rather ordinary—no giant fangs, no barbels, no luminescent organs or bizarre fins or colorful scales. It was about a foot long, dark and smooth, with a slightly jutting lower jaw and delicate undulating fins behind its gills, living and hunting in the dark zone below twenty-two hundred feet.

Coming across a red-spotted squid or a unicorn fish twice or even four times its size, the black swallower loosened its jaws and clamped onto the larger fish. The unicorn fish, its belly covered in tentacles, thrashed and swam to escape, but the black swallower hung on, walking its teeth step by step around the body of the prey until it was swallowed whole. The swallower's belly would expand to impossible, grotesque, mind-bending dimensions. As if Beebe, rather than enjoying a plate of pork chops and plantains, had detached his jaws, stretched his cheeks, and swallowed the plate, the table, the cook, the entire kitchen.

The black swallower then floated in the pressurized darkness, all its bodily attention now aimed at digesting this bus-sized creature it had just swallowed. Inside its distended belly there was space for whole schools of myctophids and ctenophores, adolescent mola mola, psenes and bristlemouths, calliste green eels and olivaceous buff octopuses. Eventually, the fish would swallow Beebe and Barton, the bathysphere and the *Ready*, the island of Nonsuch, the whole Atlantic, planet earth, everything that had ever or would ever happen. Stretched but not bursting, the entire ocean of possibilities held in the ruminative embrace of the black swallower.

Unknown Organisms

Some were not fish or any recognizable form. Some were just motes in the water, a rain of small things, one spark after another.

He saw little vertical strings like cobwebs with beads in them, a body moving in the distance, uniformly white, perhaps a squid or a fish of considerable size. He saw three tiny sparks in the distance, pale yellow. A flash, then three more. Lots of stuff moving. Then no flashes at all. He saw large, dark forms in the distance, then the plankton was so dense it refracted light.

There were fish and invertebrates moving up and down like insects. There were sparks, masses of lights, sometimes it rained light.

A large, pale white body appeared in the distance. There was a huge flash, a distinct central spark, blinding, illuminating everything around it. Light streaked through the water, then something large in the beam, perhaps a squid, a large body perhaps four or five feet long. Then there was a dead spot with no life.

The water appeared blue, and soon there were thousands of lights, pale blue to green, but brilliant, like phosphorescence. Many lights at once, moving this way and that, as a dark, unlit organism moved through, covering them up as it passed.

It's boiling with light, he told Hollister. Jet-black comets shot through, ghostly things in all directions, like meteors. Then for a hundred feet there was nothing, no lights or life. He saw something wiggling like mad, then a bit lower there was a light the size of a dime that moved toward the quartz window and exploded. When his eyes refocused, he saw a hundred brilliant points instead of one. Every light persisted as the creature writhed and twisted to the left, still glowing, and vanished. He could not even guess its phylum. They entered a black hole, no light at all. Then the biggest flash yet.

He saw a body, five- or six-feet wide, passing through the beam, perhaps a fish. He counted forty-six sparks in ten seconds, mostly pale yellow or blue, something like a huge necklace made of silvery lights. For a time there was not a flash in sight. Then one came—*flash*—but the light seemed to come and go slower at this depth, as deep as he'd ever go.

He saw lace-like things, a long slender series of lace-like things, and then another. He saw many jellies. Pale blue linuche jellies and large aurelias. He saw pteropods that looked like silvery vibrating bubbles of air, or that looked like silver balls. He saw arrow-shaped pteropods that looked like ships sailing. Some were like comets or shields. He saw three-inch shrimp that hung in the water like luminous mist. Some shot liquid light from their bodies that faded after a few seconds.

He saw copepods, strings of pale-blue luminescent copepods, a rain or mist of copepods. They were so persistent he forgot to note them, all the tiny copepods. He saw a school of brilliantly illuminated jellyfish, one three feet in diameter, like an enormous wheel.

Lots of jellyfish, he told Hollister. More jellyfish than anything else.

Life Getting Thicker

1800	Here's a fish with nothing but teeth illumined, mouth 1 inch across, does not close completely. Teeth are lighted from the bottom upward with black between.
1810	Siphonophore, 6 to 8 inches, with all network lighted up and oval in shape. Now a copepod which looks like a fish's light. 3 more fishes, 18 inches, with irregular lighting-like line around side, and another one which may be same kind.
1900	Sides of bathysphere as cold as the devil. Whole atmosphere perfect.
1950	Fish crash again and again; no, it is shrimps throwing out light, letting it go every time they hit the glass.
1990	Beam on. Big fish seen above are Lamprotoxus. Remember this.
2000	Lights here are great. 1650 pounds oxygen, humidity 60%, temperature 86°.
2030	Lots of lights that come and go.
2060	4- to 5-inch big Myctophids.
2090	Now ghostly things in every direction, like meteors in every direction.
2100	Colors of lights are pale blue, pale lemon yellow, pale green. Now 2, 12-inch fish, one

lights up the other, then both light up.
Their lights are under control. Big
cheek lights and lights along sides,
both fish elongate like Melanostomiatids.

2150   Big siphonophore, and now 4- or 5-inch
fish and something wiggling like mad.

2200   Have never seen such a dark place, it is the
darkest in the world. Can see radiolite markings
on the barometer glass in bathysphere.

Abyssal Ignorance

Beebe was at the window, looking out, telling Hollister he saw two fish moving slowly by, six or eight feet away. They were large, at least six feet long, shaped like barracudas but with shorter jaws that never closed. A single line of strong, pale blue lights ran down the side of the fish from head to tail. Beebe had seen many fish with such lines, but usually there were two. These fish also had unusually large eyes, even for a creature six feet long. The lower jaw of the fish extended further than the upper, and there were sharp fangs that shone from some internal light. It might be mucus, he thought, or some bioluminescence inside its mouth. Because the vertical fin was so far toward its tail, he thought the fish must be a kind of sea-dragon related to the melanostomiatid that had startled Hollister with its beams of light. But unlike other sea-dragons he'd seen, this one had two long tentacles hanging from its body—one from the chin and another from near the tail, each glowing at the end, either red or blue. The tentacles twitched and jerked below as the fish moved forward.

Beebe turned on the beam's yellow light to discover another fish, which appeared to float, the front half of its body illuminated. Two fins swatted idly at the water, keeping it in place. Beebe exclaimed to Hollister, and she began to question him: What was it? What had he seen? But before he answered he swung around to nudge Barton.

Look, he said. Look at this.

Barton moved forward and their two skinny bodies were side by side, each looking out one of the quartz windows.

This fish was over two feet long, with small eyes but a large mouth. It was without bioluminescence—if they hadn't flipped on the beam they would never have spotted it. Its side fins moved slightly, exposing another broad fin on its lower body that appeared to be composed of tiny threads. In the yellow light of the beam, the fish appeared to be a drab, unhealthy green that reminded Beebe of a human corpse. It had no tail, only a small knob. Instead, it had large transparent dorsal fins that reached far behind its body.

Deeper down, Beebe spotted a large, indistinct outline of a creature, but it disappeared a second later. A bit deeper, a delicately glowing jellyfish floated past. Then the indistinct outline reappeared, resolving into a large fish silhouetted in the light of the beam. Was it the same significant form he'd seen before? It was huge, or seemed to be—Beebe guessed it must be twenty feet long—a monochrome oval without distinguishing features like an eye or a fin. Was it a fish at all? How did it move? There was nothing flitting or pulsing. It simply sailed past.

In its size and monotony and effortless motion, it was like the living mirror of a blank mind. He needed Hollister to see it too, but she was not here.

Beebe grunted and nudged Barton again, but before the engineer could get into position the creature was gone.

A marine monster, Beebe thought. How much else is down here that no one has ever seen?

From his tiny perch, he'd seen hardly anything at all. And what he had seen—he didn't even know what it was.

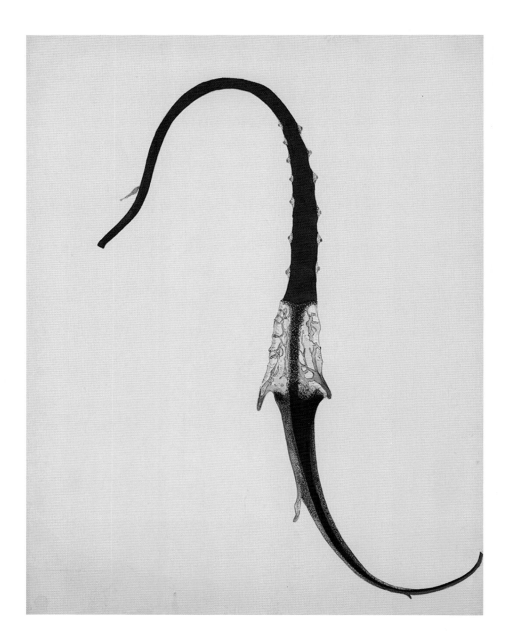

The Lowest Depth

2500	Beam off.
	Barton says not more than one-quarter-inch of hose has slipped in.
	Oxygen 1500 pounds, humidity 63%, barometer 76.
2540	Another shrimp.
	Ctenophore completely lighted up.
	Another big shrimp at window, whole thing very
	clear now about
	the luminous substance
	they shoot out.
2600	Beam on, and off.
2650	Millions of sparks when hit window.
	Big 12-inch Heropod, like Firola.
	Luminous all over but no luminous
	spots.
	Another big shrimp shooting out luminous
	material which looks like a veil.
2690	The walls of bathysphere are icy cold.
2700	Hose in about one-half-inch only.
	Oxygen 1450 pounds, barometer 76, temperature 80°.
2775	So black outside can't look, and what lights!
	A fish with long, slender, pointed tail, a big fish.
2800	Here's a telescope-eyed fish, it's Argyropelecus, and its eyes are very distinct. Something like a huge necklace of silvery lights. Now another big shrimp.
	Beam off.
	Marvelous outside lights. Water filled

with lights, more so than on our last
dive at 2500 feet.

2900 Now a curved, pale-green light under eye,
eye lighted up by it. It is crescent-
shaped. The fish is at least 3 feet long.
5-inch Myctophids, swimming so slowly
that I can see whole light pattern.
Several close lines of lateral lights, and constantly
lighted plates.

2940 Not a flash in sight.

2950 Now a light coming toward me.

3000 Siphonophore, a big one.
Oxygen 1400 pounds, barometer 76,
temperature 77°, humidity 61%.

3028 Beam on.
Beam off.
Long lace-like things again. Salpa-like with big head and long
slender tendrils.
Now another one.

A Siphonophore Manifesto

There out of the darkness of the deep appeared a long, slender, glowing shape—Beebe knew it was a kind of siphonophore. It was enormous—some twenty yards from end to end. It appeared to be a pale magenta color, but that seemed impossible given the spectral restriction down here. It had no head or legs but varied in texture and shape, a complex form with tendrils extending from its sides and gently but rapidly flagellating the water.

A siphonophore, he knew, appears to be a single organism, but it's not. It's a colony of smaller animals—polyps and other beings called zooids. It's a city adrift in the ocean, an undersea metropolis whose citizens cooperate closely to keep the bustling society harmoniously alive.

The citizens share a common ancestor that once emerged from a fertilized egg, but now they grow and clone themselves and attach their offspring to their own bodies. These new bodies are genetically identical to their parent but develop differently, acquiring finely honed skills. There is no central brain—each creature has an independent nervous system, but they share a circulatory system. This frees the small bodies to pursue whatever they might devote themselves to. Some provide protection, some are responsible for eating, for reproduction, or for producing colorful glowing light. Some absorb water and squirt it back out, propelling the siphonophore through the water.

Some absorb air or fill with gas to regulate buoyancy. The nectophoric jellies that propel the siphonophore can't eat, and the polyps that eat can't swim. They depend on each other, working together as one.

Some of the animals grow dangling limbs at the perimeter, and these can produce powerful neurotoxins that stun small shrimp or other creatures for food. The limb then enwraps the shrimp and digests it, distributing its energy to all the siphonophore's constituents.

These collective bodies can grow to be over a hundred feet long. Most are very slender, seemingly composed of a transparent, gelatinous material like jellyfish. Some have dark orange or red digestive systems that can be seen inside their transparent tissues. Some turn green or blue when disturbed. They are extremely fragile and break into pieces at the slightest touch. But in their highly organized state they are the longest creatures on earth, if they can be considered a single creature at all.

Human bodies, too, are metropolitan—not only because of the many cells that make up our tissues and organs, but the bacteria and other animals that live within us. To them we are an environment, a world. Siphonophores are complex, like humans, with organs performing different tasks. To the individuals that compose them, the integrity of the body is a social impulse that binds them in cooperation.

The siphonophore mind, Beebe thought, asks us to rethink our individuality, to consider our epidermis as only one way to measure the extent of our bodies. In that light, our furious competition, our backstabbing and fights over resources, is nonsense. Better we work together, getting closer and closer, more finely attuned to each other's needs until we are indistinguishable. Then we might draw our boundaries differently.

When some Buddhist monks meditate, key parts of their brains quiet and go still. One is the part that locates us in space—the sense of ourselves that forms as we bump into a table, come up against a wall, and so learn the extent of our bodies. This boundary is drawn over and over again as we keep bumping into things, coming into contact, feeling and moving against things and each other. But this division is only a habit of mind. There is nothing essential about it. When that part of the brain stills—requiring the quiet musing and freedom from fear that propelled the First Wonderer—we no longer distinguish between *us* and *not us*.

At such a moment, let loose from the limits of the body, as we float in a greater unity, the siphonophore might inject us with powerful neurotoxins, to remind us there is no answer.

Medusa

Dangling at depth. The only others who had come before had all been corpses. Corpses falling from above, food for these gliding creatures with their soft, pressurized tissue.

He knew the old English *bwg* was the word for monster or mystery. But he didn't know if he was the bug or if the bug was out there.

He thought of Immanuel Stewart and his daughter Priscilla on Medusa Island, pointing to the horizon where Alabama slave-raiders used to disappear, their holds full of abductees. Except the rare one who escaped and jumped overboard, preferring the horizon of death to that other horizon.

All those ships going this way and that, and all those bodies overboard, drifting down. Another kind of abyss.

The sea is a record. Even its absences are records.

It was impossible to keep his mind trained on that blank, to speak from it, of it, not only those who had jumped from the ship and swam toward Medusa Island. Also the density of the water, his own vulnerability, like the argyropelecus, a creature that looks up while its light shines down.

His only contribution to science and literature, he thought, was to be able to testify: "At a depth of a quarter of a mile. A luminous fish is outside the window."

What would the luminous fish outside tell him, that he could not hear or smell, that he was cut off from? His tissue insufficiently soft, insufficiently scarlet-black. Instead, he was held in a steel bubble with Barton, seasick and jealous, while these subtle and fearsome creatures illuminated the darkness outside, as if signifying something.

But no, that was just his imagination. Like he imagined he was the only one to see this. He was wrong about that, too. They had all seen this, those who swam for Medusa Island rather than disappear over the Alabama horizon. They were here too.

All the ways he'd learned to identify, enumerate, count, and describe, distinguish, it was nothing.

A luminous fish, a solitary zooid.

Trapped in the steel bubble with Barton, he sank further, to a place where his charts and lists fell deader than the dead of Medusa Island. Surely the ocean knew something, and the luminous fish knew something, but he, alone with Barton, knew little.

What would it mean to know what the ocean knew? To think like the ocean? To have enveloped and seen the falling bodies from Medusa Island, to have seen Columbus come and go, to have seen the bathysphere come and go, to have watched as pale, skinny men with their pointy heads and knobby knees, dangling by a delicate thread, made lists and distinguished one thing from the other?

Submerged within that luminous cloud, that absence he could not penetrate, that fecund vacuum of unknown creatures, were the eyes of Medusa Island and those living ghosts for whom Beebe's century was a blink of an eye, who had been there long before he'd arrived and would remain long after the bathysphere and Beebe and Barton had been swallowed by oblivion.

In those pressures and depths: the illuminated bodies of the abyss dwellers, the mucous-smeared fangs and glowing tentacles, the face that is no face, body that is no body. The ultimate logbook encompassing all others, that knows when your time has come, when it's time for the steel ball to drop, the oceans to dry up.

The cable tightened and the weight of the ball increased. As risks grew, animal light proliferated, the suction of the seafloor accentuated, as Barton's heaving and sighing, the falling and wanting that was below the white seasnakes of Hollister's fantasy, beyond the personal death of the persons of Medusa Island, words repeated: *let us go down.*

It was like the words of Wordsworth that Roosevelt wished he'd write of the Pleistocene horse: an imaginary alp, a stand-in for an absent God, the distant God that watched the bathysphere dangle indifferently only to turn away, a dream that had died and left him making lists, overturning rocks for a follower to turn right side up, chasing ants.

Perhaps here in the deep was a luminous ant that would teach him something worth knowing, or that would crack his consciousness brightly in two, scoop out his brains and carry him off into another world of interpretation and thought, where he was the ant and the rock and the zooid and the sickness of Barton and the voice of Hollister. Between the insect mind with its speed and opacity, the grip of the leaf-cutters on his train of thought, and the delicacy of the marine bodies with their softness and grace, led a narrow walkway beyond human limitation. The fish face he'd seen on that first dive—terror and hunger and jaws so wide there were no eyes.

And there, though it remained unspeakable, he would be united with an unthought field, a thing that was not place or mind or creature at all, a contactless mind that subsumed all matter but was itself immaterial, or was the sum of matter, which saw and reflected and did not comment.

Or the luminous ant would shine its insect eye and remind him that nothing was worth knowing.

Beebe in the steel bubble was a neurotoxin as absurd as Buffon in the trees.

As usual, a grunt from Barton interrupted his musings.

The tank is low, the engineer said. We're running out of oxygen.

And with that Beebe could suddenly feel the thinness of the air. He realized that through all this he'd been speaking into the phone to Hollister, listing fish.

He reported that it was black as hell, but then the inadequate air infected his speech—he dropped adjectives and adverbs; his similes dried up.

He could only say *black, black, black*—the staccato repetition practically an end in itself—*black, black, black*—as they hovered in the density and she sat above in the bright blue sun.

He gazed out the window, knowing their time at this depth was short, and saw another whirl of animal light, a carnival of creatures that had never been named and might never be seen again. And if no one could see what he'd seen—and he didn't even know what he'd seen—then what was the point of even looking?

His countless articles trying to convince readers in the comfort of home that the jungle is nothing to be afraid of. Snakes and spiders—no, the jungle was an enveloping world, always alive. The legends that had meant to scare children, what was in the dark forest, the heart of the jungle. He was proud to report that he felt safe and secure in the jungle. He had done the same with the kingdom of the helmet. Come and see, he wrote. There are underwater gardens to tend, colorful fish to shoot, it's just at the edge of your American home.

But the eye of the deep was not like that. It saw him with iron sight. His pitiful excursions. His collected specimens. His underwriters' delight. The admiration of citizens.

He saw himself between microbe and cosmos, between cave dweller and Einstein, between copepod and whale. He saw ice ages like waves crashing against a shore—repeated, rhythmic movement.

Barton flicked on the beam and it shone a distinct yellow. Beebe sat soaking in that color, as weak as it was, trying to draw it into his being. But then the light switched off, and it was as if it had never been. There had never been daylight, no streaks of illuminated clouds in twilight, or any relative darkness of a midnight in the jungle.

If the blue he encountered on the first dives was so blue as to permanently alter the yellowness of the sun, here was a black so black it called his very existence into question. The sound of the blower, the shifting and murmuring of Barton, were absorbed into this fecund and hungry vacuum.

Having arrived at his ancestral home, at what appeared, to the best his mind could conceive, as something universal, he felt the terminal quality of the embrace, the mercilessness of the glare, and the impossibility of moving away.

The Turn

2750   Mass of Copepods and other plankton, can see them
       about 40 feet out away from bathysphere.
       Barton sees a big body with 1 light on each
       end, it may be a Melanostomiatid.

2630   Beam on.

2540   Saw a fish with literally hundreds
       of lights, about 8 inches long, from
       head to tail its body was peppered with
       very brilliant but small lights. Color
       of lights was pale lemon-yellow.

2500   Oxygen 1200 pounds, barometer 76
       Barton photographing. Light at 110 volts, very hot
       and dazzling.

2490   Beam out.

2430   Lovely outside now. Fish with light
       below eye, when light went out rest
       on head not lighted up at all.

2380   Going through kind of a desert—darkness,
       just a black hole because of lack of animal light.

The Only Borneo in the World

Beebe felt the change in momentum, and already with their slow rising his mind scrambled to make sense of things.

There were three moments, he thought, that had defined his time here. The first was his initial witnessing of bioluminescence in its native place, a wholly new vision of life and color that had never been described by humans.

The second moment arrived in the aftershocks of the explosions of animal light: a recognition of the unfathomable darkness of the deep sea, a zone where sunlight had never and would never penetrate. Below two thousand feet, where the heat source of the planet, the life source, was cut off completely, where life was supported by tiny bits of decomposing organic matter drifting down into the abyss. A darkness that split logic into impotent flagella, detached from the bodies they were meant to move. Where the comparisons of the human mind, its clawing after orientation—for a table to bump into—evaporated.

But then there was the third moment, when a glow floated into view and pulsed with its strange light. Stranger than anything he could have conceived, and in this illumination, the contour of a body emerged, a shape with fins or pulsing membranes, eyes or teeth or threadlike networks of tissue: the simple thrill of spotting a new species. His scientist mind lit up with delight as he struggled to render the unknown to Hollister in language, as best he could, before the creature swam off or drifted from view.

But he returned to the frailty, even absurdity of his situation: he was but a *bwg* beneath the *Ready* rocking on the surf south of Nonsuch, a strand of steel and wire leading down through the vanishing reds and yellows to their lonely perch, sealed against the crushing pressure of the water, like a capsule in distant space about to be extinguished by a galactic explosion.

Beebe remembered the first palm tree he'd seen, his first visit to the circus. He remembered his first reading of *Alice through the Looking Glass*, which had set the stage for all that was to come. He remembered his trips chasing pheasants around the world, when he'd sat on a rock and known he was in the only Borneo in the world. Later he would strive to revisit those experiences, not only to remember and relive that astonishment, but to integrate a sense of beauty that was right before his eyes, to make that contact with the world permanent.

"Just one moment of actuality," he thought, "so that this or that could be seen again."

And there at the edge of his mind was what had come just before, the fourth moment, not included in his list, less discrete and compactly charged than the sighting of a new species, even the contemplation of the eternal darkness of the water outside the bathysphere. It would revisit him, he knew, days and weeks after the dive, as he lay in bed or sat in the shade at the field station, as he lectured an interested roomful in some city somewhere.

He pictured in his mind a creature a few inches long he had seen dart toward the quartz pane.

He knew the creature, knew what was about to happen. He readied himself, concentrated intuitively on the periphery of view allowed by the small window—and in that moment a luminous fluid shot from the creature, causing a flash bright enough to light up his face and the inside of the steel sphere. He knew by now that its use was not illumination but obfuscation. It was a light that attracted in order to confuse. But by having trained his mind to keep his attention dispersed—*the oblique glance*—for a moment he could see the world in the light of that glowing fluid. It was like a flashbulb: as soon as it happened it was gone. But it left a trace engraved in his memory, sole record of the otherwise perfectly dark depths. Glimpsing those traces, brightly etched but nearly imaginary, was the culmination of a lifetime's training.

Now ascending, he felt an emotional-cognitive itch, a sense of dimensionality that gave way to flickering insight. His mind detached from his human form and dispersed until he returned to that moment when he had, or hadn't—he had, hadn't he?—seen what the ocean saw, felt, and even understood life and death under the crushing weight of the depths. From that unfathomable moment emerged threads of causality, a reason, a planetary reason older than the Pre-Cambrian hole he had strived to claw out of.

Submerging or arising into that bodilessness, blank and without language, it was as if all the infinite interconnectedness was revealed, why and how in their eternal, unexplainable play. It was not what any Roosevelt hoped he'd assemble, conclusions based on careful observation, experimental outcomes, and broad strokes of dynamic thought. It was sensed through the pure swoon of blackness, beyond light, with nothing to observe and nothing to recover. When he eventually did come back, with that void in the black of his eye, it would cultivate a corner of his perception, but it would not help him. It proved nothing at all.

And now, after all that, they were alive, and barring an accident they would reach the surface. If there was something beyond the decomposed bodies of the dead, the only humans ever to pass that way before, the best response, probably, was a respectful silence. They had completed their trip through the underworld, an idea that had haunted humans for thousands of years. Now it was done, and reasoning about it, even talking about it, was useless.

8.

Underwriting

1934

The summer of the deepest bathysphere dive, the Depression started to abate but the Dust Bowl still raged across the Great Plains—temperatures reached 117 degrees.

Bonnie Parker and Clyde Barrow stole a car in Dallas and went on a spree, robbing and killing and jailbreaking until they were gunned down in Louisiana.

John Dillinger broke out of jail in Indiana, stole a police car, picked up his girlfriend in St. Paul, robbed a few banks, ducked the FBI in Wisconsin, was fingered by a madame in Gary, and got shot outside the Biograph Theater in Chicago.

Shirley Temple and Donald Duck appeared that year; Cole Porter ruled the pop charts. Bergdorf Goodman's chicest dress was a satin gown called "Shining Climax."

A wealthy London brewer was kidnapped in Canada and ransomed for $150,000—it was billed as "Canada's first Kidnapping."

German sportswriters covering the heavyweight bout between Walter Neusel and Max Schmelling were instructed to tone down their reports "to a note of seriousness in keeping with the Nazi spirit."

A British gynecologist shot a picture of the Loch Ness monster, the first record of the beast in centuries.

Stalin began the Great Purge, a cavalcade of random executions that included some of his closest collaborators. One of them addressed Stalin affectionately, by his nickname:

"Koba," he asked, "why do you need my death?"

Back at Headquarters

Half Mile Down was dedicated to Madison Grant, a wealthy New Yorker descended from Walloon Huguenots and Scottish Jacobites. By the time he was born in 1865, every family member for one hundred and fifty years had come into the world within fifty miles of New York City Hall.

An ovoid etching from 1913 portrays him as a bald man with a swooping handlebar mustache, in a stiff collar and tie pin. He was a lifelong bachelor who lived in a finely appointed apartment on 5th Avenue.

He was friends with Herbert Hoover, and it was Grant who'd introduced Beebe to Roosevelt. He and Roosevelt helped found the New York Zoological Society in 1895. They were already part of the Boone and Crocket Club—dedicated to "promoting manly sport with the rifle"—and regularly went on hunting trips together, where they killed moose, elk, and bison.

Grant also founded the American Bison Society, co-founded the Save the Redwoods League, helped establish Yellowstone and Everglades National Parks, and was an important supporter of the Sierra Club. He was the force behind the Adirondack Deer Law and the Alaska Game Law. He worked to save zebras, koalas, white rhinos, Congolese gorillas, Spanish ibex, and the giant tortoises of the Galápagos.

In 1931, the tallest tree in the world was named in his honor.

Grant joined the American Defense Society and the New York branch of the General Society of Colonial Wars, and he was a key player in the Immigration Restriction League. He was president of the Galton Club, named after Darwin's cousin. The club's mission sprung from Galton's famous quip: "If a twentieth part of the cost and pains were spent in measures for the improvement of the human race that is spent on the improvement of the breed of horses and cattle, what a galaxy of genius might we not create!"

167

Grant became known internationally after the publication of his book on eugenics, *The Passing of the Great Race*. The director of the Natural History Museum wrote the preface, and it was endorsed by Roosevelt. The book argued for the superiority of a Nordic race—strong and virile men with wavy hair and straight noses—and advocated segregating populations into racially defined ghettos.

Adolph Hitler wrote a letter to the author, saying, "The book is my Bible."

Karl Brandt, who served as Hitler's personal doctor and oversaw the killing of hundreds of thousands deemed "unworthy of life," submitted passages from Grant's book in his defense at Nurnberg. Citing passages arguing for "exterminating the insane or incapable," Brandt claimed the Nazis had been merely implementing concepts and plans devised by prominent Americans.

Grant advocated for US laws limiting immigration from southern Europe, and for intelligence tests that would prove the superiority of white Americans. He lobbied for laws against interracial marriage and promoted contraception in Black communities. He worked with Margaret Sanger to promote birth control and Marcus Garvey to promote race purity.

He served as treasurer of the Second Eugenics Congress, hosted by the American Museum of Natural History in 1921. The event included President Hoover, Alexander Graham Bell, and Darwin's son Leonard.

In 1930 Grant wrote a chapter for a racist polemic called *The Alien in Our Midst, or Selling Our Birthright for a Mess of Pottage*, which drew on statements from George Washington, Thomas Jefferson, and James Madison. But by then his ideas had fallen from fashion. With the rise of the Nazis, his stock sunk lower.

It was that Grant, the fading, outmoded Grant, to whom Beebe dedicated *Half Mile Down* in 1934. Beebe still considered the old racist a friend and mentor.

Three years after Beebe's last dive, Grant's kidneys began to swell up. On his deathbed he called for a secretary from the Zoological Society. In a barely audible whisper he asked her:

"Are we winning?"

A near life-size portrait of him still hangs in the executive conference room at the Bronx Zoo, not far from the sea lion pool.

A Memorial

William Sheppard, a Black West Virginian and student of Booker T. Washington, left the United States as Reconstruction gave way to lynching and arrived in Congo to witness hands severed, ears cut off, men castrated, women raped, children captured by officials of the Belgian government. He documented these atrocities and also found his way to the Kuba Kingdom, the first American to visit that sophisticated, elusive, quasi-mythical civilization.

Sheppard's dispatches from Congo were read with interest in the US. Bronx Zoo Director William Hornaday wondered why the curse of God was not brought down on King Leopold, after such inhumanity was perpetrated in his name.

When another American, a white man named Samuel Verner, arrived to fill a position with the Presbyterian Church and was put under Sheppard's supervision, Sheppard's wife welcomed him with southern fried chicken and biscuits. Verner came from a North Carolina slave-holding family; he was appalled by Reconstruction, tormented by mental illness, and confounded to find himself eating his native cuisine, answering to a Black man.

Verner skipped out on his duties, roamed and schemed and sought advancement. His activities were mostly unclear, but in 1904 he boarded a steamer to Leopoldville, crossed the Atlantic to New Orleans, and made his way up the Mississippi, bringing with him a young man known at times as Mbye Otabenga, or more commonly, simply, as Ota Benga.

The pair disembarked in St. Louis, site of that year's World's Fair, where visitors were dazzled by electric light and moving pictures. Ota Benga, like hundreds of other captured and trafficked men and women from around the world, including the Apache chief Geronimo, was held for view in a decorated cage, ogled by visitors eating the world's first ice cream cones.

When it was over, Verner and Ota Benga arrived together to New York. Verner wanted to head home to South Carolina, so he got in touch with Hornaday and asked if he could leave Ota Benga in his charge, to which Hornaday, now unafraid of the curse of God, was only too pleased to agree.

Hornaday wrote a press release—*An African Pigmy, Exhibited at the Zoological Park:*

> A genuine African pigmy, belonging to the sub-race commonly miscalled "the Dwarfs," is now on exhibition every afternoon at the Zoological Park. His name is Ota Benga, and he can be seen, during his working hours, at the Primates House, working with the chimpanzees and the orang. His height is 4ft 11 inches, he is about 23 years old, and has been married twice. His first wife was stolen by a tribe of unneighborly savages, and his second wife died from the bite of a poisonous snake . . . He is quite pleased with his temporary quarters in the Zoological Park, and the Park people like him quite well.

A *New York Times* reporter filed a story about the man in the monkey house, and soon huge crowds of New Yorkers came out to see Ota Benga, following him around and shouting taunts at him (the grounds of the Bronx Zoo, built over the slave-owning Delancey family's former plantation, had seen trafficked men before).

Within a week, Hornaday was complaining to Verner—"Boy has become quite unmanageable. Will not obey keepers and resists control"—pleading with him to come back.

In letters to Verner, Hornaday describes Ota Benga finding a knife in the feed-room of the Monkey House and walking through the zoo "flourishing it in a most alarming manner." He then went to the soda fountain near the Bird House, and "got into a great rage and started to disrobe on the spot"

(Hornaday thought this was because he'd been refused a soda). It took three guards to drag him back to the Primates House.

In a letter to the mayor, Hornaday described this as "comic opera material," but meanwhile, he was begging Verner to come back for him.

Verner did not appear, but wrote messages in a transliterated language, asking Hornaday to read them out to his captive:

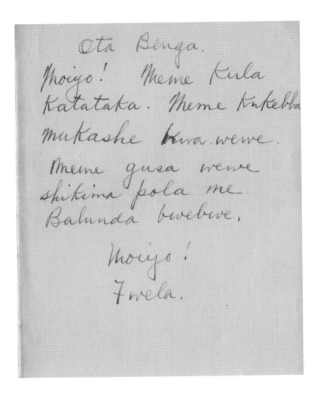

Scholars Pamela Newkirk and Saleh Mwanamilongo identified the language as Tshiluba, and said the messages implore Ota Benga to stay calm, to help Verner find a particular woman but not to mention the woman to anyone. Hornaday reported that when he read these letters to Ota Benga, "he seemed pleased."

A Black beautician on 59th Street offered to come out and give Ota Benga a manicure, and the owner of the Hippodrome off Times Square offered to arrange a theatrical show. Hornaday thought neither was a good idea, and wrote to Verner once again.

Despite Hornaday's urgings, Verner did not appear, and the scandal increased by the day. A community of Black ministers, led by Reverend James Gordon, sought to have Ota Benga released. Reverend Gordon was not only outraged by the fact of a Black man in a cage for animals. He was also offended at the suggested continuum between ape and human, in approval of Darwin:

"The exhibition evidently aims to be a demonstration of the Darwinian theory of evolution. The Darwinian theory is absolutely opposed to Christianity, and a public demonstration in its favor should not be permitted."

Reverend Gordon's Howard Colored Orphan Asylum in Weeksville, Brooklyn offered to take Ota Benga in, but refused to surrender him to Verner whenever the white man might reappear.

Hornaday was resistant to give away what he still understood to be Verner's property:

"They are not willing to take Ota Benga at all unless they can own him absolutely and for all time, and of course I know this would not be in accordance with your wishes."

Madison Grant insisted that the Zoo staff "not even <u>seem</u> to be dictated to."

Hornaday agreed: "I would rather keep him here for the whole month than to be brow-beaten by a Committee of negro ministers who are only anxious for newspaper notoriety."

Eventually, with no sign of Verner, Hornaday had had enough and surrendered Ota Benga to Weeksville.

Reverend Gordon, along with Rev. Gregory Hayes, took Ota Benga from Brooklyn and brought him to Lynchburg, Kentucky, where he was housed and cared for by the Black Baptist congregation there. His teeth were capped and his name Americanized to Otto Binga.

In Lynchburg, Ota Benga befriended Anne Spencer, who went on to be an important poet of the Harlem Renaissance. In her 1922 poem "Translation" she wrote:

We trekked into a far country,
My friend and I.
Our deeper content was never spoken,
But each knew all the other said.

In Kentucky, Ota Benga took up smoking a pipe and shaking hands with his neighbors, saying, "How de do." He briefly worked in a tobacco factory, and in his off hours lolled in the Spencer garden surrounded by flowers. He taught neighborhood boys, including Spencer's son Chauncey, how to sharpen a hickory wood rod into a spear for fishing, how to gather blackberries and other roots, and how to make sassafras tea. He amazed the boys by gathering honey from a hive without disturbing the bees.

The boys noted that on certain nights Ota Benga preferred to stay alone at the fire, at times dancing and singing a song he'd learned at the Virginia Theological Seminary: *"I believe I'll go home, / Lordy, won't you help me."*

On the night of the vernal equinox of 1916, after six years in Lynchburg, he made his customary fire, then stood up to sing and dance. Sometime before dawn he went behind the store to the hayloft where he'd been staying, grabbed a gun he'd stowed there, and shot himself in the heart.

The Names of Others

The year between the St. Louis World's Fair and the detention of Ota Benga in the Bronx Zoo, as a follow-up to his article "On the Keeping of Ducks for Pleasure," Beebe published an article called "Savages and Children."

It described people he had come in contact with over the course of his travels. The fishermen of Sri Lanka, for example, were "contented with their monotonous lives and governed by simple desires," and the people of the island's interior were "slow in thought and speech, and incurious."

Certain Tibetans, he wrote elsewhere, were "stupid, with that impregnable stupidity which far transcends the reputed stupidity of animals." Even so, the porters he hired in the Himalayas, were "boisterous, good-natured, jolly, indefatigable, frank and outspoken . . . They seem to have acquired some rough, instinctive philosophy which gives a bright color to the world."

Most Sikhs were "handsome, as Greek gods were handsome." He explains this by supposing they are descendants of Alexander's armies.

Bornean Dyaks were "splendid and naive" and possessed of "great mental quickness and receptivity . . . honest and straightforward in all that they do." Their drums were "low and resonant, perfect primitive instruments for the expression of primitive emotions. Their rhythmic beat, minor and inevitable, seemed to embody every savage ideal."

Beebe praised an employee called Drojak for his theatrical storytelling: "His quickness was marvelous, his hands and his arms moved faster than the eye, every lunge and thrust was the very essence of savagery."

When he set up the field station in Guyana, Beebe lamented that the cook they hired, reputed to be the country's fastest sprinter, was "too good-looking and too athletic to last . . . his stay with us was like the orbit of some comets, which make a single lap around sun never to return."

He wrote a special article to praise men who had helped him. He called them *super-servants*, and they included "Aladdin the Singhalese, Tandook the Tibetan, Delgado the Mexican, Shimosacka the Japanese" and Samuel Christopher, "a young Negro" in British Guiana.

"When our river steamer was in flames at midnight off Trinidad, with Sam alone on board, it was by his single-handed efforts that the large collection of living animals and my five years' accumulation of notes were saved. . . . Our friendship was of the kind which is developed by months and years of association in a tropical jungle."

Madison Grant belonged to a lineage of racists terrified and scandalized by polyglot urban realities. Albanians in Vienna, Jews in Dresden, Italians in New York—the mishmash, the unknowability of it, the fact that others have angles you don't, have expertise you don't—rather than take pleasure in the growing and changing city, Grant found the new realities disturbing, to be stopped.

Bellamy's *Looking Backward* attributes capitalists' acceptance of inequality to "a singular hallucination . . . that they were not exactly like their brothers and sisters who pulled at the rope, but of finer clay."

That was Grant's hallucination.

Beebe, with all his prejudices and privileges, was used to being around all kinds of people and often relied on people he could not understand. He also knew the people he encountered had a self they did not reveal to him— "the Indian's medicine plants, like his true name, he keeps to himself." At the same time, he was confident he could see exactly what was going on and recognize who was who—he had the confidence that came from never questioning his sense of superiority.

Beebe liked to say he was aware of his own ignorance—he knew no amount of aviation would tell him anything about the soaring experience of a vulture.

"Etymologies do not grow in the jungle."

Learning about the experience of others, human or non-human, required experiential knowledge. And that entailed hardship:

> Before we have the complete solution of the whys and wherefores of herding and flocking and schooling, there must be a great deal of uncomfortable climbing and diving, hiding in unpleasant places, getting wet and hot and cramped and weary. And then, after we have tried to be sandpipers and ants, silversides and mackerel, we may attain to the honor of such knowledge as our prejudiced, but humbled minds will permit.

If Madison Grant had had the curiosity and courage not to head west seeking the sublime among tall trees, but to hide in unpleasant places like the tenements of the Lower East Side, getting wet and hot and cramped and weary, he might have had a better idea about the people who lived near him, who disturbed him so much. He might have developed some love for them, he might have given up some of his guiding illusions, he might have torn off his high-collared shirt and gotten down in the trenches, discovered the pleasures of redistributing wealth. He might still have saved the redwoods.

Instead, by the time he died, over thirty thousand Americans were forcibly sterilized under laws he'd campaigned for.

Beebe's friends and sponsors were not simply men of their time. They represented a side in an ongoing debate with a body count. They were actively fought by others like Reverend Gordon.

Franz Boas had once trafficked several Inuit Greenlanders and housed them in the basement of the Natural History Museum until all but one had died. But over the course of his career he grew into a fierce opponent of Madison Grant's racist pseudo-science. As head of anthropology at Columbia, Boas published a stack of articles against what he called Grant's "Nordic nonsense."

Grant believed his notions of eugenics were rooted in the indivisibility of humans from nature: the same laws govern humanity as govern three-toed sloths and leaf-cutter ants, and the merciless grind of *survival of the fittest* ensured the modern horse was more highly developed than its Pleistocene predecessor. Some humans were also higher than others, he thought, and it followed that just as horses were bred for success, so must be humans. To deny such truths was weak-minded sentimentality.

It was all nothing but Grant's unquestioned sense that the world belonged to him, a wealthy white man of 5th Avenue. What he saw as laws were simply outcomes of violence he took for granted. Horses were for people to ride, and forests were for powerful men to experience the transcendent effects of their supremacy.

Boas, humbled by his vulnerability in the cold north, pointed out that biology was inseparable from history and culture. Any claims to the contrary were examples of exactly such a culture and history. Although the indivisibility of nature was not as Grant believed, nature was indeed indivisible. So was humanity.

Are we winning?

Beebe's self-image had been formed after his mother took him to a phrenologist as a child, and he was an avid measurer and comparer. But he also understood that leaf-cutter ants were inseparable from the leaves, the trees, the soil, the rest of the plants and animals of the jungle. Still, he would continue counting, measuring, distinguishing, believing he could see from the outside, not understanding that the leaf-cutter ants, and his ability to look at them, were aspects of the year, the continent, and varying attempts to name such things.

"Play, among animals," he repeated, "is a much less certain subject than fear."

As Beebe got older, his sense of human hierarchy loosened. He felt differences between the people he met as he moved through the world, but he began to see that "if superiority and inferiority entered into this, we divided them equally between us."

In 1941 he signed a letter from the American Refugee Committee along with Boas, Countee Cullen, and Richard Wright. It not only expressed solidarity with England, the USSR, and China against Hitler, but called for improved workers' rights and an end to racial discrimination in the US.

Trawling on the *Gladisfen*, he mentions "a native crew of five Bermudians." They can be seen in photographs—Black, brown, and white men in overalls and flat canvas caps, tying up, winching, settling the bathysphere—and as risky as some of the bathysphere work was, his life at times depended on them. But their roles in the operation are not detailed and their names do not appear outside a staff list at the back of the logbook:

R. Robinson, J. Stovell, A. Smith, M. Roberts, E. Pascoe, J. Richardson, H. Bradgo, T. Green, H. Douglas, J. Bishop, E. Brown, G. Casey, C. Dowling, F. Duerden, C. Hayes, H. Paynter, A. Riley, G. H. Smith, W. Swainson, M. Thompson, H. H. Trott, L. Bascome, M. Bishop, C. Caisey, H. Waller, H. Whitehead, L. Baxcome, H. Waller.

They were paid two to five dollars a day, depending on skills.

9.

Surfacing

Surfacing

800	Shark, a small one, which turned obliquely upward, and it was about 4 feet long.
730	Strange cold color in this light; looking up can see brilliant blue; looking downward it is a grayish black.
700	5 sparks.
660	Few more sparks.
630	Beam on.
600	Beam off.
590	3 little dim flashes. Have seldom seen sparks so high up before.
500	Oxygen 800 pounds, barometer 80, humidity 74%, temperature 68°.
300	Rapid increase of daylight in water so bright it makes my eyeballs ache. Nothing in water.

Untouchable

The bathysphere surfaced. The winchmen clamped the cable so it dangled a few feet while they hauled the sphere out of the water and onto the deck of the *Ready*. The air was cool at the lower depths, but now that they were back in the light of the tropical afternoon, the sun's heat beat against the steel, turning it into an oven. Beebe and Barton sat inside while the staff slowly unscrewed the bolts on the four-hundred-pound door. They did their best to withstand the heat and airlessness by futilely waving a couple of palm fronds they brought along just for this purpose.

Once the last bolt was off and the door was lifted and removed, the two men could crawl out. Moving from the heat of the bathysphere to the breezy warmth of the afternoon was an enormous relief. They had been sitting in the tiny space for hours, and it took a while for them to regain the use of their creaky knees. Shaking and stomping until circulation returned.

Then once again the light—Beebe never got used to the return to the plain light of day. His eyes, having adapted to the darkness of the deep, were blinded and tearing for a few minutes, until the equipment on the decks, Hollister's face, the outline of Nonsuch and Bermuda in the distance came into focus. Now he remembered who he was—the director of the Department of Tropical Research, operating from the field station on the small island of Nonsuch. He was back on the surface of the earth, an astronaut who had returned from space.

Else Bostelmann was there, too, sketchbook in hand, and as soon as he regained his senses he and Hollister and Bostelmann sat down together. Beebe began right away to detail the shape and color of what he'd seen, how one organism interacted with another. As he spoke, Bostelmann began to sketch.

Like this?—she showed the outline of a fish.

No, Beebe answered. More elongated. And the maxillary extends further beyond the eye.

She sketched again, and their conversation continued as the ship returned to harbor, as they made their way back to the field station, and there Bostelmann continued her sketches, now adding color. Beebe looked at her progress, advising and correcting. Finally, after several tries, they settled on a version.

There it was, the strange pair of toothy, six-foot fish with their red and blue lanterns swinging below their bodies. The bathysphere was in the picture too, to provide a size reference. The image was as if viewed from some outside perspective, as if the ocean were looking at itself. But it was as close to an expression as was possible of what Beebe had seen. Something no other person had seen before, as far as he knew. And as Barton had been behind him fiddling with instruments or checking the aperture on his useless camera, he was unable to corroborate.

Hollister could say, yes, he really had described it like that, but otherwise Beebe was alone with the image he carried in his mind. He, for one, was sure he'd seen it. If he could be sure of anything. And now, somehow at least, it had been rendered. He named the fish the *Bathysphaera intacta*, the untouchable bathysphere fish.

It has never been seen again.

Most of the animals Beebe saw out the window of the bathysphere were species they had hauled up in nets or seen in shallower dives. He might not have glimpsed them in their native depths, but he knew what they were. They were species that had been named and classified and entered into zoological encyclopedias. He spotted many unfamiliar creatures as well, and over the course of the dives, the team registered thirty-seven new species of fish and eighteen deep-sea organisms.

Bostelmann sketched many without having seen them, but in subsequent years they were verified.

There were five species that Beebe saw only once, and which no one has seen since. The only evidence we have of their existence is his description, written down by Hollister and rendered by Bostelmann or one of the other DTR artists. These images—like the portrait of the pair of large fish called *Bathysphaera intacta*—were published along with other images in *National Geographic*, in the *New York Times*, in the bulletin of the *New York Zoological Society*. But did Beebe even have the right to name them?

At nineteen hundred feet he had seen a large fish that resembled a butterflyfish or a surgeon fish, but this one had five glowing lines of yellow and purple photophores down each side of its body. Beebe called it the *Bathysidus pentagrammus*.

He named the corpse-colored fish, shaped like a torpedo, the *Bathyemebryx istiophasma*. A six-inch fish that lived below twenty-four hundred feet, with protuberances like fishing rods from the top of its head, a kind of angler fish, no doubt, was called *Bathyceratias trilychnus*. He referred to a long-beaked fish with a scarlet head, blue body, and yellow tail as the *abyssal rainbow gar*.

The discoveries of these species, if they can be called discoveries, were met with much suspicion by the scientific community. What right did Beebe have to claim discovery? Anyway he was too popular, too present in the newspapers to be taken seriously as a scientist. Him with his bubbling prose, his novelist wife, and their modern arrangement. At a costume gala in New York he was photographed with Rube Goldberg in a gorilla suit. His discoveries were no doubt as fanciful as Goldberg's crazy inventions. Who knew the mental effects of prolonged submersion? Barton himself claimed the air pump was open too wide on certain dives.

He and Beebe, Barton said, had been on an oxygen jag.

So the untouchable bathysphere fish, the abyssal rainbow gar, and the other three fish entered the history of crypto-species and mystery animals. With no evidence beyond Beebe's questionable perceptions to verify to existence, they were included in lists along with the vegetable lamb, the dog-fanged frog, and the unicorn hare.

Bloop and Bristlemouth

Explorers of the deep ocean can't help but wrestle with the extent of abyssal ignorance. All the forests and mountains, deserts and plains of the earth's surface account for only one percent of the planet's habitat. The seas and oceans cover seventy percent of the surface and descend for miles.

They contain at least ninety-nine percent of earth's living organisms. We know so little, and the ocean is so huge, that the chances there are species, even large and wonderful fish, that we have never seen or seen only once, is overwhelming. Recent ocean explorer Robert Ballard believes we might as well assume the *Bathysphaera intacta* and Beebe's other four species are real.

In the waters around Bermuda, the Department of Tropical Research encountered a small bioluminescent fish with a wide-open mouth full of needlelike fangs called the *cyclothone*.

Cyclothones are within the family *Gonostomidae*, commonly known as bristlemouths. They live in the mid-oceanic depths, and Beebe and the other bathysphere divers were the first to observe them in their natural habitat, eating tiny copepod crustaceans. The bristlemouths were caught in dredges, stained by Hollister, and painted by Bostelmann. They appeared again and again, a ubiquitous character on all the bathysphere dives. As ocean exploration continued over the rest of the century, the bristlemouth appeared everywhere. All throughout the middle depths of the ocean around the globe, the bristlemouth is there in force. Its population is estimated in the hundreds of trillions or even quadrillions. The little fish, unknown to humans until the nineteenth century, turned out to be the most numerous vertebrate on earth.

During the Cold War, the US Navy traveled the world sending signals down to map the floor of the ocean in order to discover potential submarines or submarine routes. At one point they realized what they had taken as the seabed seemed to change depths—rising at night and sinking during the day.

But this turned out not to be the seabed at all, but a layer of living things so dense that it interrupted the penetration of the signal. Who knew what all was in there?

In 1997, receivers three thousand miles apart registered a very low and very loud sound with rapid variations in frequency. It indicated the presence of something occurring deep in the ocean, but no one was able to determine what it was. It became known, for lack of a better name, as "the bloop."

We now know of about two million species on the planet, but we still know so little of the ocean depths that as exploration continues, the number can only increase. We have only seen a sliver of the ocean and must assume an ignorance much larger than everything we know. The oceans are rising, but the planet's center of gravity keeps shifting down.

They Were

After that season of deep dives in 1934, Beebe never again descended in the bathysphere. He had encountered something, perhaps the riddle at the heart of the fourth moment—when he'd dissolved and intuited what the ocean might see—that left him powerless to express what he as a scientist, a mere person, had observed out the quartz windows of the steel sphere.

Although he had always imagined his work as ranging from explorer and collector to observer, with intentions that were partly aesthetic, still, it had all ultimately been in the name of science. But the dark depths he saw from the bathysphere were a thing apart. The purity, the boundlessness of his ignorance and powerlessness. It was not simply that he did not know certain facts, that there were creatures he could not name. It was a more unsettling suspicion about the coherence of any point of observation, the coherence of his body, of any body. The delicate lattices of the siphonophores, the illuminated tips of angler-fish tentacles—who was he?

He knew he would go on writing, talking, and closely watching the world he encountered, but there was an inherent flaw—a gap at the bottom of all he did.

He could see his career unfurl before him. He would go on writing book after book, and they would be successful, sold and read and translated across the world. But there was a joke within them that he was unable even to laugh at:

"All these words in type . . . but I have given no more idea of the real happening than if I had attempted a description of the single peacock, the one opal, the solitary sunset which I had seen and you had not."

Beebe thought of this inarticulacy—the nontransferability of experience—as the "penalty man must pay for rushing into new dimensions."

There was just no substitute for being there, and even being there—what had happened? All of this set him circling a central mystery that contracted to the size of a fish's glowing eyeball, then expanded until he was unsure of the solid ground he stepped on through the island at night.

When he had seen the volcano erupt on the Galápagos, he knew that everything he had learned and studied was useless:

"We had been brought close to the beginning of things—and this could not be written or spoken, hardly thought."

Language grew thin and questionable, its usefulness—perhaps the usefulness of empiricism and science, the pitiful naming of creatures—was revealed to be vacant. It was all devoid of sense.

When his mind sunk with the bathysphere, he returned to this state of affairs. A tower of mirrors that at times led into other worlds, but at times simply reflected a pale man in a crown of cut glass.

Goethe had moved his prism between light and dark, concluding colors were only in the mind. But if this mind was short of oxygen, questioning the reality of the phenomenal world itself, what words could possibly be spoken? Perhaps it was better to signify the contents of the deep ocean with inarticulate grunts and blubbers, by singing nonsense syllables or clapping one's hands.

What difference did it make to call these fish, or whatever they were, anything at all? The frail faith that speaking at all made any difference. His voice traveling up the line to Hollister did not mean he knew anything, only that his heart continued to pump, his lungs inflate and deflate as he stared at a world he would never understand. To speak about it, to think about it at all, implied a kind of faith. In what, he was not sure. Perhaps it was what was meant by the word *mystical*—an inadequate, even hopelessly fraught word, a placeholder for the inexpressible, whatever lay beyond thought and language. It meant to be confronted with the bare miracle that we exist at all. It said nothing about the *how* of things, just rested for the moment in the fact that they *were*.

And if they were, and if this were beyond words, we might remain forever in a stunned silence. But if we don't, if we come out of it, we might start to babble hysterically, write book after book, trying to communicate something about the luminous fish, the opal, the stone corpses of Medusa Island.

Listening to language, like Hollister hearing Beebe pointlessly repeat *black, black, black*—perhaps she felt something. Who knows in what way it was causally related to Beebe's moment of vision, but it was there, too.

Perhaps the inadequacy of words could be their strength. The color and sound, the patterns and enunciations, black marks on white paper, indicate an elsewhere that is also here because it's at the base of things, not only the beginning of things but also their continuation, the flux and fate of phenomena. To try to say something about these flashes of vision, these deep-sea dragonfish we don't know if we dreamt, is to animate the world. *Black, black, black* becomes a spell, pronounced rhythmically, that hopes to raise the dead by finding meaning in what we go through. Right at the intersection of what was and what wasn't.

New Species of Deep-Sea Fish

Chaenophryne draco
    a surface which looks like the nap of black velvet
    lips which are smooth and dark brown
    low and inconspicuous and probably not at all
    the anterior profile of the elbow
    translucent, pale purplish blue
    a large, round pad of pinkish-white, silvery spicules
    beneath this is an ebony plaque
    transverse like the fin of a squid

Dolopyihthys gladisfenae
    an inwardly stretched, dark, dermal vellum
    useless for swimming
    the core is dark and upon its tip is placed the bulb
    the bulb is jet black
    there is a misty, pale green tissue
    like a puff of pale green smoke
    The lemon cap is split
    and the green mist disappears into
    this crevice, where it becomes a deeper emerald green.

10.

Summer

Grand day, grand time, perfect day, clear calm day, uproarious time, grand time. Clear and warm, clear and bright, a dead calm, we took it easy in the morning, hot, dead calm, and clear, terrific thunder and lightning, feel as well as ever in my life. Hot, hot, slight breeze, heat of a shower at mid-day, hot, taking it easy all day, then to cocktails.

An Afternoon with the Sea Devil

Count Von Luckner's yacht pulled into the port at St. George's. Beebe knew him. He'd been in Bermuda in 1929 when Beebe and Hollister were just getting started. Else Bostelmann was setting up her underwater painting studio and drawing the reef, and Von Luckner had donned the copper helmet and explored the reef as well. And now, with the expedition complete, he was back. Beebe wrote to Harrison Williams, knowing his friend and benefactor would be amazed to hear the famous seaman had returned.

Von Luckner became known during WWI as captain of the *Seeadler*, a tall-masted sailing vessel that had slipped through the British blockade meticulously disguised as a Norwegian timber freighter bound for Melbourne.

Von Luckner had crewed the ship with the wrestling champions of Saxony and Westphalia, the most well-built man in Bavaria (his ideal muscular development making him much in demand as a model for sculptors) and—knowing Norwegian skippers like to bring their wives along on voyages—a beardless man of delicate features named Schmidt, who he dressed in a blond wig and passed as his wife Josephine, fooling the British inspector when they sailed out of Hamburg.

Once they made it into the open Atlantic, Luckner tossed the timber from their deck, revealing racks of guns. The *Seeadler*'s strategy was to approach British or French steamers asking for the correct time, a common practice to help with navigation. Once the steamers were close, Von Luckner would show his weapons and demand the captain surrender, taking his crew captive and sinking the ship.

The German was proud of treating his captives well, and throughout his legendary pirate career lost only one.

When they happened upon the ninety-eight-thousand-ton British steamer the *Horngarth*, they lit a small magnesium fire, which made a lot of smoke.

They let the smoke billow and ran up a distress signal. The *Seeadler*'s crew hid, and only Schmidt was visible, strutting in his Josephine outfit, hips swaying through the smoke as he called for help.

Once the *Horngarth* drew close, Schmidt threw off his silken dress and tossed his blond wig aside; someone ran a German flag up the mast, and the entire crew rose from behind the rail, rifles ready.

Von Luckner ordered the ship's gun to fire at the *Horngarth*'s radio. The whole cabin went up in smoke.

"Lay to," the German shouted. "Or I will sink you."

He ordered his men to prepare the torpedoes, and the British captain surrendered.

Later Von Luckner admitted it had all been a bluff—he had no torpedoes—and the Brit pleaded with him not to report that he'd been outwitted.

Von Luckner assured the captive captain he'd behaved admirably.

The Germans went aboard the *Horngarth* and found the steamer outfitted with candelabras and big club chairs. They also discovered a grand piano, a violin, a guitar, a melodeon, and a ukulele. Von Luckner knew a few of his sailors had come from German conservatories and ordered the instruments brought over. They went down to the hold and found five hundred cases of rare cognac and twenty-three hundred cases of Veuve Clicquot.

That night Von Luckner sat under the moonlight on the deck of the *Seeadler*, draining goblets of champagne and listening to music that sounded better than the Stadt Opera in Berlin.

"How remote the war seemed then!"

The Wind

Then the wind rose and blew over Nonsuch for days on end. The sky was dark and brooding, with low-hanging, swift-moving clouds. At sunset, Hollister wrote, the western horizon "flared up with a glorious intense rose peach sunset." She left after dinner to walk to South Point "to really feel the wet, dripping wind."

The beach gleamed pink under the glow of the sunset, then as puffs of clouds rolled by overhead it turned a sickening green. Hollister stood watching heavy waves crash against the cliffs. She went to the edge and felt the wind press against her. It was so strong she could lean into it, teetering out beyond the precipice, supported "on the breast of the breeze."

It started to rain, and she headed back to the lab. She pulled the swinging door open, and saw everyone was at work. She sat at her workstation and joined them. It must have been an hour or so later that she heard someone shouting.

Come down! The boat's underwater!

She and Beebe bolted outside together and ran down to the dock holding flashlights. They saw gasoline barrels, diving helmets, chain ladders, everything being washed away. The deck of the *Sea Fern*, usually two feet above the surface, was now submerged under three feet of water, and the tide was still coming in. Vessels thrashed in their moorings, and they struggled to gather whatever they could. They were still at work at midnight, and the rain and wind were increasing. At 3 a.m. they saw a red light from the signal station—a hurricane was coming. They ran back to the laboratory and started stowing microscopes and lab equipment and nailing down the blinds and doors.

The wind and rain increased until dawn, when Tee-Van and several others crowded into the *Skink* and headed to the big island. Hollister was left alone with Beebe and seven other staff members, now completely cut off from the rest of the world. Waves piled up higher, crashing over Gurnet's Rock. Great sheets of white spray blotted out the cliffs where Hollister had leaned euphorically just hours before. Now she was saturated and salt-streaked, under still menacing skies. At 10 a.m. Beebe poured them both a double shot of rum.

Dr. Barry

They couldn't stay on Nonsuch with the hurricane threatening, so Beebe and Hollister moved to St. George's and stayed with Beebe's friend Mary Hunter. Her house lay just up from a protected bay, and they could see the harbor and also Nonsuch in the distance. They sat around the table as Mary poured tea and talked. She talked about Bermuda, about her father and grandfather who had brought the family to Bermuda.

Her grandfather had been British Commissariat General during the Crimean War, stationed in Malta. His wife, Mary's grandmother, had fallen ill, and the only available doctor was James Barry. Her grandmother told Mary she'd been nervous to be treated by this doctor, because she'd heard he'd once been found dead. He'd been sealed up in a pine box, but his little dog had barked so much the onlookers opened the coffin and found the doctor alive.

Despite her trepidation, Mary's grandmother was treated by Dr. Barry and recovered. Mary hadn't thought of the story in years, until reading an issue of *The Lancet*, she'd come across an article about the doctor's life and career.

James Barry had enrolled in the Edinburgh University medical school at age fourteen with the support of the Venezuelan revolutionary Francisco de Miranda, who he'd met in London. The dedicated young student dressed in an old-fashioned surtout and graduated with a thesis on femoral hernias.

Lord Charles Somerset, governor of the Cape Colony of South Africa, hired Barry in 1816 as a surgeon. Appearing in three-inch platform heels, red-haired and beardless, with an extravagant sword attached at his waist, the talented young doctor proposed some changes to the water system in Cape Town, performed the first successful Caesarian section, and cured Lord Somerset's daughter of a serious illness. Thoroughly impressed, the governor made Barry his personal physician and installed him in a house on the grounds of his estate.

Barry lived with Lord Somerset for ten years, meeting the governor at the Round House to shoot leopards. Their relationship was so intimate it aroused suspicions, and a placard appeared in town accusing the pair of *buggery*—punishable under British law at that time by prison, pillory, or death.

Barry was not cowed by accusations. Brilliant and hot-tempered, he seemed to enjoy making enemies, shooting the cap off one adversary's head in a duel. He was a consummate professional as a doctor and improved sanitary conditions wherever he worked. He scandalized white South Africans by speaking to Black patients directly. He advocated for humane treatment for the mentally ill and insisted that hospitals treating female sex workers hire female attendants.

When Lord Somerset was away in England in 1828, the acting governor, jealous of the doctor's position and influence, had Barry removed. Barry then set out on a peripatetic life, his only constant company an African servant named John and a toy poodle named Psyche. Barry was vegetarian but traveled with a goat for fresh milk. He didn't drink but advocated bathing in wine as a disinfectant.

He worked in Mauritius, Jamaica, the Windward and Leeward Islands; he was dispatched to Saint Helena and then Malta in 1846. It was there that he treated Mary Hunter's grandmother. He ended his career as Inspector of Hospitals in Montreal, where he liked to wear an ox-fur cape and go around in a sleigh.

Florence Nightingale called him the most hardened creature she had ever met.

Forced into retirement not only for ill health but due to his "uncontrollable temperament," he returned to London, where Lord Somerset's daughters took him for carriage rides.

Barry left explicit instructions that when he died, he be buried in his clothes without inspection, but such wishes were not respected. His landlady contracted a woman to prepare his body for burial, then stiffed her, so she went to the press, saying she had discovered Barry's body to be "a perfect female."

Mary Hunter had read this story and dropped the journal in disbelief. There was no mention at all of the doctor being buried alive.

I

"I spit a curve in the wind"

Cradle of the Deep

In the evenings, Beebe read to Hollister from Joan Lowell's recent autobiography, *Cradle of the Deep*. Hollister found it "very jolly and gay." Lowell had been a silent film actress who'd appeared with Chaplin, but her memoir told of her childhood at sea with her father, captain of the *Minnie A. Caine*.

The book described Lowell taken aboard at eleven months old. She wore a flour sack dress and slept in a hammock. She was weaned on goat's milk and the first words she spoke were "goddamned wind." She grew up the only female aboard and developed a fear of women. Instead, she cursed and spat and harpooned and gambled and hung out with shellback sailors with names like Stitches and Slop. The *Minnie A. Caine* freighted soap and tinfoil from San Francisco and traded for guano and coconut meat from the South Seas. Her girlhood misadventures included trying to get whales to cough up ambergris by feeding them pea soup cooked with dead cats and spit from a spittoon.

She was assaulted only once and learned to be cagey and tough as any man.

She learned to make shoelaces from shark intestines. She learned about clandestine traffickers who called the slave trade "blackbirdin.'" She learned to speak Samoan and Marquesan and Gilbertina but struggled with French. At fourteen her father dropped her off in California with her mother, but she couldn't manage to behave and ran away back to sea. She caught scurvy and gorged on porpoise blood. Her first love jumped ship to get away from her. She rejoined the *Minnie A. Caine* and sailed with her father until the ship splintered and sank and she had to swim for shore with a bunch of kittens on her back.

Cradle of the Deep sold a hundred thousand copies, was picked up by the Book of the Month Club and optioned by D.W. Griffith. Then interviews with neighbors in California began to appear. Lowell turned out to be not so much a hardened seafarer as a daughter of the Boston Lowells. Her father had indeed captained the *Minnie A. Caine*, but only for a year or so, and whenever Joan had been aboard she was accompanied by her brothers and her mom. Mostly she'd gone to private school and grown up in Berkeley, and the *Minnie A. Caine* was safely docked in Oakland.

In the wake of the scandal, Lowell's booking agent took a swing at her and was sentenced to fourteen months. She moved to Boston, where she got a job in the tabloid press. She wrote a second memoir in 1933 called *Gal Reporter.*

In 1935, lost and alone, she sailed for Rio de Janeiro. She struck up a conversation with the captain, a man named Leek Bowen, and by the time they caught sight of Sugar Loaf Mountain they were in love. They bought land in central Brazil, cleared it themselves, and cultivated coffee. Lowell drove all across the Amazon in an old Volkswagen and wrote a third memoir about that, called *Promised Land.* It was optioned by Joseph Kaufman, with Lowell's part to be played by Joan Crawford. The *New York Times* criticized the book for "excessive sobriety," and the movie never got made.

Kong

The film of the season was an unexpected blockbuster by their old friends Shorty Schoedsack and Ruth Rose. Mordaunt Hall wrote the review for the *Times*, titled "A Fantastic Film in Which a Monstrous Ape Uses Automobiles for Missiles and Climbs a Skyscraper."

When Beebe had first arranged to let Schoedsack join the crew of the *Arcturus*, the filmmaker was just back from Southeast Asia, where he'd made a hybrid form drama-documentary about a Laotian family battling a leopard. He'd brought his camera out into the jungle to shoot rural life, but later had staged scenes to try to recapture what he'd observed.

This new film was a quintessential Hollywood fantasy. It portrays a New York filmmaker who, like Schoedsack, shoots in far-flung locations. The producers insist his next picture—a film within a film—include a love story. Annoyed, but about to set sail for the Pacific, the fictional filmmaker finds Fay Wray shoplifting in Times Square and hires her on the spot. The next sequence has the ship sailing to an unknown destination, which turns out to be Skull Island. The filmmaker himself has never been there. He only heard about it from a Norwegian captain in Singapore who'd claimed to have rescued an islander alone on a canoe some years before.

Schoedsack had been struggling with the script when he met Rose, and she rewrote all the dialogue:

"Some big hard-boiled egg gets a look at a pretty face and bang he cracks up and goes sappy."

Schoedsack said Rose's talent was in watching situations, especially animals, and writing according to what she'd observed. She wasn't proscriptive in her writing, and that made the films easier to shoot. She modeled the female lead, a character called Ann Darrow, on Fay Wray's offscreen personality. One imagines the filmmaker based on Schoedsack and the ship based on the *Arcturus*. Skull island, with its treacherous bays and unknown animals, seems like a nightmare version of the Galápagos. Rather than giant tortoises, here we have the gorilla-god Kong and a host of dinosaurs.

The islanders are played by Black Americans with natural hairdos and white face paint, dressed in wooly shorts and coconut brassieres. They abduct "the golden woman" in outrigger canoes and marry her to Kong.

"Blondes are scarce around here," the filmmaker observes.

The crew gives chase and finds the island in full torchlight celebration outside a wall that had recently served as the Temple of Jerusalem in Cecil B. DeMille's "King of Kings." Trying to save the woman, men are eaten, stomped, drowned, devoured by giant crabs and an octopus.

Kong takes the golden woman to his lair, gingerly removes some of her clothes, tickles her belly and sniffs his finger. A sailor rescues her, the filmmaker drugs the gorilla-god, and soon, like DeMille's King of Kings, he stands crucified. Rather than on the Mount of Olives, he's on a Broadway stage.

The filmmaker, now turned sideshow impresario, announces:

"He was a king and a god in the world he knew, but now he comes to civilization, merely a show to gratify your curiosity."

But mistaking camera flashes for rifles, Kong rips free of his shackles, grabs Fay Wray, and climbs the Empire State Building. The skyscraper was only two years old when the film was made.

Clutched by a mad and magical beast, a white dream of savagery, a monstrous product of colonial violence, the ape-god climbed the craziest, most grandiose and futuristic thing in the world, a monument to capital and ambition rising from the bitter ash of the Depression. Then fell to his death in a sea of fedoras.

To Mona Williams

Il Fortino, a fortress once occupied by Tiberius, rested on the cusp of the island of Capri, overlooking the Bay of Naples. In the summer of 1983, the palace *Vanity Fair* once called a "monument to luxe, calme and volupte" was surrounded not by fedoras but magnolias. Inside, dressed for burial in a pink-and-black Givenchy dress and matching shoes, lay the body of the great twentieth-century dandy Edmona Travis Strader Schlesinger Bush Williams von Bismarck-Shönhausen de Martini. Her ninety-eight-carat sapphire necklace, designed by Cartier, would soon be shipped to the Smithsonian.

Not long before she died, she received a visit from her old friend Cecil Beaton. The photographer had once rhapsodized about her eyes—"the color of sea water"—like "wild birds in flight"—and her hands—"the deftness and control of a pianist or a surgeon" and "the restraint of violin, no matter how 'brio' the melody." But now he found her a ruin.

Her luxurious hair, which had matured from red to silver decades ago, but always remained crisp and lively, was now a "dried frizz." Worse, her elegant and restrained makeup had devolved into "a grotesque mask on the remains of what was once such a noble-hewn face, the lips enlarged like a clown, the eyebrows penciled with thick black grease paint, the flesh down to the pale lashes coated with turquoise."

This was Beaton's last image of one of his greatest subjects, "a rock crystal goddess with aquamarine eyes," "one of the few outstanding beauties of the thirties . . . who represented the epitome of all that taste and luxury can bring to flower."

In her years at Il Fortino, she had hosted the Duke and Duchess of Windsor, Queens Narriman and Soraya, Princess Grace and Jackie Onassis, Joan Crawford and Brook Astor, Winston Churchill, and Maria Callas.

At tables full of aristocrats, she liked to seat herself between Gore Vidal and Tennessee Williams. Truman Capote, too, was a regular visitor, especially toward the end.

Anyone wondering if her taste for bohemia might say something about her politics could consult the portrait of Mussolini that hung on her wall.

She tended the gardens around Il Fortino using fresh water boated in from the mainland and dressed in couture smocks designed by Balenciaga. When the designer closed his shop, she shut herself inside for three days of mourning.

Mona was the daughter of a Kentucky Irishwoman named Bird O'Shockeny and Robert Sims Strader, a horse trainer at Churchill Downs. They divorced when Mona was young, and she was sent to a grandmother, but her grandmother was institutionalized along with an uncle, and another uncle shot a sex worker, then himself.

Mona was visiting her father, hired to train horses for Arthur James Schlesinger, heir to a great steel and coal fortune, when she caught the wealthy young man's eye. She had a son with him, but their marriage didn't last. It would be the first of five marriages. When it ended, Schlesinger got custody and Mona got a half million dollars. In 1920 she married another rich man, James Irving Bush, but he turned out to be a mean and violent drunk who liked to piss in the fireplace. When they visited Paris together, she left him.

An ice queen with a piercing gaze and red hair already turning silver, she had a boyish body that made clothes look perfect. In 1933 she was the first American to be voted Best Dressed Woman in the World.

Cole Porter sang about her. Dalí painted her (first naked, then in rags).

Vacationing in Venice, she dove into the water near a beautiful yacht only to have the top of her swimsuit come undone. She shrieked in embarrassment while struggling with the ties. Mistaking her scream for a cry for help, a man dove in to rescue her, adding to her mortification.

Soon they were on his yacht, laughing about the misunderstanding. The erstwhile savior turned out to be Count Albrecht Edward von Bismarck-Schönhausen, grandson of the German chancellor. He told Mona to call him Eddie. He was tall, blond, beautiful, and gay. They were soulmates, and a few years later they married. He was her fourth.

Exquisitely attired, hung with discreet but priceless jewels, the newly titled Countess von Bismarck affected a British accent and shuttled between Capri and Paris. After their wedding, she and Eddie converted to Catholicism.

When Eddie died, Mona was devastated, but soon married his doctor, a Neapolitan named Umberto de Martini. Fourteen years younger than Mona, Umberto soon appeared walking her dogs and serving surprisingly rustic wines at her parties. But before long he raced his Alfa Romeo off a bridge, an event immediately dubbed *Martini on the Rocks*. After his death, she found out he was already married and had been siphoning funds from the countess to support his other family.

Perhaps that's when her dissolution began.

Mona's third marriage—after she left the drunken Bush but before she was rescued by Eddie von Bismarck—had been to the utilities magnate Harrison Williams, who fancied himself an explorer and had partly underwritten Beebe's trips to the Galápagos. Williams was nearly wiped out in the stock market crash of 1929, but still managed to help pay for the Bermuda expedition. In a letter to his benefactor, Beebe said he longed to give Williams something "small and oblong and pink" that money couldn't buy. Beebe dedicated his book *Nonsuch: Land of Water* to Mona.

11.

Invisibilities

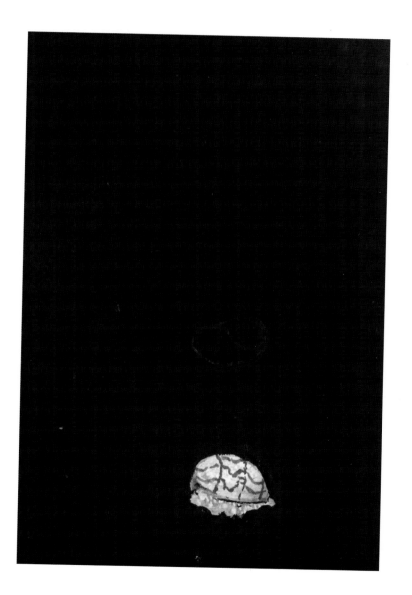

Passing of the *Gladisfen*

It's her time, Captain Sylvester said. Time to put her away.

The captain had a strong mustache and a loud voice, and Beebe had hired him to take care of the tugs and barges and all the shipping-related tasks of the expedition.

It was the captain who doubted the winch from the *Arcturus* would be strong enough to lift the original, five-ton, 1929 version of the bathysphere. He set them back a year and maybe saved their lives.

He okayed the winch on the *Freedom* in 1930, with a smaller bathysphere and stronger mast. But when they went out to lower the ball, he discovered a hole in the hull of the *Freedom* large enough for grouper to swim through. He ordered the tug back to harbor.

He eyed the winch's naked drum when it unrolled 3028 feet of cable, leaving the barrel open to the sky. He told Hollister to pass word to Beebe and Barton: time to come up.

He'd been dubious, enthusiastic. He'd laughed and scowled and given the thumbs up. He was proud to have been part of it.

The expedition complete, as they set to pack up the field station at Nonsuch, Captain Sylvester informed Beebe it was time for the *Gladisfen*, the old tugboat that hauled the *Ready* out to sea, the engine of the bathysphere dives, to be put to rest.

It was her time.

The ship had served in the Spanish-American war. She'd carried the first American flag to be flown over the Morro Castle Liner from New York to Havana. One of the bathysphere fish—jet-black, with a huge mouth and a single illuminated tentacle—was named *Dolopichthys gladisfenae*. They sank her near the site of the record-setting half-mile dive.

It was a clear and perfect day under the yellow sun, and the ship rocked on the swells as the sea-cocks were opened at 10 a.m. and water rushed into the hold.

Beebe waited aboard the ship about fifteen minutes, the sea rising, "a heavy, dead feeling about every movement," until water surrounded her engine. Then he jumped onto a launch where Hollister stood watching, and the captain motored them a hundred yards away.

For a while, nothing seemed to happen. A loose metal door banged. Beebe imagined the ghosts of dead officers and sailors moving in and out. Then, lifted by a swell, the bow rose up and the ship slipped beneath the surface without a splash.

They stared at the surface of the sea where the ship had disappeared. For a long moment there was nothing, just a green-blue emptiness. Then the sea began to spit up planks and gratings. Finally the mainmast shot up. It stood above water, straight and still for a second, then toppled into the floating debris.

Beebe had seen a ship burn up, he said, "but never before have I seen a vessel sink in cold blood."

Half-light

It had rained all night and only stopped now with the morning. Hollister was still sleeping, and Beebe stood at the jalousie slats of the field station window. He'd watched the bobbing mast of the *Gladisfen* shoot up and then fall. Now he wondered, if he watched closely enough, if he could see the last drop of rain evaporate in the sunshine of the day. He thought of that drop as *the last living bead on an elemental abacus*.

A delicacy of time, like practicing how slowly you could close your eyes, watch the shaded darkness fall under your eyelids. In that darkness, he might wake up to another timescale.

He could feel his brain shrink inside his head as his muscles grew. His haunches thickened, and he dropped to all fours. His coccyx extended, bone by bone, and grew fur. His ears lengthened and his teeth shrank and sharpened. His nose grew into a snout and became exceedingly sensitive. The scent of insects sparked his hunger.

His legs faded and disappeared as the fantasy continued. His skin coarsened until it was scaly, and, bone by bone, his ribcage extended. He slithered on the ground until he came to the water's edge, felt the liquid envelop his form. He turned to glance at land one last time before sinking into the water. The liquid flowed through his gills, the vestiges of his limbs were now spiny fins. But those vanished, too, until his backbone, the last thing that once separated him from jellyfish, amoeba, bacteria, was a dot, then an inkling. And in the penumbra of the last evaporating dewdrop, he disappeared completely.

Jalousie slats, the last drop of rain.

From that incipient nothingness, he reverses the fantasy until he is a man again, standing in this room, with the lab next door, where he keeps specimens in cages. He attempts to project himself forward into the future, to feel what his nose will grow into, what his limbs will become. But no image emerges.

It is not a deficiency, perhaps, but simple mechanics. Our blindness is our dynamism.

Out the window in the damp morning, his gaze settled on a periwinkle snail, insistently moving up a branch.

My little snail, he thought, is eternal, crawling up the branch as it has for eons.

He imagined himself here, in the house with the furniture and the lab. The snail must be *previous* to him. But then, the snail was probably like the sea. It had moved on without him. Perhaps, like the sea, it was three times saltier than it had been when they parted ways in the well of the past.

He tried to imagine a time when he'd never seen a snail. What would he think of it?

If he saw a mermaid and a seahorse for the first time, he was sure he'd be much more surprised by the seahorse. But perhaps that was only because of the name. If he didn't think of it as a version of a horse, but just as the animal it was.

But seahorses were remarkable not just because of their names. They had been known to call and answer each other, even when held in separate aquariums.

Who's to say that's remarkable? What feats could he do if someone put him in an aquarium?

How do they even know the other one is there?

He projected himself into the body of a minnow in a large school, darting and changing course in unison. His limbs might shrink into fins, but could he, a man, become a school, or part of a school? Could he extend his nervous system beyond his body, feel an intelligence finer than water? Somatic cells of the body politic, like the leaf-cutter ants in Guyana? His whole sense of Rooseveltian manhood rebelled against the thought. But the evidence was all around him, and within him.

Like the blue shark he had dissected, with the pilot fish attached to the body, copepods behind the fins, embryos within, not to mention all the microbial life. It was actually over a hundred creatures. Who gave him the right to call the shark *one*?

But still, out in the water, he was sure the blue shark felt singular and masterful.

Invisibilities

Beebe sat on dry land on the cusp of Nonsuch, looking at cedars.

The island, the archipelago, had sprung up alone in the middle of the ocean, a spasm of geology, a whim.

The sleep of plants must be very light, he thought, and stirred by ambitious dreams.

The jungle is an abstraction. It's an effusion of details, multiplicity on multiplicity, from beneath the soil to above the canopy. So dense the mind cannot hold it.

Here on Nonsuch, however, he could count every cedar tree. Not to know how many there were, but to spend time with each one, to learn of the character and fate of each tree.

Cedars formed, interacting with wind. The wind itself was invisible, only its effects could be seen. Its unseen action recorded in the cedars.

The ability of the invisible to shape the world—a theme worthy of consideration, Beebe concluded. Later, he sat at his desk with his pen hovering over blank paper.

"The moulding power of the invisible," he wrote.

His ideas were gusts of wind in his mind, and he could feel an itch in his arm, in his wrist, but there was nothing to say about it.

Instead, he thought about cedar wood, what it's used for:

"Cradles, wedding-chests and coffins," he wrote. "Ducking stools and gallows."

He went back to the beach to watch the cedars. He saw those nearest to the water as hunching their shoulders, crouching, stretching out their fingers to compete for light and air.

He pictured cedars as soldiers who'd fallen to their knees, and tried to describe them: "blue-green, close-scaled."

He imagined all the plants of Nonsuch as a choir singing together every morning. He wanted to hear this chorus, which included not only the blue-green cedars, but sage and goldenrod, lavender and tassel-plant, sea rocket and star-of-the-earth.

All these plants must have been brought to the island by wind or tide, or were carried by birds.

He went on naming them, appreciating the names people used for them, so much prettier than the names in his botanical texts: hairy horseweed, scarlet pimpernel, rosy primrose, poor-man's weatherglass, match-me-if-you-can.

When Beebe was a teenager, he used to sit on the roof with his notebook, trying to describe the sunset. He learned to write without looking at the paper, in order to keep his vision trained on the colors. They changed so fast that his description, if he'd looked away, would have been inaccurate.

Trying to record the permutations of a sunset, he concluded, was like reporting on a three-ring circus.

He sat now facing the ocean from the shore and imagined a moment when the earth had been created but hadn't yet begun. He thought of a pause just as it was about to set in motion. The winds were ready to blow, but they weren't blowing yet. All the strife and success that would set natural selection in motion existed only as possibilities. The cedars were just ideas. The sea was dead calm. You couldn't call it stagnant; it was too recent, too incipient. The horizon suggested a sunrise held in suspense. Nothing drifted in the wind, no leaf or feather or particle of dust. There was no breeze yet, no breath. The air itself was unthinkable. The earth was not yet spinning. There was no summer giving way to fall. No pressure from above, no pull from below. At any moment it all might spring into action, but until then he felt caught in a momentary embrace, held close.

It was not *oneness*. That word had been spoiled by belief. It was something more concrete and definite—time and space compressed; Beebe and the cedars, the sea and the sky held together. In the future lay raging hurricanes, winter storms of icy wind, the endless search to eat and mate. But all of that was still to come.

He picked up one of the green spheres that dotted the beach. This one's scientific name was pleasing—*halicystis*. Each was a single cell, the largest cells in the world. Minute copies of Beebe and Barton might be crouched inside, looking around at what creatures lived in the open air.

Beebe held one in his palms—*they are green like emeralds*—then hurled it seaward—*and bounce like rubber balls off hard sand.*

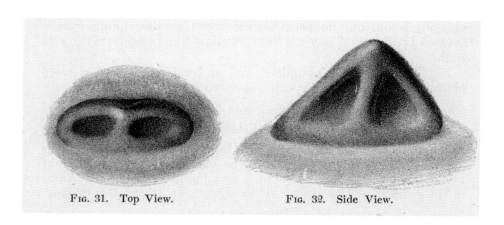

Fɪɢ. 31. Top View.   Fɪɢ. 32. Side View.

Marble

Bags packed, equipment in boxes, Beebe thought approvingly of his peripatetic life. He hoped it might give him some insight into what it felt like to migrate. But beyond shipping out from Bermuda back to New York, he wished he could shed his house and clothes and his human body, to feel himself covered in feathers. He wanted to feel the wind in his wings. But more than that, he wanted to feel the instinct for flight, to feel compelled to fly. It was there at the edge of his imagination, and sometimes he felt he could grasp it for a moment.

He had trained as a pilot and flown planes over Europe. He recalled a night when he'd lost his way. Everything was covered in fog, and he was running out of fuel. He kept making low, swooping passes, trying to see something that would indicate a safe place to land. He scared birds from their roosts as he passed and felt fear and need and the sharpening of the mind as he calculated risk. But nothing of that tin can in the air had taught him how birds fly.

He'd hoped to inhabit the mind of the luminous fish he'd seen from the bathysphere, too, to feel covered in scales, to know a wave and a reef the way fish knew them, not as a man in a helmet or a steel ball. But there was no substitute for being as they were, being at home there.

How could he understand the fish that jumped and flipped, achieving a few seconds in the air above the ocean as the tide receded? Or his own ancestor who, at one point, dragged his body onto land?

He felt the restlessness of his mind, flitting from this to that, as a kind of blindness. I look and I look, he thought, but I see only a fish, a wave, a bird, and a beach.

Most animals are Babbitts or John Smiths, he went on. Solid middle-class citizens. Most fish had hardly heard of the seashore. It was like a myth or a legend.

Only what he thought of as *the gloriously discontented* learned anything new.

He remembered Roosevelt saying he'd rather be a saber-toothed tiger than a field mouse, and Beebe knew what he meant: there was something more important than comfort and contentment, safety and sanity.

But the gloriously discontent didn't often end up swashbuckling US presidents like Roosevelt.

Often, they ended up in tide pools, left to dry up and die when the tide receded.

Evolution was not a progress upward. It could just as soon lead down. Down to the deep like the luminous fish. He thought of the sea creatures, like the periwinkle snail, as previous to him, but just as he had wriggled free of his scales and learned to stand on land, even to climb mountains and fly in airplanes, so the deep-sea fish had strived downward, had become softer in order to go deeper, had learned to withstand cold and heat and pressure that would destroy him.

When he sat to write all this in his notebook, Beebe thought of Lucifer, that angel of light who had refused to bow down. Cursed, perhaps, but certainly easier to relate to than the other angels, mere wisps of transcendence.

He could understand Lucifer, he wrote, as a "monophyletic, mammalian combination of artiodactyl, chiropeterian and human."

Awake again, with the ink dry in his pen, he stepped out of his house and made his way back to the rocky shore, laying on a crest of rock under the stars. After gazing into the sky, his mind was caught by the chirp of birds.

In the crags and crevices all around him he sensed those birds tending their young. Nonsuch now appeared to him not as the site of his laboratory, or an island in the Bermuda Archipelago, but as a chunk of marble implanted with hundreds of baby birds. Within a few months the rock would issue forth these chicks ready for flight, and they would scatter over the Atlantic.

He rose to go back to his room, and felt, for a moment, overcome with love.

12.

Ink Spills Everywhere

Feedback from Readers

John Healey in Cork, Ireland, pointed out that Beebe mistakenly described a gibbous moon as occurring within a day or two of a total solar eclipse, which everyone knows is impossible.

A reader named Jean Coleman pointed out an error in *Half Mile Down*: "On page 108 at the end of the second line. Lt. Commander Edward Ellsberg raised the S-51 and not the S-57 as you have stated in your book."

Upton Sinclair corrected his Latin.

Dr. Pilászy György wrote to inform him of the events of 1052, when a Hungarian named Zotmund, "of his own free will" dove below the invading ships of the Holy Roman Empire, which were barricading Pozsony ("now under the new-fangled name Bratislava") and bored holes in the ships, so that "dawn saw the vessels sink with men and engines." And "Emperor Henry was forced to leave Hungary."

"I hope I made you acquainted," the doctor wrote, "with a little story, that may be a new fact for your collection of divers' deeds."

Another Hungarian, Dr. Geza Entz, at work on a translation of *Half Mile Down*, was struggling with nomenclature, because his language, developed in a landlocked country, had no names for the wondrous fishes of the sea.

A man who'd known him as a boy in East Orange, New Jersey, recalled a time when, as kids, they were "skylarking about," until Beebe got smacked on the nose and started to bleed. They rushed inside to the bathroom to clean him up, but Beebe was still bleeding profusely when a firetruck passed and the boys abandoned him to chase it down the street.

"I remember how wrathy you were."

Hollister's Honors

Before she found work with the DTR, Hollister had worked in cancer research at the Rockefeller Institute. She knew it was meaningful, but her heart wasn't in it. She longed to be out of the confines of the laboratory and live in the wilderness, which she believed would strengthen her reason.

The Girl Scouts of America named her their annual leader in 1934, but she declined the honor.

She could trace her family back to Major General Sir Thomas Shirley, from the ancient Sussex family of Shirley. Thomas fought in the Seven Years' War, became governor of the Bahamas from 1768, governor of Dominica in 1774, and governor of the Leeward Islands in 1781, where Dr. Barry would work a century later. In 1786 he was awarded a baronetcy as "Shirley of Oat Hall" and buried in Bath Abbey.

To observe her record-setting dive, *Modern Mechanix & Hobbies* honored Hollister, among other women scientists. Alongside Henriette Swope, who viewed a solar eclipse at Ak-Bulak, USSR; Edith M. Wallace, who had spent twenty-seven years making daily drawings of vinegar fly mutations; Hollister, having just made the deepest dive of any woman in history, was pictured panning for gold in Guyana.

The Society of Women Geographers that honored Hollister was cofounded by Beebe's first wife. When Hollister made her record-setting dive in 1934, she affixed the flag of the society to the bathysphere's cable. Before her, the flag had been brought to Greenland by Marie Peary Stafford.

Later the flag would be loaded up with Amelia Earhart in preparation for her circumnavigational flight. Hollister had made her last dive and cleaned out the Nonsuch field station when she heard her friend had disappeared.

Earhart had already announced she was more afraid of growing old than dying. She wrote a letter to be presented to her father, a religious man, on the event of her death. It began:

"I have no faith that we'll meet anywhere again."

Odds and Ends Left at Nonsuch

Bromide tablets
Castor oil
Licorice flavored cough lozenges
Epsom salts
2 tubes of K-Y lubricating jelly
Rhubarb and soda

Winter of 1934

Beebe toured university towns, usually alone, giving lectures. In Notre Dame he had a nice crowd but "no hospitality." In Sioux City he took himself to the movies, watching *The Meanest Girl in Town* with Zasu Pitts and *Roman Scandals* with Eddie Cantor.

Zasu Pitts, from Parsons, Kansas, married a boxing promoter and was the model for Olive Oyl. "Bully," Beebe concluded.

He lunched at the Rotary Club and lectured in Pittsburgh. Some days, the only activity recorded in his diary was *cocktails.*

A home-cooked meal in Cincinnati, lectures in Chicago, Detroit, Indianapolis.

He sailed to England, where he observed the filming of *Stanley and Livingstone.* He visited his friend Iris in Tunbridge Wells and played with the little dog she'd drugged and made to look like her pregnant belly in order to smuggle it into the country. He visited A. A. Milne again, another cup of tea among sculptures of Pooh and Tigger and Piglet.

Riding the train back to London, he read Dorothy Sayers's *Gaudy Night,* wondering what kind of book he might write if he really tried.

In California he visited a cousin of the queen, a talented botanist named Mary Hood.

He had lunch with a man named Kiesling at MGM studios, surrounded by actors dressed as pirates. He stopped by the filming of *Strange Cargos,* where Clark Gable and Joan Crawford marched across a re-creation of British Guiana. When they both stumbled forward and fell flat in a faint, Beebe told the director that's not how people faint. First their knees buckle, then they fall.

The director ordered another take, commenting that Beebe was "the only man who had ever brought Clark Gable to his knees."

Later he went to hear a lecture by an astrologer, who predicted the war would end in 1941 and the last great battle would be fought near Turkey. And that after the war Germany would unite with England and France to fight Russia.

Finally, due to the many eclipses: "a continent would rise in the Pacific."

The Other Beebe

Hollister set off to lead her own team, mapping Guyana, while Beebe and a few staff worked out of a fishing boat, sailing south from San Diego. They inspected fish habitats along Baja California, then continued until they got to Acapulco. They pulled into the harbor and went into the old port city looking for a drink. They stopped for beer at a place called El Hotel Tropicale. It turned out the proprietor was named Beebe, from Dayton, Ohio, perhaps a distant relation.

This other Beebe's wife had recently been horseback riding along the edge of a cliff. At a misstep, Mrs. Beebe was thrown. She went landward and ended up bruised but unharmed, while the unfortunate horse was thrown over the cliff and dashed to pieces. Just a trick of fate and it could have been her.

The other Beebe brought out a painting on a small sheet of metal. It depicted the scene: woman one way, horse the other, with a cloud of smoke rising from the dead horse. Emerging from within the smoke was the image of a bearded man.

"That's the saint who'd saved my wife," the other Beebe said.

They left El Tropicale for a place called The Seven Seas, where they met "several gangsters and other notables." Then they went to Los Cocos, where a marimba band lit by a single bulb played under a palm tree. Men went to invite girls in bright-colored clothes from some chairs across the way and danced with them for ten centavos. At the end of the song, the pairs split immediately and returned to their seats.

They danced well, Beebe thought, but without gaiety. He marveled at the great variety of men's hats.

The proprietor here was a man with plucked eyebrows and heavy eye makeup. He had a graceful sway when he walked and long eyelashes that would have made a Hollywood star crazy. Beebe found him perfectly sincere and unselfconscious.

He brought a round of drinks for them, told them he was fresh out of jail.

Every once in a while the police came around, took him down to the station and fined him forty pesos, and the girls had to raise the money to get him out. After garnishing their wages for the house, and for such fines, they made a centavo and a half per dance.

No one was drunk, Beebe thought, but it was still early.

What struck him most was everyone's naturalness. No one displayed any shame at being the proprietor of a lowly dancehall, or of working in one, or of patronizing one. The dances were decent, the clothes were decent. And some danced for pure pleasure.

The next day they flew to Mexico City, and from the sky Beebe watched a hammerhead shark in the sea as pelicans scattered in their wake.

The Sunset of Luisa Velasco

In Manzanillo, Beebe and his crew sat to watch a performance of *La Dama de las Camelias*, with the part of Margarita played by Luisa Velasco. In her prime she'd been famous but was now on a downward slide toward oblivion.

They paid a peso and sat in some bleachers. Stray dogs roamed the aisle. Among the crowd, he saw faces "scarred and stamped with the fear of life."

You could hear the creak of stairs from out of view—someone was mounting the stage.

Luisa Velasco emerged—she was blond, platinum, reminded Beebe of Lillian Russel with a few extra pounds *avoirdupois*. She was dressed in a tight silver gown.

The crowd gasped, and the floorboards bent under the weight of the star as she stalked the tiny stage.

She gave all her energy to the performance, "wholly undisturbed by her audience of desperados, Indians, babies, and dogs, as well as itinerant gringos."

Another actor spilled wine on a chair Velasco was meant to sit in. While delivering her monologue, the star "deftly dropped her handkerchief, a newspaper, and the cover from a small table onto the chair before she trusted her frock to its damp seat."

The costumes were ill-fitting. The leading man could hardly fill his suit. When he needed to gesture vehemently, first he shook his hands free from "the enveloping sleeves."

Whenever there was a stage kiss, someone in the crowd would call *¡otro!* Applause was enthusiastic.

"The sunset of such an actress is not pleasant," Beebe thought, "and yet the sincerity of the whole—bands, performance, audience—made it all admirable."

The Names of Things

The bathysphere expeditions were over. Hollister was elsewhere. Beebe found himself on the deck of the *Zaca*, leaning on the railing and looking down at the Pacific, as they steamed from Mexico back to California.

When the ocean's surface is calm, Beebe thought, we see it as a single identity. When we see waves, we think of them as individuals moving through the sea, eventually splashing against a palm at shore. But a wave as a quantity of water does not move. The water stays mostly where it is. Only the movement moves through it. The water that will eventually splash against the palm is already right near the palm, simply waiting for the energy to come and give it lift.

Like a whirlpool in a stream, the particles of water approach, are caught in this movement and swirl around each other before loosening and heading off downstream. In that case it is the water which moves, and the movement which is still.

Either way it is movement, energy, that has identity, not water.

That's what we are, Beebe thought: "a few particles of material substance entangled in and passing through a bodily whirlpool for a brief space of time."

Whatever swirls of thought may be brought on by the waves, their presence was indisputable as they rolled back and forth aboard ship. When Beebe walked, he pressed the walls or reached for railings. He had to brace himself in order to type, and attempts to use a microscope immediately led to a black eye and smashed lens.

In the afternoon, someone caught a *dorado*—what the English call a *dolphin-fish*. Beebe preferred the Spanish name, because indeed the fish was "a vibrating sheet of pure gold."

This fish entered the record as *Coryphaena*, named by Aristotle because it reminded him of a golden helmet. Linnaeus called the smaller dolphin fish *equisitus*. Then a Swedish copyist copied the name as *equiselis*, so the fish they caught, due to the copyist's mistake, went by the moniker *Coryphaena equiselis*.

With all these twists of observation and error, Beebe thought, after two thousand years since Aristotle named these fish, "we can add little to the Whys and Hows and Wherefores of their lives."

It was not the fish that had changed, but the names. Eventually, perhaps, to be dashed against a palm and forgotten.

When they were back in port in San Francisco, Beebe showed a collection of shells to a conchologist. She named two of them after uncertainty.

Flight rhythm of pelicans, of cormorants, and of the
two when flying together

Last Visit

On his last visit to Nonsuch, in 1941, he found the sea full of silt from an oil spill. He hunted down the coil of cable that had been used to lower the bathysphere and found most of it had been stolen. Back in town, he walked the waterfront surrounded by Scottish soldiers who'd fought at Dunkirk, then been sent to Bermuda to get over the trauma.

They had the unfocused gaze of drunks, Beebe thought.

At dinner, he told of the time when Tom Dill was accosted by a sex worker in Piccadilly. Dill tightened up and said: "Do you know I am the Crown Solicitor of Bermuda?" The girl responded: "Blimey, that's nothing. I'm the 'alf-crown solicitor of Piccadilly."

He thought the joke was hysterical.

Beebe left Bermuda by plane, rising to nine thousand feet. From that height, he thought, the surface of the sea looked just as it did from below, without so much as a crinkling. "It was dull and oxidized and absolutely solid."

With his eyes trained down, he made out that the snow-crystal flecks he saw were huge swells, and that a tiny chip was a freighter heading to port. He saw Cuba, where Hollister had bounced a tarantula from the nightclub, now: "flat as paper, ruled with near rectangles of sugar cane, stippled with asterisks of coconut palms."

He wanted to write about the world from above, but found it as futile as describing wind through cedars, or the deep ocean for that matter. It was like a eulogy to emerald and turquoise reefs, malachite waves, an ivory sailboat floating—

No, he stopped himself: "So tame and humdrum are any combination of twenty-six letters."

When he looked up, the blue sky darkened to black. He thought of the Himalayas, of the clean space above earth's dirty atmosphere.

He ordered an old-fashioned and fell into conversation with another passenger, who turned out to be the Yugoslav ambassador. Someone tried to use a fountain pen, but pressure made the ink spill everywhere.

Titans of the Deep

With the bathysphere retired, Otis Barton went on to invent new submersibles that could reach deeper depths. A vessel called the Benthoscope went down to forty-five hundred feet, a temporary win in the game of record-breaking Beebe found infantile.

Barton wrote him in 1938 complaining he was short of funds for his new deep-sea plans—it seemed the engineer's personal fortune wasn't enough to finance his increasingly ambitious projects. Displaying stark ignorance of economic realities, Barton asked Beebe for a job doing "dirty work" in the lab, as if that would pay enough to cover the costs of deep-sea exploration.

Holding the note in his hands, Beebe scrawled across the top "utterly absurd." He wrote a curt note in reply, explaining that the lab was closed. Anyway, he had more help from grad students than he could use.

"You don't realize how lucky you are to have an income of your own. None of us have such a thing and have to work every moment to get enough to merely live and carry on with."

Later the same year Beebe received notice of a film to be released called *Titans of the Deep*. It was billed as a Hollywood cross between science and adventure. Beebe didn't respond at first, but was taken aback when he saw an ad for the film in New York that featured his own name, indicating he had participated in the film. He sat in the theater to watch and was horrified. It was a mishmash of old bathysphere footage Barton had salvaged, most shot in Panama without Beebe's presence. There were underwater shots of bathing beauties in diving helmets and wet suits, always narrowly escaping the jaws of a shark or tentacles of a hungry octopus. This was what Barton obviously thought of *girl scientists*.

Oh God, Otis!

Beebe dashed off letters to the *Times* and to *Science* magazine:

"Together with my staff, I would like to completely dissociate myself from this motion picture and to have it known altogether as the work of Mr. Barton."

13.

Silence and Solitude

World's Fair

The bathysphere starred in two World's Fairs. As Beebe and Hollister had steamed around the Caribbean in 1933 stopping to meet Priscilla on Medusa Island, Barton's sphere sat in the Century of Progress Exposition in Chicago. Beebe liked to think about the fact that it would outlive all of them, even the oceans themselves. All humans would drop dead, the abyss would evaporate, while the bathysphere's quartz eyes would keep watch.

Beebe agreed to participate in the World's Fair again in 1939. This time the plan was more ambitious. The bathysphere would be on display, but he also hoped to steam out to the Hudson Gorge and do some dives and trawls during the exhibition. In 1928, trawling on the way back from the *Arcturus* expedition, Beebe had brought up fifty-five species of deep-sea dragonfish, their richest haul ever, right there.

They would rush the catch to the display, trying to keep as many alive as possible. He hoped to show the gorge's rich and varied abyssal life, to impress visitors with "amazing creatures living in the least known area of exploration left on the planet, all captured within one hundred miles of City Hall."

This impetus was dear to Beebe: reveal the wondrous unknowns of our everyday surroundings. Having traveled the world from the depths of the sea to the highest mountains, tramped through jungles and flown across continents, Beebe was more and more adamant that wonder was not produced by swashbuckling adventures—it was a way of seeing, an attitude toward experience that was always available. At every turn, the world's marvels were right before our eyes.

But there were other forces at play in this confluence of interests:

The 1939 World's Fair was conceived and designed by Edward Bernays, nephew of Freud, progenitor of public relations (which he called *the engineering of consent*) and a major inspiration to Joseph Goebbels. A brochure tells what else was on display:

One corner was the home of *Voder*, a synthetic human voice, which answered questions in what sounded like a German accent.

Elsewhere two chairs were comfortably positioned on a platform, surrounded by tulips. You could rest there to chat with your companions. When you stood up, you'd be surprised to find the platform sliding out of the way. Now the chairs were occupied by dummies, whose painted mouths spoke words you'd just said, in your own voice.

The Borden Building was dedicated to "scientific dairying." Visitors could admire "a fluorescent phial of lactoflavin" and watch cows milked automatically on a Rotolactor.

In the Budd Exhibit, visitors interested in "viscose acetates" could watch rayon thread being manufactured.

Other exhibits showed an early fax machine, a television receiver, cellophane, plastic toothbrushes, plastic combs, and a machine that processed soybeans into flakes that could be used for paint, enamel, buttons, gear shifts.

General Motors presented its history of the world:

(a) Morse invents the telegraph; Bell invents the telephone; Marconi invents the wireless (b) Boessemer erects the first modern converter to make steel out of iron (c) The Wright brothers fly at Kitty Hawk (d) Drake sinks the first oil well (e) Olds pioneers mass production of the horseless buggy (f) Benjamin Franklin, Faraday and others give the world electricity (g) Arkwright patents the yarn-spinning frame (h) Goodyear learns how to vulcanize rubber (i) Wolf patents a mechanical refrigerator.

Visitors could admire plexiglass and Bakelite. The Playground of Science exhibit included a Wilberforce pendulum, a self-balancing bicycle, a cathode ray oscillograph, and music sent over a beam of light.

Finally, we come to the exhibit of the New York Zoological Society:

It begins with a diorama of the Hudson Gorge, illustrating how it was created by glacial movements, walked over by mastodons and saber-tooth tigers.

The bathysphere is there, along with preserved specimens of angler fish, hatchet fish, and a black swallower. At the end was a model of Barton's futuristic "Bottom Gazer," meant to descend to six thousand feet.

The bathysphere was used to test the impacts of underwater explosions during WWII, and then its trail goes cold. In 2005 it turned up at the Coney Island aquarium, where for a time it served as a redoubt where young staffers could smoke clandestine joints. It now sits at the entrance to the Shark House.

Rancho Grande

When Beebe and his pet monkey Chiriqui arrived at the concrete structure in the high jungles of Venezuela, the site had been abandoned for fourteen years. It had been under construction, intended as the getaway home for Juan Vicente Gómez, when the man Beebe thought of as "the last great South American dictator" died in 1935. At the news of their patron's death, the construction team, consisting of almost two hundred workers, dropped their tools and went home, leaving a maze of half-built oval, semicircular, and triangular rooms.

Beebe and Chiri found huge salons meant to be elegant ballrooms for dancing that were bare concrete. Some lacked walls, hovered in mid-air, appeared out of nowhere. Without ever being used, these rooms had become a ruin of rusted fixtures. Cubist murals and brightly painted walls were overlaid with fungus, lichens, slime, and mold.

Beebe pulled out Robert Ridgway's color key and matched "auricula purple, rainnette green, hathi gray, chamois, dark dull gray, apricot orange."

Pools of water gathered in the concrete pools, full of "protozoa, coelenterata, platyheminthes, nemathelminths, and rotifera."

Rancho Grande was usually enswathed in cloudy mist. He thought of it as an enormous question mark.

Beebe worked closely with George Swanson and Jocelyn Crane. Crane, an assiduous assistant and talented scientist, had joined Beebe's team in Nonsuch. She was in the background while Beebe was focused on Gloria Hollister. But now Hollister had permanently returned to the US, married, and left scientific exploration for conservationism.

From now on, Crane would be Beebe's closest companion.

They worked in a makeshift laboratory frequented by ocelots. Beebe studied lichens, mold, and orchids that grew in the jungle outside. He considered that somewhere, somehow, they all, we all, shared a single ancestor.

"Even today there are one-celled lives," he knew, "which are animals at night and plants in the sunlight."

Having survived the crushing pressure of the ocean depths, in the relative calm of the Venezuelan highlands, he found himself preoccupied with death. Death might come for him right there at Rancho Grande, or elsewhere, at some unanticipated moment. He wondered how it might arrive. A car crash? An explosion? A train wreck? A house fire? A crime of passion? A confident dive into a shallow pool?

"A time comes," he wrote in his journal, "when there develops a feeling of superfluousness, a redundancy of self, a surfeit of ego."

Shorter Works

BY WILLIAM BEEBE

WHAT HAPPENS AFTER WARMTH IN THE NORTH AND MOISTURE IN
THE TROPICS

Two hundred and fifty years ago Leeuwenhoek found that gutter
dust when moistened awoke lowly creatures to life. Decades later
round worms were revived after twenty-seven years. The museum
snail, after four years of being glued to an exhibit card, revived
when placed in water.

LEARNING TO LIVE

Like a naked grub; no wings, no beak, nothing but a shapeless
body, naked, and a cavernous gaping mouth.

Tadpole from gooey egg, to a fish, to a leaping land animal.
Compare with an egg, a worm.

SLEEP

Butterflies hang like leaves.

1520   Ger. Swanson

Moth Wings

It was 1940, the depths of a New York winter, and Cathelat was performing his debut in Defrère's production of *Pelléas*. At intermission, the audience streamed out into the lobby, and soon George Swanson's cheeks flushed with the gin in his martini. He turned to his friends and made an announcement: I'm going to paint in the jungle.

Swanson had joined Beebe for the last season at Nonsuch. Now, Beebe wanted him to depict specimens at the field station at Rancho Grande. He had studied under John Grabach, a proponent of the Ashcan style, whose paintings reflected "the innately disconsolate aspect of the human condition."

No doubt the tropics, and the nonhuman condition, presented an attractive alternative. Swanson had never been to the jungle or South America and imagined it all out of storybooks.

He was saddened, when he arrived, to report an absence of "floating ladies aloft on sea foam under the full moon." Instead, he found a yellow-spotted snake in the garden, frogs in the kitchen, and spiders everywhere.

He painted "carnivorous grasshoppers with blue legs, emerald tree snakes and alabaster hylas with jade popeyes." And as Isabel Cooper had, he rushed to render animal colors before they were swept away by death.

Swanson, with his sense for mise-en-scène, gathered moss-covered bits of bark to serve as backdrops for his scenes. "*Enterolobium* seedpods like something in the window of a French confectioner, and twigs from mellow-trunked old trees with miniature forests of young ferns, mosses and seedling epiphytes."

Then he rushed to paint, before the orchids bloomed themselves to death, trying to capture the grandeur of a caterpillar that reminded him of Bakst's design of the chief eunuch in *Sheherezad*.

It was nearly impossible to invoke the unimaginable creatures of the insect world with ordinary paint. He longed for a palette that was heaped with "smoldering gems and minerals and stuff made of moths' wings."

But as he worked *al fresco* in his jungle studio he came to feel at home among the vines and strangler figs. He sketched the toothy red zigzag of the heliconias, as all around him he heard bellbirds with their resonant calls, the hum of gold and purple wasps, and red howling monkeys, which he imagined singing from some paradisiacal mountaintop.

"A song like some Latin chèvre-pied piping on a reed," he learned, "would be a small brown bird sitting on a rose-tinted spadix of an aroid blossom."

He imagined enough time like this and his feet would turn into hooves, his thighs would cover with hair, and he would prance off through the thick draperies of thorn-covered vines.

He filled trunks with exquisite illustrations to be shipped back to the zoo for publication, depictions of the great diversity of flora and fauna in the high Venezuelan jungle.

When his contract ended, he returned to New York stripped of the austerity of the ashcan style.

He applied his newly zestful eye toward the opera stages that had been his first love, and made his name painting "sensuous and lustful" portraits of the male dancers of the Ballets Russes.

Things We Do in Moments of Pensiveness

BY GEORGE SWANSON

1. Putting dead chaparro trees in milk cans filled with stones.
2. Stuffing dead leaves from a butterfly net into a milk can.
3. Winding dead pygmy anteater's tails around tree branches
4. Holding dead pygmy anteaters against the sky.
5. Bathing rhinoceros beetles.
6. Poking sloths with sticks and pulling them off rafters.
7. Running after Chiri.
8. Taking dead rats out of the refrigerator.
9. Putting dead rats into the refrigerator.
10. Chopping termite nests.
11. Stroking lizards' backs.
12. Enticing sphinx caterpillars out on the ends of branches.
13. Waiting for the sun to come out with a lizard in one hand and a toad in the other.
14. Watching Iggy eating yellow Puoi flowers.
15. Wishing we were macaws.
16. Blowing baby nighthawks out of their eggs. (Horrors!)
17. Stuffing bananas down baby orioles' throats.
18. Cutting the gables off the 3 hole Excusado.
19. Cutting pieces out of butterflies' eyes.
20. Helping Jocelyn catch runaway spiders.
21. Cleaning Chiri's ick off the front steps.
22. Idling away the golden hours. (O, Yeah!(.

Animals and Men

Beebe was a social gentleman. He loved cocktails and costume parties and tennis. But he preferred the company of the nonhuman. He collected extensive notes on this in a file called "Animals and Men."

"Whenever a horse and I look each other in the eye," he writes, "I feel I am closer to his feelings, to his real being, than most men."

He compiled a list of famous horses, from Alexander the Great's Bucephalus to the legendary Black Bess who one night sped the highwayman Dick Turpin two hundred miles from York to London. He listed Napoleon's Marengo, Muhammad's Buraq, the reigning thoroughbred Man o' War, the immortals Xanthus and Arion, and Don Quixote's Rosinante. To that list he hoped to add Satan, a Tibetan pony with saffron eyes who he rode through the Himalayas in search of tragopans and blood pheasants. Satan made him feel like the Sahib of Sahibs, he said, like Mahbub Ali himself.

He had a special love for camels, those contradictory creatures with melting eyes, Hollywood lashes, and quivering nostrils, whose voice, he mourns, "should end all human attempts at swing."

Beebe was of the opinion that when Jesus said it was easier for a camel to fit through the eye of the needle than for a rich man to enter the kingdom of heaven, he was not referring to the tiny eyelet in a sewing needle. Beebe thought Jesus was instead referring to a door or opening in the old walls of east Mediterranean cities, large enough for a person to pass through but too small for a horse or camel. Such openings were known as "needle's eyes," Beebe claims, and in good news for rapacious capitalists (such as the underwriters of his annual program budget) he tells of a time in Cairo, when he saw a camel kneel and inch forward on its knees through exactly such a threshold.

Solitude

In 1939 Beebe received a letter from the writer and biologist Rachel Carson, who was at work on a book about the ocean. Although she had a master's degree, she thought of herself as an autodidact like him. She worked for the department of fisheries but was most at home on a small island in Maine where she gazed at the sea and walked along the shore and listened attentively for the sound of a hermit thrush at nightfall.

She intended to write a lyrical and contemplative book of science, and was considering spending some of her advance on a trip to Bermuda to go diving. She wondered if there were a chance to go down in the bathysphere.

Beebe wrote back to tell her the expedition was finished. The field station was closed. Carson would have to find another way of witnessing the world beneath the ocean's surface. But she was not put off and kept in touch.

Carson wasn't ever much of a swimmer and only ever went underwater a few feet. Unable to dive off Nonsuch, she went helmet diving in a protected area in Biscayne Bay. She was surprised by the sudden lightness of the helmet underwater and by the rhythmic whooshing sound of air entering and leaving.

Even that brief submersion, she said, changed her writing forever.

The Sea around Us reached back to the very formation of the solar system. Carson imagined our planet still a cluster of cooling gases, when "a tidal wave of earthly substance" had been spit out into the atmosphere, forming the moon. The Pacific, she wrote, was a scar reminding us of what had left us. And the moon was a chunk of early earth frozen in space.

Life, she thought, was an impossible thing that troubled lines of distinction. Think of a single-celled organism, she suggested, somewhat like bacteria, a halfway state between organic and inorganic matter. Like Beebe's creatures who were plants during the day and animals at night, the first creatures to move onto land, a kind of prehistoric arthropod, were also natives of border country. Now, after millennia of adaptation, we still carry the sea in our veins. But we're unable to inhabit it as our ancestors did. As the sea has moved on without us, we have to devise complicated technologies to spend time there.

Watching mostly from the shore, Carson was able to send her imagination through the entire ocean. It was Carson who first pictured as *marine snow* the "steady, unremitting, downward drift" of decaying plankton that feeds the depths. She was able to visualize the vast area of the north Pacific floor covered in red clay, where nothing remains but shark's teeth and the inner ears of whales. She marveled that the earth's processes of creation were so destructive and catastrophic. With few exceptions, she wrote, every island in the world—and Bermuda is her model here—is a result of the violent eruptions of submarine volcanoes.

Watching mostly from the shore, Carson contemplated the tides. She'd read that the ancients attributed the sea's movement to the breathing of an abyssal monster. But she knew tides to be an effect of the moon and the sun and the earth's own gravitational force. As pervasive as they seem, she pointed out, they are not always the same. The tides in Tahiti ignore the moon almost completely. And as permanent as they seem, they are not fixed or eternal.

"As with all that is earthly," she wrote, "their days are numbered."

The movement of the sea was an irregularity across the planetary surface. It created friction and slowed the rotation of the earth. Since Babylonian times the day had slowed several seconds.

Earthquakes sped the spin infinitesimally, but they would never compensate.

Instead, she predicted, the earth will continue to spin slower, and the moon's gravitational attraction to us will weaken. Eventually a day will be two months long, and the moon will drift away.

Silence

Carson had spent the war years monitoring fisheries. She knew how much research had been done, how much technology had been unleashed. In the 1950s, with her own body wracked with cancer, she sent out letters to field stations and researchers and analyzed reports.

Much of the damage was permanent.

By 1960, when she started writing her last book, Strontium 90 from nuclear explosions had already cycled through the planetary systems until it was in our bones.

Like nuclear fallout, insecticides were biproducts of wartime research into the technology of mass killing. Findings originally used to develop nerve gas were now used to produce DDT.

Carson imagined nerve gas sprayed over fields of alfalfa, the alfalfa fed to hens and cows. Now there was nerve gas in our eggs and milk and butter. We ate it every day.

These were chlorinated naphthalenes that had been shown to cause hepatitis back in the 1930s.

Dieldrin and aldrin—a pile on your pinky fingernail could kill four hundred quail.

Parathion that made honeybees bellicose.

A chemist set out to experiment on parathion himself. He set out a trace amount with an antidote on hand. After ingesting it, paralysis set in so quickly he could not administer the antidote. He died reaching for it.

Florida children found an empty bag of parathion and used it to make a swing and also died. Orange pickers fell to the ground, retching, and became temporarily blind.

It was a world of unintended consequences. A flea bites a dog and the dog's blood becomes poisonous, killing it. Insects die from fumes rising from poisonous plants. Bees carry poison back to the hive and produce poisonous honey.

Her prophecy was dire: "Chemicals kill every insect, still the song of birds and the leaping of fish in streams."

She saw chains of poison, "this ever-widening wave of death that spreads out, like ripples when a pebble is dropped into a still pond."

In the genes of the poisoned, it became part of our inheritance. She described a scene at Tule Lake in 1960: dead herons, pelicans, grebes and gulls gathered into piles to be disposed of.

Silent Spring provided the foundational image of the US environmental movement:

"Spring now comes unheralded by the return of the birds, and the early mornings are strangely silent where once they were filled with the beauty of bird song."

The silence Carson conjured, in a noisy, difficult world, became not the resolution of babbling mysticisms, the wordlessness of Beebe's infinite deep. Now it was the silence of self-inflicted desolation and ruin, a haunting that was just beginning.

Final Exchange

Hollister wrote Beebe in 1949, on the fiftieth anniversary of his employment with the Zoological Society—twelve years after they'd stopped working together. One can imagine it was John Tee-Van, even Jocelyn Crane, who suggested she write.

He'd love to hear from you. It would mean a lot.

In the letter, Hollister reminded him of a night they spent reading by the light of a kerosene lamp in the house on Nonsuch, waking up to "the rush of wind through cedars carrying bird calls."

And remember, she wrote, when the English prince came by, and the barge and diving ladder dragged over a reef, nearly killing him, "while his Royal Highness unconcernedly continued his explorations below."

Remember the *Gladisfen*, she wrote—its passing.

And her little dog Trumps. He was with them on Nonsuch, too.

Remember the pirate-themed birthday we gave in your honor, she wrote, when "you were made to walk the plank and to land, blindfolded, on Castle Island where, from the dungeons, Al Donohue and his orchestra struck up 'Happy Birthday to You.'"

Beebe wrote a short letter back in response:

"I hope the new home is all that you hoped and want."

Trinidad

The last field station was up in the hills of central Trinidad. Beebe named it Simla after Kipling. He came and went from New York less frequently. His constant companion was Jocelyn Crane. She accompanied him while completing a study of crabs, disappearing occasionally for expeditions of her own.

He and Crane passed the time imagining a Beebe autobiography, making lists of stories that might go in it. Crane suggested his mother taking him to the phrenologist, and "the minister who couldn't remember the Lord's Prayer."

Beebe listed titles of unwritten stories:

How a Beetle Laid Waste to a Tropical Isle
How I Met a Danish Flapper and What Ensued
How I Sat in the Lap of a President's Wife and What Resulted
What Oil Did to a Great City

In 1950 he found himself alone in Port of Spain, sharing his hotel with the Jamaican cricket team. Back at the field station, he entertained a group of young women with his binoculars, surrounded by birds called pour-me-ones.

He flew to St. Thomas on a small plane called the *Sea Gypsy*. When he climbed into the co-pilot's seat his stomach started to turn. He hadn't been in the cockpit of a plane since WWI.

His brows and jowls grew heavier, his expression haggard and exhausted, but he retained the same posture and focus.

On stray newspaper clippings: a mugging downtown, the USSR paying seven-hundred thousand dollars to the US after shooting down a US plane over the Bering Sea, the reconsideration of a capital case involving three men sentenced to hang for murder, an editorial complaining about "the run down condition of certain premises in the city in which liquor is sold."

The rains came and lizards hatched. His journal entries became short and staccato and typos proliferated.

"If you know how, you can pick up a scorpion by its stinger."

"A bat falcon, crying 'ke-ke-ke-ke' flies by with an emerald hummingbird in its claws." "caught a Celeus elegans woodpecker. but issed a bellbird."

He pisses all night long.

After breakfast his lips pucker and he speaks as if he had a baked potato in his mouth. His right hand suddenly trembles—stops when he "gets mad at it."

Hernia seems to get no worse. Constipated, takes laxatives every three days.

What "passes as his brain . . . seems to click on as well, or poorly, as ever."

If he stands up suddenly his head spins and the world is decorated with "a multitude of beautiful violet specks."

On April 18, 1958, he hears of the death of his first wife.

In June, as he was walking through the lab, he began to see events "as separate points or tableaus of shining light." It was as if he had scratched through and seen reality for the first time. He saw "the cup of mountains; the plague of flies, each fly as a not unpleasant entity."

He saw "the Wedding of the Snows as a detail-less church," and he was moving up the aisle toward the minister. A butterfly flapped around the wire screen. Outside, he could see flowers. And beyond that, "the wide spreading repercussions."

Between Day and Night

Among the piles of papers Beebe left behind after his death in 1962, Jocelyn Crane found a couple of typed pages, titled "Between Day and Night," opening with the line: "There is a certain hour before dawn when men die."

His old friend, the reactionary ranter Lord Dunsany, had written in his *Book of Wonder* that there was an hour "when sick men mostly die, and sentries on lonely ramparts stand to arms, exactly half-an-hour before dawn."

Beebe must have been remembering, or half-remembering that line, when he sat down to write:

> Day is hope and light and life in the sun is a fair give and take; night itself is a challenge, a worthy gamble. I stumble trustfully through black, slimy, tropical palm swamps in deepest night, with only the excitement of interest in strange beings; but as I float quietly along in a canoe on rippleless water, a cold terror sometimes creeps over me as the afterglow dies down.

He describes the moment when sunset has given way to darkness, when he starts to sense not only "tooth and fang, poison and thorn" but "electric shock" and "fatal amoeba." Then he hears the calls of familiar birds and "the death hour is past."

These moments of fear heighten his awareness, and he finds them "of superlative interest."

It had happened to him recently, floating through a mangrove swamp. A sudden silence fell, and Beebe sensed the "transparent luminosity of the world."

Then "the mobile mirrors of the mangroves changed" and fearful thoughts arose from his memory. He remembered hiding in a tree from an elephant in

Sri Lanka, and it was as if it were happening right then. He could smell the elephant's "hot strong breath." Its trunk, searching for him, was just there. He was easily within reach, staring at the two searching nostrils. He could not understand why the animal, which he had angered by entering its territory with a shotgun, hadn't grabbed him, pulled him to the ground, and trampled him to death right then and there.

At that thought, he abandoned the essay.

If I Come Up

Beebe had imagined a last chapter of *Half Mile Down* called "If I Come Up." A contemplation, no doubt, of the possibility of dying in the deep. Over the course of the bathysphere dives, there had been leaks, broken windows, oxygen shortages, tangled cable. It was not unreasonable to contemplate that one misfortune too many might lead to his annihilation. Beads of water like lead pellets tearing his body apart, shards of shattered quartz flying into his eyeball, the steel sphere crumpling under pressure and him falling to the ocean floor in an eternal embrace with Barton, that unlovable colleague whose puke he had lived with during the engineer's bouts of seasickness.

He must have imagined the absurdity of an eternal Bartonian embrace. It might have scared him more than the bullets of water and shards of quartz, certainly more than the sharks and squids.

He left no explanation of why he changed his mind, but the chapter was never written.

New Species of Deep-Sea Fish

Linophryne arborifer
    post-brain
    apex of snout
    the summit
    arising from the skull
    covered with an infinity
    a sparse scattering of numerous
    short, stout, vertical
    a sparse network of white meandering nerves
    roofed by thin invisible skin

Melanocetus murrayi
    brownish black, dead black
    a buffy orange
    the inner body is broken
    the anus is at the summit
    no glow was seen

Aceratias edentula
    invisible in the fresh
    more deeply stained
    negatives the idea
    this bone with its nine teeth
    degenerate, if not atavistic

14.

Leaving the Body Behind

The Hospital Ceiling

In the rage of battle in WWI, a young German conscript named Alfred Wegener took a hit and was wounded. Medics evacuated him from the front and he convalesced over several months. He lay on his back on the medical cot, drifting in and out of consciousness, tormented by memories of war that slowly gave way to troubled dreams. He saw the bullet that flew through the air penetrating his body. He saw movement of soldiers and armies across the continent.

How had all these bodies come together from so far away to kill and torture and blow each other up?

They had come from Poland and Belgium and as far as Russia and America. The war had raged on other continents. It was something larger than any human decision, like a natural force at play.

Before the war, he had spent the winter in Greenland studying atmospherics and had almost been crushed by a glacier. Now, through visions of that inhospitable cold, he saw swirls of motion, bodies and countries, shifting borders. Lifting from the earth's surface, he saw the continents too, shifting and moving like the armies, attacking and retreating.

Yes, he thought. It's happening on every level. It's not just us. The whole planet is in motion, crushing up against itself. How could it all have started?

He pictured the earth in some primordial state, where all the land was joined together. A vast green pasture that swept from Tierra del Fuego to the top of Japan. It had been one. Until these same forces that now entrenched battalions in the drizzle of northern Europe, that brought death and flight, had cracked the continent, fragmented it, and set the parts adrift.

He pictured the map in his mind. He could see the bulge in Brazil fit snugly against West Africa. The eastern seaboard of the US came rushing east, pressing England against the low countries until it was a single steppe from

Siberia to the Great Plains. India returned to Somalia. Madagascar sidled up against Mozambique. It all fit together. There was no doubt—that was how it started.

Wegener regained his health, still dreaming of this original continent, and when he was released he set to work explaining it in a book called *The Origins of Continents and Oceans*—the first articulated theory of continental drift.

The scientists of the time read his book, laughed and scoffed at such a wild idea, and put it aside. Wegener was left to research on his own. In 1930, just as Beebe and Barton were making their first dives in the bathysphere, he put together funding for a return trip to Greenland to examine the coast-line. There must be some sign left in that cold place that would show how it once fit against Scotland and Norway. The fingers of ice enlacing with the western fjords. But, just like before, the cold of Greenland was worse than they'd planned for, and the crew suffered from exposure. On the trip home to Germany, Wegener froze to death before he could set down what he'd learned.

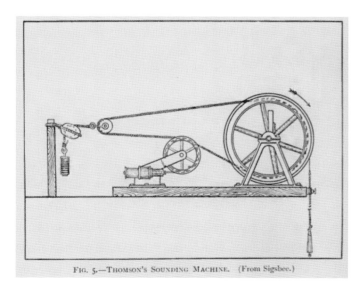

FIG. 5.—THOMSON'S SOUNDING MACHINE. (From Sigsbee.)

Reimagining

Her father was a surveyor who mapped soil for the department of agriculture. From him she learned to "read nature." Marie Tharp hardly spent a full school year in any one place. In Florence, Alabama, she had a crush on a boy named Xenophon. In Cooperstown, New York, she was punished for wearing pants. In Oneonta she caught the whooping cough and took up the violin. She earned bachelor's degrees in English and music and math and a master's in geology.

In 1948 she was hired as a researcher for Columbia's geology department. Their project was the bottom of the ocean.

In the nineteenth century, to find out how deep the sea was, you dropped a cannon ball tied to a hemp line off the side of a ship. The ball plunked to a stop at the bottom and the line went slack.

Then you measured how much rope had unrolled. Hemp rope became twine. In 1870 Lord Kelvin used piano wire.

Echo sounding started in the 1920s. An engineer sat with his head pressed to an earphone listening for the echo of an amplified ping, watching a clock and noting the echo's timing as best he could. During WWII, the US Navy fitted ships with new echo sounders using microphones and spools of paper. When the mic registered the ping's echo, the echo sounder burnt a mark with a stylus. After the war, a ship called the *Atlantis* crisscrossed the Atlantic, making thousands of these readings. The Navy filled boxes and shelves with marked-up spools, raw data on ocean depths where the ship passed, fraught with glitches, called *fathograms*.

Tharp and a colleague named Bruce Heezen worked for Dr. Maurice Ewing out of a converted mansion in the Palisades. Tharp worked upstairs in one of the bedrooms. In the basement was a man trying to prove creationism. When that failed, he started collecting bones and experimenting with radioactive material. Tharp suspected he jettisoned spent cadavers into a nearby pond.

Tharp and Heezen began unspooling fathograms, noting measurements, trying to make sense of the information they contained. By 1952 Tharp had laid out the spools alongside each other, crunched numbers, and created an image of terrain. No one had ever synthesized data about the ocean like that before.

She plotted the edges of continents and the drop-offs to mid-ocean depths. She plotted inclines and recesses, surprising shallows, volcanic islands with their stark slopes. She had a lot of information about the sea around Bermuda, because the *Atlantis* had stopped there many times to fuel up. Her information radiated from the archipelago like a spider web.

As Tharp's map started coming into focus, she wasn't surprised to see a mountain range rise in the middle of the Atlantic, but she was surprised to discover that in the middle of the mountain range was a valley, a trench. Tharp knew that Alfred Wegener's accursed theory, which she'd been educated to laugh at, predicted such a trench. It meant continents drifting and opening up, there in the middle of her map; in the middle of the ocean, ripe new earth emerging between two plates drifting apart. She recognized it as the result of seismic activity. She checked all her calculations and it was still there. Wegener had been right all along.

Heezen famously called her discovery *girl talk*. Five years later, he and Ewing published an article about it without crediting her. It was two years after that, with the publication of a volume of maps called *The Floors of the Oceans I*, that Tharp's named started to appear.

In the 1960s she found another mid-ocean ridge in the Indian Ocean. Matching its location with seismological data, she showed that the ridge coincided with a fault line. As predicted: spreading plates with earthquakes along the seam.

Tharp and her team created another set of maps, some of which ran in *National Geographic*. A few months later, the magazine received a letter from a girl in Austria:

"I've been looking at your maps," she wrote, "and my father can paint better than you can."

Unbelievably, the magazine dispatched their best topographer to Innsbruck to meet the girl's father. The topographer found Heinrich Berann painting panoramas of the alps for tourists. He had developed a style that exaggerated spatial features very slightly to make the images more readable.

National Geographic hired him, and for many years Tharp and Heezen traveled to Austria, bringing data to Berann. In 1977 they published the first complete map of earth's ocean floor.

Their maps soon hung in classrooms all over the world. Within a few years, students took them for granted. We already lived in the world they created. Like Else Bostelmann's views of the bathyspheric depths and NASA's first photo of the earth from space, Tharp's work produced an entire reimagining of the planet.

The Big Dive

In 1934, Beebe and Barton had gone deeper than anyone else, but they hadn't reached the bottom of the ocean. Barton kept trying to go deeper into the 1950s, but it was Jacques Piccard and Don Walsh who followed Tharp's maps to the very nadir, and finally reached the bottom of the Mariana Trench in 1960. They went down almost thirty-six thousand feet, ten times deeper than the deepest bathysphere dive. Piccard wrote about the dive for *National Geographic.*

Without the subtle pings and styluses of Dr. Ewing's researchers, Piccard and Walsh brought a destroyer out into the middle of the ocean and bombed the sea floor, firing tons of TNT straight down and listening with radar detectors to gauge depth. When the pair of divers located the lowest point and approached in a submersible called the bathyscaph, they found everything covered in lead pellets, remains of the destroyer's munitions. When they closed in on their target—the deepest point in the global ocean—Piccard looked out from the window of the bathyscaph. In that very spot, he claimed, he saw a flatfish, its two round eyes facing up. The same flat fish that kept Gloria Hollister awake at night lay resting at the bottom of the world.

As the bathyscaph hovered, the flat fish lifted off its spot of sea floor and gently swam away.

Their spotlight only reached about ten feet, and the darkness of the deep soon swallowed it. Piccard and Walsh watched the point where the fish disappeared, stared for a while into nothing, before guiding the bathyscaph back to the surface.

Vents and Chimneys

When expeditions took samples from the Marianna trench, they found young, freshly minted earth pouring out of submarine volcanos. The ridge was forty-two thousand miles long, and continuously productive. At the bottom of the ocean, as Wegener had imagined and Tharp had identified and finally deep dives had verified, was the world's largest geological feature, as if we'd found the origin of the planet itself.

Despite the flatfish at the bottom of the world, ocean explorers still expected the deep to be relatively devoid of life. Below three hundred feet, oxygen already builds up in the blood of humans, rendering it poisonous. And as Beebe had witnessed, the sun never reaches below two thousand feet. At further depths, the sea grows colder and the pressure builds. The pressure compresses sound, so the water is loud with reverberations. Photosynthesis is impossible, and any marine snow would disintegrate or be eaten before it reached that far down. It was supposed to be an inhospitable desert of cold, dark, crushingly heavy water and nothing else.

In 1977, a San Diego oceanographer named Robert Ballard, spurred on by watching humans explore the moon, took a small team down in a vessel called *Alvin* to explore the Pacific near the Galápagos, about as deep as the home of Piccard's flatfish. As they approached, they found vents in the sea floor spewing out water so hot it threatened to melt the vessel. Inside *Alvin*, it began to smell of sulfur.

Nearby they found a strange vista of rock towers spouting hot blackish fluid. The darkness was due to high concentrations of mineral salts, but it looked like the fumes from a smokestack burning coal. There at the bottom of the sea they found a subaquatic factory town with chimneys belching liquid smoke at 662 degrees. And like the vents, the regulated atmosphere inside

Alvin smelled of sulfur. One of Ballard's comrades said it all seemed "connected to hell itself."

But there in the heat and pressure, as far from the sun as possible, the ocean was teeming with life. There were fish and crabs among ten-foot worms that looked like giant white seagrasses. They captured a few of these worms to bring back to the surface. When they cut the worms open, they were full of red, hemoglobin-rich blood. And inside their white casings they looked strangely like a penis attached to a vagina.

On the earth's surface, the heat of the sun converts carbon dioxide into organic molecules, forming the basis of all life. But here was a system thriving in a place where the sun never reached, completely cut off from that life-giving force. Ballard found that the worms were feeding off bacteria that could metabolize the sulfur-rich stew that spewed from the vents and chimneys. This was more than a new species—they had discovered an entire life process. Cut off from the sun, whole communities of animals, an entire ecosystem, lived off the heat of the earth.

Ballard imagined a moment when the sun quit shining, when the earth broke off from the solar system and drifted out into empty space. Life on earth would be extinguished in a flash. There would be nothing left.

But undisturbed in the darkness of the deep ocean, animals would continue to feed off this metabolized hydrogen sulfide. Natural selection would go on unabated. New species would emerge, to live and thrive and reproduce in the darkness. In the acoustic rich atmosphere of the deep, perhaps languages would emerge, a new literature. A history of the earth would be written that knew nothing of what had gone on above—no continents to crash and drift, no Himalayan peaks, no New York and Bermuda. No Baal, no Zoroaster, no God of Light.

The tubeworms, with their blood-red sexual centers, adapted to live at the highest temperatures and under unimaginable pressure, end up fossilized in the rocks near the ocean chimneys. In 1983 scientists found such fossils in an old copper mine in the Arabian desert.

Eventually, the entire ocean cycles through the vents. The water comes out rich in iron, copper, zinc, and manganese. These elements can be traced all across the planet, even within the cells of our bodies. The chemosynthetic process of the deep ocean, it turned out, is a simpler, older way of life. It preceded us, and it will go on without us.

Black Bottom

The plates shift, the continents drift. Mountains are pushed up from below. Ice and water and wind wear them down from above. Seismic push and erosional pull caught in an uneasy balance.

There is no such rising tension and catastrophic release on Mercury, Venus, or Mars. This shifting and pushing, grinding stasis punctuated by euphoric cataclysms, is an aspect of Earth.

The Atlantic spreads at about the rate that fingernails grow. The Pacific spreads faster, at about the rate of human hair. Pushed and pulled by these pressures, India moves three inches a year.

The Boxing Day earthquake of 2004 moved a significant amount of mass slightly closer to the earth's center, like a figure skater pulling her arms in, speeding up the planet's rotation by 2.67 microseconds.

We think we know the range of earth's motions—volcanoes, earthquakes, erosion—but written in the body of the planet are rare and dramatic occurrences. Seventy-three thousand years ago, a tsunami near the Cape Verde Archipelago hurled one-ton boulders thirty miles through the air, so they landed six hundred feet up the side of one of the islands. In Wyoming, a rock one-mile thick and as wide as Rhode Island slid thirty miles down a slope, traveling sixty miles an hour, on a bed of hot gas.

Descending along the submarine volcano beneath Bermuda, marine biologists located fossilized reef a hundred feet below sea level—where the ocean's surface had idled during the last ice age. As the waters rose, continents were rewritten. When the sea broke through the Dardanelles and the Bosporus jerked open, flooding the lake in the Black Sea basin, the salt-laden seawater trapped fresh water beneath it—lighter, warmer, devoid of oxygen.

At times, anoxic water gathers deep in the central Pacific. When it surfaces every decade or so, due to changes in wind patterns or other factors not well understood, this anoxic upwelling releases quantities of ammonia, contributing to the phenomenon known as El Niño. Waves crash and storms rip through the South American coast, inundating towns, destroying crops, and washing away houses. Marine animals sicken and die, and birds go hungry. Weather patterns across the hemisphere devolve into chaos. You can walk across the Brooklyn Bridge in January in a T-shirt.

The anoxic cloud at the bottom of the Black Sea is many times larger than what gathers in the Pacific. If it were disturbed and bubbled to the surface, Istanbul and Odessa would be water-drenched wreckage. Havoc would reign across Europe and the Middle East, far out into Central Asia.

Another peculiar effect of this bubble: without deep ocean vents of the open ocean, there is no chemosynthetic life in the Black Sea. Because there is no oxygen down there, nothing at all is metabolized. The dead of the Black Sea simply fall to the bottom, never to decompose.

When he realized this state of affairs, Robert Ballard had moved on from the study of thermal vents' chemosynthetic life systems and was delving into undersea archaeology, exploring sunken ships in the Atlantic. He made headlines across the world when he and his team finally located and explored the wreck of the Titanic. They found a tea set with silver tray and china cups sitting upright, bottles of wine, and a pair of shoes with nickeled steel button hooks.

But the shoes were empty; there were no remains of tea-drinkers; all the bodies had been devoured by the ravenous life of the deep. It occurred to Ballard that at the bottom of the Black Sea they might find the bodies of sailors and passengers, Russian and Byzantine and Pontic Greek mariners, all perfectly preserved as if they'd died moments before.

They mounted expeditions and set off in search of them. But as yet they have found only dead dolphins that lay resting on the ocean floor as if asleep.

Leaving the Body Behind

At the height of his career, Ballard wrote a book about sea exploration called *Eternal Darkness*. The last chapter tells of the limits of submersibles carrying humans into the lower reaches. The atmosphere of the deep ocean, so antithetical to our bodily needs, makes it expensive and dangerous to visit. And though humans have continued to descend, like Victor Vescovo who recently visited the deepest points in all five oceans (hardly bothering to look out at what was around him), more and more submersibles are robotic, guided by humans in remote locations like the Inner Space Center in Rhode Island.

Ballard is fond of these drone explorers. They gather data, make detailed scans of the sea floor, and take acoustic recordings of the noisy depths. Our knowledge increases, but we descend less and less:

"We can cut the ultimate tether—the one that binds our questioning intellect to vulnerable human flesh."

Kipling had foreseen this. After hearing of Beebe's first dives, he wrote a letter to his friend, predicting, "The time will come when we will draw the curtains of the back parlor, turn on the television, and see the wonders of the Tuscarora Deep."

But like Beebe having seen a solitary opal that we had not, despite the incommunicability of the deep, there is still no substitute for being there. Ballard knew this too:

"Nothing can match one's first mind-boggling, gut-wrenching immersion in the deep ocean—as everyone who has tried it from Beebe onward can attest."

Still, hunger for greater mobility, to see more, to gather more data, had inevitably led Ballard to subtract his organism from the equation. After 1934, Beebe abandoned completely the impetus to go deeper. He left it to others to build better machines. The last section of Ballard's *Eternal Darkness* is called "Leaving the Body Behind"—which is something Beebe never did.

The trouble, the risk, the fleeting nature of those hard-earned observations was inseparable from their impact. What Beebe saw by the glowing liquid of confusion could not be seen without going through what he went through to be there. It was not only the ocean he saw, but the world reflected in the mirror of fixation and contingency and grace, a mute glow from the intersection of wonder and vacancy, meaning and meaninglessness. He stopped there and went no further, perhaps to breathe in the encounter more deeply. Perhaps the only thing Beebe brought back from the deep, etched in the corner of his eye, was that wizened fleck of futility.

Hollister's world was one of interpretation and thought. Beebe's, despite his many blindnesses, was one of marvels that reflect back on themselves. Ballard's method opens to a world of achievement and information. It has no place for the blank of cognitive breakdown, the sudden eclipse of the yellow sun that enwrapped the Nonsuchian need for the deep.

15.

Recent Sightings

The Destiny of Ships

When marine drones passed the Titanic in 2019, they found that monument to opulence and ambition corroded by salt, eaten by bacteria, swept by ocean currents. The ship's bow was covered in icicle-like forms made of rust. Tiny iron-eating organisms were rendering the enormous ship into fine powder. Within ten years, perhaps, there will be nothing left.

After WWII, Beebe had sat meditating on the fate of the *Brooklyn Belle*, which sunk in the Pacific. He imagined it digested by clouds of microscopic pre-shrimps, barnacles, and phalanxes of other sea creatures, until it became an expression of some beauty that is "wholly inhuman."

He saw "permanent animal blossoms," and "inorganic everlastings."

He saw worms carving catacombs into every board and eventually secreting acids to consume each sheet of copper and lead. He saw millions of polyps embalming and ingesting the great hull. He saw a coral formation surrounding the place where the ship had been, like its shadow—"the intaglio of the Brooklyn Belle."

Then he turned his attention to the sinking of the *Tai*, a Japanese submarine that had a fatal encounter with a whale. He imagined the chambers and corridors swamped with seawater, steel and copper and iron and lead compressed and sinking. He saw the telescopic eyes of the marine creatures wondering at this plummeting form.

"Soon," he pictured, "the twisted hull was filled with shrimps and fish glowing with port-holes of unearthly blue and green cold light, or clouds of sheer luminescence."

The steel began to corrode and rust and dissolve. Wood first petrified, becoming as hard as iron, before disintegrating. Leather and canvas were protected by the cold for a while, but they, too, soon turned to dust and were swept away.

"Over the course of what we call time, a few distorted fragments of the submarine came gently to rest on the bottom ooze."

In its fatal home on the abyssal floor of the Pacific, where human time and human measures are meaningless, it ceased to register, "not even a mound." Like ultra-black fish that absorb even darkness, it was not even a memory. An absence of an absence rained on by "tiny dead shells."

"Everything that fell from the world of warmth and light dissolved in the alchemy of salt water."

Of the submarine, there was nothing left. All that remained were the ear-bones of a great whale and the triangular, razor-sharp teeth of sharks—"scattered over the face of the ultimate red clay."

King Neptune's Whiskers

Among Beebe's final, disorganized notes on marine subjects are a couple of typewritten pages on superstitions. He describes the legendary shipyard at the bottom of the sea where wrecked ships go when they sink. It's run by an old sailor, he writes, who sits biding his time, playing quoits with Neptune and hoping that one of the newcomers who show up will bring him some dry tobacco, which is the only thing he misses in the life of the deep. Sailors sometimes claim an old ship might be brought down to be ransacked for their parts and keepsakes and booty—after they've "gone into the unknown and the vast unknowable."

The sea angel Amphitrite swoops down for the sailors who have served her faithfully, and takes them to the court of King Neptune, who judges whether they've lived by the laws of the sea, whether they've been worthy.

Others end up in a harbor in the far north where lost ships go. Some vessels crossing in the northern seas encounter these ghost ships, appearing and disappearing, flagless, unresponsive to salutations or threats. The Harbor of Lost Ships is locked in by high, barren, icy cliffs. In their shelter lie thousands of hulls, pressed together. Their ghostly crews walk the wharfs or stand still, as if they would sail off the next day, trimming sails and swabbing decks in the icy mist.

A ship sailing through the Caribbean was caught in a hurricane. All the crew were lost except three hands, who found themselves clutching the skylight of the main cabin. They floated on the wreckage, cupping their hands in the rain to stave off thirst fired by the hot sun. After five days, a mass of seaweed came up against them, called King Neptune's Whiskers. It looks like sargassum, but inside it are little red berries. The shipwrecked sailors grabbed at the berries and ate them and survived. They floated another five days, picking the red berries in the seaweed, before a Portuguese vessel found them and took them aboard.

These men were not true sailors. They were just hired hands who'd been picked up in the port, needing work. They did not belong to the sea, so the sea would not accept them. So King Neptune sent his whiskers to keep them alive. Not truly belonging to the sea, they were turned away.

Others, no matter if they've resolved to head for the hinterland, will always end up before their king at the threshold of the deep. It makes no difference how far they've strayed, the sea always claims its own. Sailors who believe in the laws of the sea, who know they're betrothed to Amphitrite and Neptune, will always find their way back to where, deep down, they've always belonged.

Recent Sightings

The deeper you go, the less you can see and the farther sound travels. The strongest spotlight is absorbed within meters, hardly offsetting the enveloping darkness. But the grindings of container ships travel far, the hollers of whales, the blurp-blurp of simmering vents. The frying oil sound of shrimp clacking their claws. The crack, thump, and vomit of oil exploration and mining. The infinitely slow exhalations of tectonic plates.

The room tone of the abyss comprises rasps, creaks, grunts, rhythmic patterns like crickets in fall, the creak of an old door repeatedly opening, two balloons rubbing against each other, voices through blown speakers, the shrill grind of a dentist's drill, the occasional raspberry. Someone might identify the harrumph of sea bass, the woodblock clop of Atlantic sturgeon, dolphin thinly miewing like hungry kittens, the growl of eels about to spawn, the cacophony of all the fish in the deep shouting to each other at once.

The eloquent banter of educated aliens.

Abyssal creatures slowly come into view, bodies of mucous and mucoid substances, gelatinous bodies that undulate and pass food through tissue-filters.

If it's true that as many sea creatures as we know about, from blue whales to diatoms and flagellates, there are an equal number we have never encountered, mostly from the depths of the ocean, many will go extinct without us ever knowing they existed, arising and passing away without a trace. Others will reveal chemical compounds of unprecedented complexity. They might resemble the giant larvacean recently discovered that secretes its mouth parts into the water, a balloon-like film that expands and surrounds and digests. Ultra-black creatures, so black that even within the absolute dark of the deep, the *black, black, black* Beebe found inexpressible, their forms absorb and concentrate darkness. Animals with hundreds of genders, that switch genders, like mola mola and yew trees, out of pure delight in being alive. Color that eats color and forms that defy all categorization, that ruin systems and shatter reason, until we wallow and luxuriate in perfect darkness, beyond the reach of thought.

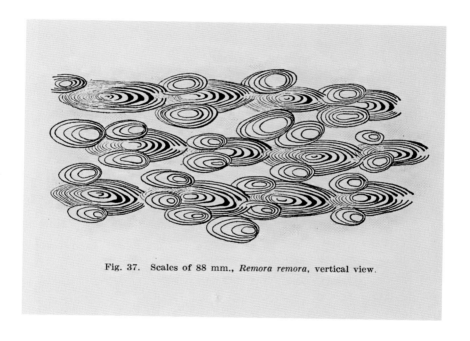

Fig. 37.   Scales of 88 mm., *Remora remora*, vertical view.

LIVE NEEDLE FISH

Endnotes

All passages labeled *Logbook* are synthesized from the original *Bathysphere Log Recorded by Gloria Hollister, 1930, 1932,* and *1934* (WCS) and the typed and corrected versions in *Bathysphere Records and Reports, 1930–1934* (WB). They are at times lightly edited for clarity or emphasis.

Archival material is labeled:

WCS—Wildlife Conservation Society, New York Zoological Society. WB—William Beebe Papers, Princeton University.

LoC—Gloria Hollister Anable Papers, Library of Congress.

Misc.—Miscellaneous archival material (detailed in corresponding bibliographic entry).

First Glimpse

FIVE MILES SOUTH OF NONSUCH

The scene is reconstructed from photos in *Bathysphere, Circa 1929–1949* (WCS), the description in Beebe's *Half Mile Down*, 99–137, and Beebe's *Bermuda Diary, 1928–1932* (WB).

"woylds and boyds"—as per recording of Beebe's appearance on the quiz show "Information Please" (see: sound files).

Logbook passages from *Logbook*, June 11, 1930.

"eel-like creature": this is a description of a creature I saw washed up on shore at Los Órganos.

"can never hereafter be as wonderful as blue": Beebe, *Half Mile Down* 113.

TRANSPARENT BODIES

Mahwah River: "Girl Explorer Extends Women's World to Ocean Bottom and Jungle Depths."

"Amazonian stature": Barton, *World Beneath the Sea*, 15.

Popular Mechanics: Beebe, "Three Hundred Fathoms beneath the Sea."

"I kissed Gloria . . .": Gould, *The Remarkable Life of William Beebe*, 279. The code actually reads, "I kissed her and she loves me": Beebe, *Journal*, November 5, 1928 (WB).

"They exchanged visits . . .": ibid., 280.

"Crystal bright . . ." Hollister's *Journal* (LoC), April 27, 1930.

"well over her sickness . . .": Beebe, *Bermuda Diary, 1928–1932* (WB), April 27, 1930.

"forever yours . . ." Hollister, *Journal* (LoC), April 28, 1930.

The Easter visit to church: ibid., April 20, 1930.

"Deity of Beauty . . . flat-faced!": ibid., May 3, 1930.

Melanostomiatid: ibid., June 2, 1930.

Diving at Gurnet's Rock: ibid., August 2, 1930.

"My whole soul wanted to get back . . .": ibid.

"I hope the Gods of Excitement . . .": ibid.

Hollister's sightings on her birthday dive: *Logbook*, June 11, 1930 (WB only—not included in the WCS logbook) and Hollister, "Birthday in the Ocean Depth."

"Down to the dark, to the utter dark . . .": Hollister, "Birthday in the Ocean Depth."

NOTHING AT ALL

Beebe, *Half Mile Down*, 103.

MY PROFESSION IS IGNORANCE

Visit to the phrenologist: Gould, *The Remarkable Life of William Beebe*, 16–17.

"masterless, rioting in the vast expanse": *Journals* (WB), August 4, 1896.

Glass-bottom bucket: ibid., March 18, 1903.

Binoculars at the field station: Gould, 388.

"chatting with a lady . . .": letter from Mabel Ingolls, undated 1949, in *William Beebe Vermix* (WCS).

Birds at play: see: Beebe, "St Francis of the Plaster Cast" (WCS).

Florodora: see: Gould, 70, and Edward Boyd-Jones and Owen Hall, *Florodora*.

New York Times on *Riders on the Wind*, see: "Unashamed Romance in Vigorous New Novel."

Thane's *modern* opinion: Gould, 280.

THE ENGINEER

On Barton, see: Matsen, *Descent*.

Pearl diving: Barton, *World Beneath the Sea*, 76.

"Oh God, Otis": Gould, 295.

CONTOUR DIVES
Logbook, October 25, 1930.

Spectral Visions

LINOPHRYNE ARBORIFERA

Note handwritten on a scrap of white paper, undated, included in Beebe, *Mid-Ocean* (WB).

ANIMAL LIGHT

The foremost authority on bioluminescence of the first half of the twentieth century was zoologist E. Harvey Newton. He visited Nonsuch in 1930 and made an unsuccessful attempt to film bioluminescent creatures. On Newton, see: Johnson, *Edmund Harvey Newton, 1887–1959: A Biographical Memoir*. This chapter is primarily a summary of Newton's *A History of Luminescence from the Earliest Times to 1900*. References with relevant page numbers are as follows: Anaximenes, 40; Vedas, 20; Chinese odes, 14; *Nyctegretos*, 110; al-Bayṭār (aka al-Baithar), 47; waxwings, 67; *liquor lucidus*, 80; Gesner, 64–70; Batman, 65; *Margarita Philosophica*, 76; Kirchner, 103; Bartholin, 107; Marsigli, 158; Kunkel, 188; Rodziszewski, 453; Humboldt's jellyfish, 223; Darwin, 235; MacCulloch, 233.

Beebe in Haiti: Beebe, *Beneath Tropic Seas*, 76.

"Stars gone mad." Beebe, interviewed in "Beebe Betters Own Mark in 3,028-ft Dive."

THE BLUE LIGHT OF THE SEA

Among the research material preserved with Beebe's papers at Princeton can be found several concerning this question of light penetration and optical effects of water. I am referring specifically to E. O. Hulbert, "The Transparency of Ocean Water and the Visibility Curve of the Eye." These documents, as well as correspondence on the subject between Beebe and Hulbert, can be found in *Bathysphere Correspondence* (WB).

Logbook passage: *Logbook*, June 19, 1930.

"Solid, blue-black world": Beebe, *Half Mile Down*, 132.

THE SCIENCE OF DELUSION

On this philosophical question, see: Henry Guerlac, "Can there Be Colors in the Dark? Physical Color Theory before Newton."

On Al-Haytham, see: Sabra, A.I., *The Optics of Ibn al-Haytham*.

On Leonardo's optics, see: Francesco Fiorani and Allesandro Nova "Leonardo da Vinci and Optics: Theory and Pictorial Practice."

Comparing the two, see: Janis Bell, "Leonardo and Alhazen: Cloth on the Mountaintop."

Leonardo describes his experiment with smoke and velvet in Codex Hammer f. 36 r (I B), discussed in Bell (ibid.).

THE LANGUAGE OF COLOR

The terms listed were pulled from the specimen cards and descriptions in *Color notes, Circa 1929–1949* (WCS) and Ridgway's self-published *Color Standards and Color Nomenclature* from 1912.

THE STUDIO

On Bostelmann, see: George Peterich, "Mrs. B Paints for Beebe," and "Else Bostelmann, Artist, Dies at 79."

Bostelmann's process is reported in "Undersea Paintings Go on Exhibit Here" and Jane Corby, "Life below the Ocean's Wave Provides this Woman Artist with Many-Hued, Fantastic Models." She describes the process herself, complete with bathtubs and reference to Diogenes, in Bostelmann, "Notes from an Undersea Studio off Bermuda."

SPECTRAL VISIONS

As in "The Language of Color," above, these color terms are pulled from the specimen cards and descriptions in *Color notes, Circa 1929–1949* (WCS) and Robert Ridgway's self-published *Color Standards and Color Nomenclature* from 1912.

On Aristotle's effects on early modern optics, see: M. Chirimuuta, *Outside Color: Perceptual Science and the Puzzle of Color*: 19–22.

On Newton's optical experiments, see: A. A. Mills, "Newton's Prisms and His Experiments on the Spectrum," and Milo Keynes, "The Personality of Isaac Newton." The exact chronology of the experiments is somewhat confused, as it is based on Newton's memories sixty years later. On that, see: Richard S. Westfall, *Never at Rest: A Biography of Isaac Newton*, 156–157.

On staring at the sun and pressing the needle into his eye, see: Keynes, 21. On purchase of the prism, see: Mills, 14.

On colors and musical notes, see: ibid., 25.

On the "untuning of the sky," see: N. Guicciardini, "The Role of Musical Analogies in Newton's Optical and Cosmological Work," 45.

"Pipes filld," see: Newton, *Of Colours.*

On occult justification for the promotion of indigo, see: Mills, 25.

On refusing last rites, see: Keynes, 53.

On Goethe's disagreement with Newton, see: D. Sepper, "Goethe, Newton, and the Imagination of Modern Science." Angèle Kremer-Marietti, "Schopenhauer, Goethe et la théorie des couleurs," and Zeno Vendler, "Goethe, Wittgenstein, and the Essence of Color."

For Goethe's interpretations of colors and color combinations, see: Eastlake, Charles, trans., *Goethe's Theory of Colors.*

On Franz Boas's early life, see: Rosemary Lévy-Zumwalt, *Franz Boas: The Emergence of the Anthropologist.*

On Boas's influence, see: Charles King, *Gods of the Upper Air.*

On the drowning of Boas's friend, see: Lévy-Zumwalt, 56.

On his dissertation, see: ibid., 47–49.

On differing blues in Central Asia and Central America, see: ibid., 54.

On Boas and psychophysics, see: ibid., 66.

On the duel, see: ibid., 51.

Measuring transparency in the Arctic, see: ibid., 96.

On Ssigna, see: ibid., 102–2; 113–114.

On the change of heart brought on by these events, see: Boas, "An Anthropologist's Credo."

Sinking Lower

AUGUST 11, 1934

Logbook, August 11, 1934.

APEX

This record of the crossing that begins the pheasant expedition is assembled from Beebe's *Journal* (WB). They visited the Portrait Gallery on Friday, January 28, 1910, and were listening to night-jars in India on May 6.

"Polaris blinked": Beebe describes breaking into the pyramids in *Pheasant Jungles*, 110.

"the very summit": ibid., 66–69.

"clear heights": ibid., 81.

"pitiful bunch": ibid., 86.

Beebe wonders about Hadzia's thoughts: ibid., 96.

On Rassul Akhat, see: ibid., 46–7.

"I hated pheasants . . . was all": ibid., 107.

"Choked a baboon": ibid., 108.

CONVERSATIONS WITH ROOSEVELT

Invited to his house in 1908: Gould, *Remarkable Life*, 117.

"My dear Beebe": ibid., 184.

French soldiers digging graves, Bosch, encounter with "Algonkins and Iroquois . . . the menace of the German line": Beebe, "A Red Indian Day."

On Roosevelt's genocidal beliefs about Native Americans, see: Hermann Hagedorn, *Roosevelt in the Badlands*, 355.

Roosevelt's reaction, "Your modesty . . . Himalayas," the Pleistocene horse: Beebe's *Journal*, September 6, 1918 (WB).

Edith Roosevelt's letter, described in Beebe's *Journal*, September 16, 1918 (WB).

Visiting Roosevelt at the hospital: Beebe's *Journal*, January 6, 1919 (WB).

"When you and I are gone . . . knowledge, wisdom, and truth": ibid.

Beebe hearing of his death: ibid.

"A diamond . . . soul to give": ibid.

ANIMAL LIFE AT THE FRONT
Paraphrased and summarized from Beebe, "Animal Life at the Front."

Upside Down

BUFFON IN THE TREES
On frogs in moonlight, see: "A Jungle Beach" in Beebe, *Jungle Days*, 90–111.
On leaf-cutter ants, see: "the Attas at Home," in ibid., 172–195.
On hammocks, see: "Hammock Nights," in ibid., 195–229.
On mournful tones, see: ibid., 109.
"Had I sat . . .": ibid., 57.
On collapsible time: ibid., 137.
"No action . . . is separate." Beebe, *Edge of the Jungle*, 97.
"In underground streets": ibid., 181.
"twenty-four hour day": ibid., 190.
"somatic cells": ibid., 191.
gashang: ibid., 191.
On leaf-cutters' ego: ibid., 192.
"for kaisers": ibid., 190.
On three-toed sloths, see: "Jungle Sluggard," in *Jungle Days*, 90–112.
"From our human point of view": ibid., 112.
"They are either a mystery": Beebe, "The Three-toed Sloth."
"One more defect": Buffon, quoted in ibid.
"Buffon clinging upside-down": ibid.

MORBID FLUX OF EXQUISITE BODIES
This chapter primarily summarizes and recombines material from Isabel Cooper's
    "Wild-Animal Painting in the Jungle."
Previous experience: ibid., 732
"the look of a mirage . . . silver gills": Isabel Cooper, "Artist at Large."
"a silly pious . . .": "Wild Animal Painting," 738.
"dim, glowing . . .": ibid.
"developed . . .": ibid.
"velvet-black . . .": ibid.
"keels of coral . . .": ibid. 737.
"with cuneiform . . .": ibid., 740.
"dusty plush . . .": ibid.
"sink utterly": ibid., 734.
"The instant": ibid.
"in one terrible ebbing.": ibid.
"as if millions . . .": ibid., 737.

"old mossback . . .": ibid.

"papier-mâché masks": ibid.

I-ON-A-CO

On Wilshire's donation, see: *Journals* (WB), February 21, 1909.

"dark and lustrous": quoted in Mark W. Nelson, "Henry Gaylord Wilshire," 70.

Wilshire declared 1887 the year he became a socialist: ibid., 45.

Joined Nationalist Club to be near the secretary: ibid., 47.

"crushing their smaller . . .": H.G. Wilshire, *Fabian Essays in Socialism.*

"a wonderful conglomerate . . . yellow journal": Wilshire quoted in Norman Etherington, *Theories of Imperialism: War, Conquest and Capital*, 32.

"let her starve . . .": Quoted in Nelson, 70.

On *Wilshire Magazine*, see: David Bell, *Marxian Socialism in the United States*, 87.

Beebe on socialism, "a sort of brotherly love . . .": Beebe, *Journals* (WB), February 21, 1909.

On *I-ON-A-CO*, see: Donald G. Davis, Jr., "The Ionaco of Gaylord Wilshire."

LOOKING BACKWARD

Looking Backward opens in 1887—perhaps that's why Wilshire attributed his socialist conversion to that year.

"The art . . . of shifting the burden . . .": Edward Bellamy, *Looking Backward*, 9.

On Bellamy's influence, see: Jerry Prout, *Coxey's Crusade for Jobs: Unemployment in the Golden Age*, 46.

On Beebe's millenarian fantasy, see: Beebe, *Nonsuch: Land of Water*, 165.

AN EPIC TALE

Beebe, *Half Mile Down*, 132.

HOW HE WAS

On Beebe's desk, see: "My Jungle Table," in *Jungle Days*, 26–48.

Blunderbuss

NEW SPECIES OF DEEP-SEA FISH

Melanonus unipennis, language extracted from description in Beebe, "Nineteen New Species and Four Post-larval Deep Sea Fish," 74.

Pseudoscopelus stellatus, extracted from description in ibid., 75.

THE HISS

Rose added to staff, driving in WW1: Gould, 122.

For an example of Rose's doggerel, see: "Lay of the Noma," below.

Rose's chapter on resources: "The Last Raid," in Beebe, *Galapagos: World's End*, 190–203.

Rose's historical chapter: "Man and Galapagos," in ibid., 332–417.

"irruption of filibusters": ibid., 343.

"on slaughter and rapine bent": ibid., 344.

"eight tons of quince marmalade": ibid.

"in the pursuit . . .": ibid., 355.

"dildo trees": ibid., 348.

"all gross Humours": ibid., 357.

"and discouraged Selkirk": ibid., 364.

"oil derricks on the beaches . . .": ibid., 365.

"No wonder that in 1923 . . . great race": ibid., 371

"Captain Porter's *Journal*": ibid., 372.

"he now remains": ibid., 375.

"The Encantadas . . . a hiss": ibid., 417.

FUMAROLES

See *Journal* (WB), April 11, 1925.

THE LAY OF THE NOMA

From *Journal* (WB), March 16, 1923.

A RIDE WITH THE SHIPWRECKED SAILOR

The body of this story is told by Beebe in "The Shipwrecked Taxi Driver," *Galapagos: World's End*, 295–309. The end—recounting the broadcast and reunion—occurs in an undated, unattributed newspaper clipping, "Gets Death Message 21 Years . . . ," found in *Correspondence N* (WB).

"as a painted ship . . .": "Gets Death Message 21 Years . . ." (WB).

"I'm done for . . .": *Galapagos: World's End*, 302.

THOMSON, KEATING, FITZGERALD, AND FLOWER

Arcturus: the yacht, donated by sulfur mining magnate Henry D. Whiton, was named by Lucretia Osborn in 1924 (Gould, 244). Arcturus is the northern hemisphere's brightest star—but it's impossible not to think of David Lindsay's early sci-fi novel *A Voyage to Arcturus*, published in 1920, in which a giant named Maskull leaves an isolated Scottish tower for the Arcturus satellite Tormance, where he grows new limbs and organs, experiences unfamiliar sexual urges, and discovers the universe to be a demiurgic mirage shaped by Crystalman.

Coded messages: *Journal* (WB), June 17, 1925.

Rose's article: Ruth Rose, "Cocos Treasure Again Exerts Its Lure."

Rose and Beebe on Cocos: "Cocos: the Land of Pirates," in Beebe, *The Arcturus Adventure*, 220–249.

THE PIRATE'S DEN

"manmangling human gorilla": Ellen NicKenzie Lawson, *Smugglers, Bootleggers, and Scofflaws: Prohibition and New York City*, 80.

Seuss playing polo with rats: Theodor Seuss Geisel, "The Beginnings of Dr. Seuss—An Informal Reminiscence," 20.

The Pirate's Den accoutrements: "Fire in Pirate's Den Ruins Relics of the Sea."

Pickle Puss Armstrong: Armstrong's granddaughter commenting on Jan Whitaker's blog post "Anatomy of a Restauranteur: Don Dickerman."

"fearsome looking . . . blameless mouths": Stephen Graham, *New York Nights*, 33.

Falling

NEW SPECIES OF DEEP-SEA FISH

Parabrotula dentiens, language extracted from description in Beebe, "Nineteen New Species and Four Post-larval Deep Sea Fish," 81.

Chaenophryne crossotus, extracted from description in ibid., 83.

THE POND BUREAU

On Pond, see: *Biography* at James B. Pond Papers, Clements Library, University of Michigan. Invitation to 1930 Christmas party: *General Records, 1878–1962* (WCS).

BETWEEN EXPEDITIONS

Up to the night out in Havana, this is reconstructed primarily from Gloria Hollister's *Journal* (LoC). They are hungover on June 20, 1933. The night out in Havana is July 23, 1933.

The meeting with the Stewarts on Medusa Island is reconstructed from Beebe's *Journal* (WB) and Hollister's *Journal* (LoC), July 11, 1932.

"Go on, Priscilla," Hollister, *Journal* (LoC), July 11, 1932.

"The night closed down . . ." Beebe, *Journal* (WB), July 11, 1932.

"A superior race," Hollister, *Journal* (LoC), July 11, 1932.

FALLING

Visiting Milne: see eg.: *Journal* (WB), August 11, 1936.

Letter from Kipling: *Correspondence K* (WB), September 18, 1934.

Letter from Conan Doyle: *Correspondence D* (WB), undated.

On Dunsany and Yeats, see: Laura Miller, "Minor Magus."

Dunsany's stories: Plunkett, The *Book of Wonder*.

"Even as the firm found fault": Plunkett, The *Book of Wonder*, 112.

Dunsany eating the redwood: Beebe's *Journal* (WB), October 23, 1919.

"What wonders . . .": Letter from Dunsany to Beebe, September 6 (no year), *Correspondence D* (WB).

"The back valleys . . .": Letter from Dunsany to Beebe, March 12, 1922, *ibid*.

"pale before ink . . .": Beebe to Dunsany, April 10, 1922, copy in ibid.

"on the wonders of the world . . . entertainment": Letter from Dunsany to Beebe, February 19, 1928, ibid.

"slobbered shirt . . . feed on offal": Beebe to Dunsany, July 2, 1920, copy in ibid.

On Dunsany's lack of prophetic power, see Rex Butler, "Re-reading 'Kafka and His Precursors,'" where such an opinion is attributed to Borges.

"through the unreverberate . . .": Plunkett, 35.

The Deepest Dives

1930

On the revolution in Spain, see: Britannica, Editors of Encyclopedia. "Miguel Primo de Rivera." On the meteor crash in the Amazon, see: Huyghe, "Incident at Curuça."

NONSUCH DAYS AND NIGHTS

196 cases: Beebe's *Journal* (WB), March 13, 1929.

Hollister born again: Hollister's *Journal* (LoC), May 8, 1931.

"alyssum grains": ibid., November 5, 1928.

Hollister's pajamas: ibid., July 8, 1931.

Invitations: *Gloria Hollister Anable Correspondence* (WCS).

Yeats and Kipling: Hollister's *Journal* (LoC), May 13, 1931.

Coded writing: Beebe's *Journal* (WB), May 31, 1930.

Hollister's version: Hollister's *Journal* (LoC), May 31, 1930.

"blackness without form": ibid., September 11, 1931.

NEW SPECIES OF DEEP-SEA FISH

Chirostomias lucidimanus: language extracted from description in Beebe, "Nineteen New Species and Four Post-larval Deep Sea Fish," 52.

Omosudis lowi: extracted from ibid., 71.

Saccopharynx harrisoni: extracted from ibid., 63.

ACROSS THE LOOKING GLASS

"today the ocean . . .": Beebe, *Half Mile Down*, 14.

"we are made to feel at home": ibid., 72.

"I knew that I had added": ibid., 66.

"newly conquered realm": ibid.

"after you have made . . . amazed": ibid., 67.

"shoot what particular fish": ibid., 69.

"kingdom of the helmet": ibid., 66.

DIVE 30

Logbook, August 11, 1934.

THE BOHEMIAN CLUB

"*de-luxe* position": Beebe, "Exploring a Tree and a Yard of Jungle," 1307.

On the oblique glance: ibid.; Beebe, *Jungle Peace*, 4; also see especially Katherine McLeod, "Beyond the Biological: William Beebe, the Bronx Zoo, and U.S. Biological Field Stations in British Guiana."

"condemned to solve problems": William Morton Wheeler quoted in Beebe, *Half Mile Down*, xii.

"fragrant asphodels . . .": Wheeler quoted in ibid.

"The First Wonderer": ibid., 4–5.
"Like the monk's coffin": ibid., 12.

DROPPING

Continuation of *Logbook*, August 11, 1934.

OF SUBMERSION AND SUBMERSIBLES

Vengeful incomprehensible powers: Beebe, *Half Mile Down*, 16.
Necho II: ibid., 17.
"The study of life . . .": ibid., 20.
"When I have descended . . .": ibid., 22.
"like strings of onions . . .": ibid., 25.
"Proto-bathyspheres": ibid., 42
"aquatic corselet": ibid., 44.
"as though it were a bearded lady . . .": ibid., 48.

GOING DOWN

Continuation of *Logbook*, August 11, 1934.

THE WASTES

Kite flying scene: Beebe, *The Arcturus Adventure*, 341.
"an infinite and unsympathetic waste . . .": Beebe, *Half Mile Down*, xi.
"The phone is broken": ibid., 114.

ANIMAL LIFE

This scene is synthesized from the *Logbook*, August 11, 1930, and Beebe, *Half Mile Down*, 121–132.

ON DARKNESS

Hneiwan: "Deep-sea Dragons," in *Mid-Ocean* (WB).
Naturalist's assistant: in "The Mystery of the Black Swallower" ("Deep Sea" in ibid.) Beebe mentions "the kind-hearted entomologist about whom Prof. Wheeler once told me, who followed Wheeler in his search for ants, and carefully replaced every upturned stone."

IN THE BEAM

Continuation of *Logbook*, August 11, 1934.

THE PRESSURE

Bullets . . . earthrise: Beebe, *Half Mile Down*, 133.
New York: ibid., 198; and see Beebe, *The Unseen Life of New York*.
Sin of boredom: see Gould, *Remarkable Life*, 386.

UNKNOWN FISH

From Beebe, *Half Mile Down*, 328.

TO THE THRESHOLD

Continuation of *Logbook*, August 11, 1934.

MONSTERS IN ETERNAL NIGHT
Paraphrased from *Mid-Ocean* (WB), individual sections as listed below.
astronesthes: "Deep-sea Dragons."
chaste squid: "Monsters in Eternal Night."
hatchet fish and *argyropelcus*: "Small Fry."
scarlet as shade of black: "Deep Sea."
angler fish: ibid.
black swallower: "The Mystery of the Black Swallower."

UNKNOWN ORGANISMS
Summarized from "Unknown Animals," in *Bathysphere, Records and Reports, Fish and Animal Data, 1930–1934* (WB).

LIFE GETTING THICKER
Logbook, August 15, 1934.

ABYSSAL IGNORANCE
On the two-tentacled sea-dragon: Beebe, *Half Mile Down*, 173.
On the other marine monster: ibid., 205.

THE LOWEST DEPTH
Continuation of *Logbook*, August 15, 1934.

A SIPHONOPHORE MANIFESTO
This chapter is a response to an email from science historian Katherine McLeod suggesting we imagine siphonophores as a "model for a commune."

MEDUSA
Corpses falling: Beebe often returned to this notion of only dead men falling. See e.g.: *Half Mile Down*, 100.
bwg: Beebe, *Edge of the Jungle*, 284.
The dead of Medusa Island: this meditation inevitably relates to Drexciya, a mythological Black aquatopia not far from Nonsuch, created by the unborn children of pregnant women who either jumped or were thrown overboard as sick cargo and whose ability to draw oxygen from amniotic fluid prepared them to do the same with seawater. This legendary civilization of aqua-humanoids, survivors of the Middle Passage, was elaborated in the unattributed liner notes of the 1990s duo called Drexciya, consisting of James Stinson and Gerald Donald and released by Underground Resistance. See, especially, liner notes to *The Quest* (1997); also Kodwo Eshun, *More Brilliant Than the Sun: Adventures in Sonic Fiction*, 83–85.
Immanuel Stewart: Beebe's meeting with the Stewarts is described in his *Journal* (WB), July 11, 1932.
Argyropelcus: "Small Fry" in *Mid-Ocean* (WB).
"At a depth . . .": Beebe, *Half Mile Down*, 135.

"*let us go down*": *Logbook*, August 11, 1934.

On struggles with oxygen and language, see Beebe, *Half Mile Down*, 163.

Ice ages like waves crashing: "There Were Giants on the Earth in Those Days" (WCS).

Impossibility of moving away: In *Edge of the Jungle*, Beebe writes: "All our stories are the middles of things—without beginning or end; we scientists are plunged suddenly upon a cosmos in the full uproar of eons of precedent, unable to look ahead, while to look backward we must look down" (289).

THE TURN

Continuation of *Logbook*, August 15, 1934.

THE ONLY BORNEO IN THE WORLD

On the three moments, see: Beebe, *Half Mile Down*, 216.

"Just one moment of actuality": Beebe, *The Arcturus Adventure*, 75–76.

Underwriting

Image of Eugenics exhibition at the state fair from my home state of Kansas.

1934

"Shining Climax": from an advertisement in the *New York Times*, August 12, 1934, the same issue announcing the new record-setting half-mile dive by the bathysphere.

"Canada's First Kidnapping": see: *The Royal Gazette and Colonist Daily*, Hamilton, Bermuda August 17, 1934.

"a note of seriousness . . .": ibid.

"Koba, why do you need my death": "*Koba zachem tibye nushna maya smerth*," said by Nikolay Bukharin. See: Simon Sebag Montefiore, *Stalin: The Court of the Red Tsar*.

BACK AT HEADQUARTERS

On Grant: Jonathan Spiro, *Defending the Master Race: Conservation, Eugenics, and the Legacy of Madison Grant* and Charles C. Alexander, "Prophet of American Racism: Madison Grant and the Nordic Myth."

Etching: William Hornaday, *Our Vanishing Wildlife: Its Extermination and Preservation*, 271.

On the Boone and Crocket Club, see: Darrin Lunde, *The Naturalist: Theodore Roosevelt, A Lifetime of Exploration, and the Triumph of American Natural History*, 139.

Tallest tree: Spiro, xiii.

Galton's quip ("If a twentieth . . ."): quoted in ibid., 121.

Hitler, "The book is my bible": quoted in ibid., xi.

Brandt's defense submissions at Nurnberg: "Extract from a book concerning eugenics" (Misc.).

Grant and Sanger: Spiro, 190–194.

Grant and Garvey: ibid., 258–265.

Second Eugenics Congress: ibid., 211.

"Are We Winning": quoted in Alexander, "Prophet," 74.

A MEMORIAL

On William Sheppard, see: Benedict Carton, "From Hampton '[I]nto the Heart of Africa': How Faith in God and Folklore Turned Congo Missionary William Sheppard into a Pioneering Ethnologist."

Hornaday reading Sheppard: Newkirk, *Spectacle: The Astonishing Life of Ota Benga*, 34.

Sheppard and Verner's meeting: ibid., 104.

Verner under Sheppard: ibid., 110.

Hornaday's press release: Hornaday, MS of press release in *Materials Related to Ota Benga, 1906–1924* (WCS).

"Boy has become . . .": Letter from Hornaday to Verner, September 17, 1906, in ibid.

"flourishing it in . . .": Letter from Hornaday to Verner, September 17, 1906, in ibid.

"comic opera material": Letter from Hornaday to McClellan, September 12, 1906, in ibid.

Newkirk and Mwanamilongo's identification and translation: Newkirk, *Spectacle*, 328.

Beautician's invitation: Letter from Gray to Hornaday, September 23, 1906, in *Materials Related to Ota Benga, 1906–1924* (WCS).

Hippodrome invitation: Letter from Hornaday to Worm, September 18, 1906, in ibid.

"That the exhibition . . .": quoted in Spiro, *Defending*, 47.

"They are not willing . . ." Letter from Hornaday to Verner, September 17, 1906, in *Materials Related to Ota Benga, 1906–1924* (WCS).

"not even <u>seem</u> . . .": Letter from Hornaday to Osborn, September 13, 1906, in ibid.

"I would rather . . .": ibid.

"Of course I shall stipulate . . .": Letter from Hornaday to Verner, September 17, 1906, in *Materials Related to Ota Benga, 1906–1924* (WCS).

Spencer's "Translation": In James Weldon Johnson, *The Book of American Negro Poetry*.

"How de do": Newkirk, 247.

"I believe I'll go home . . .": ibid., 294.

THE NAMES OF OTHERS

See Beebe, "On the Keeping of Ducks for Pleasure," and "Savages and Children."

"contented with their monotonous lives . . . and incurious": Beebe, "Pagan Personalities."

"stupid, with that impregnable stupidity . . .": ibid.

"boisterous, good-natured, jolly . . .": ibid.

"handsome, as Greek gods were handsome": ibid.

"splendid and naive . . . to embody every savage ideal": ibid.

"His quickness . . . the very essence of savagery": ibid.

"too good-looking and too athletic . . . to return": Beebe, "Patten Jackson."

On *super-servants*, see: Beebe, "Servants and Super-Servants."

"When our river steamer . . . in a tropical jungle": ibid.

"a singular hallucination . . .": Bellamy, *Looking Backward*, 13.

"the Indian's medicine plants . . .": Beebe, *Edge of the Jungle*, 132.

Aviation incapable of teaching him about flight: Beebe, *Jungle Days*, 6.

"Etymologies do not grow in the jungle": Beebe, "A Chain of Jungle Life."

"Before we have the complete solution . . .": Beebe, *Nonsuch: Land of Water*, 252.

Boas's first paper, see: Franz Boas, *Beiträge zur Erkenntnis der Farbe des Wassers*.

On Boas and the trafficked Inuit, see: Kenn Harper, *Give Me My Father's Body*.

"Play among animals . . .": Beebe, *Nonsuch: Land of Water*, 248.

"if superiority or inferiority . . .": Beebe, *Pheasant Jungles*, 114.

Letter from the American Refugee Committee: The letter was read out in Congress by Hon. Adolph J. Sabath of Illinois in the House of Representatives on Thursday, August 7, 1941, as a "Statement by Outstanding Authors and Scientists" (See: Sabath, "Statement . . .").

"native crew of five Bermudians": see: *Bermuda Oceanographic Expeditions 1929–1930* (WCS).

Photographs: *Bathysphere, Circa 1929–1949* (WCS).

Staff list: *Bathysphere log recorded by Gloria Hollister, 1930* (WCS).

The only name I was able to attain any further information on was F. Deuden. This appears to be Floyd Deuden, who would go on to work as a police officer in the 1940s. His son Colin Dueden is a mystery writer. His novel *Bloodwater*, based on his father's stories, appeared in 2016 from Moonshine Cove.

Surfacing

SURFACING

Logbook, August 15, 1934.

UNTOUCHABLE

Palm fronds: e.g., Beebe, *Half Mile Down*, 111.

On Bostelmann checking with Beebe when drawing what she hasn't seen, see: ibid., 228. For more on Bostelmann's process, see: George Peterich, "Mrs. B Paints for Beebe;" "Undersea Paintings Go on Exhibit Here;" and Jane Corby, "Life below the Ocean's Wave Provides this Woman Artist with Many-Hued, Fantastic Models."

On newly identified species of fish and deep-sea organisms, see: John R. Dolan, "The Neglected Contributions of William Beebe to the Natural History of the Deep-Sea," 1623–1624.

Bostelmann's image of the *Bathysidus pentagrammus*: see: Katherine McLeod, Mark Dion, and Madeleine Thompson, *Exploratory Works: Drawings from the Department of Tropical Research Field Expeditions*, pl. 62.

Bathyemebryx istiophasma: Beebe, *Half Mile Down*, 208.

Bathyceratias trilychnus: ibid., 327.

Photograph with Rube Goldberg in a gorilla suit: Beebe Papers, *Photographs 1929–1953* (WB) (thanks to Katherine McLeod for pointing it out).

Vegetable lamb: see: Thomas Brown, *Pseudodoxia Epidemica: Or, Enquiries Into Very Many Received Tenents, and Commonly Presumed Truths*, 227.

Dog-faced frog: see: "Human Oddity Photos," 86.

Unicorn hare: see: Zakariya al-Qazwini, *Marvels of Creatures and the Strange Things Existing.*

BLOOP AND BRISTLEMOUTH

Ballard on Beebe's unobserved species: Robert D. Ballard, *The Eternal Darkness: A Personal History of Deep-Sea Exploration* (2000), 25–30.

On the bristlemouth, see: Brian W. Coad, *Marine Fishes of Arctic Canada*, 302–305 and William J. Broad, "An Ocean Mystery in the Trillions."

On the bloop, see: National Ocean Service, "What Is the Bloop?"

THEY WERE

The title of the chapter and the passage on the "mystical" refer to Proposition 6.44 of Wittgenstein's *Tractatus*: "Nicht *wie* die Welt ist, ist das Mystische, sondern *dass* sie ist."

"All these words in type . . .": Beebe, *The Arcturus Adventure* 145.

"penalty man must pay . . .": Beebe, *High Jungle* 8.

"We had been brought close . . .": *The Arcturus Adventure*, 133.

NEW SPECIES OF DEEP-SEA FISH

Chaenophryne draco: language extracted from description in Beebe, "Nineteen New Species and Four Post-larval Deep Sea Fish," 84.

Dolopyihthys gladisfenae: extracted from ibid., 86.

Summer

TODAY'S WEATHER FORECAST

Detail of *The Royal Gazette and Colonist Daily*, Hamilton, Bermuda, 1934. undated, found in *General Records* (WCS).

[GRAND DAY . . .]

Phrases lifted from Beebe's *Journal* (WB), summers 1934–1937.

AN AFTERNOON WITH THE SEA DEVIL

Von Luckner's 1929 visit: see: "1929" in *Bermuda Reports, 1929–1931* (WB).

1935 visit: *Letter from Beebe to Harrison Williams* (Misc.).

On Von Luckner, see: Thomas Lowell, *Count Luckner, The Sea Devil.*

The Josephine ploy: ibid., 123.

Capturing the *Horngarth*: ibid., 171.

"Lay to . . . or I will sink you.": ibid., 173.

"How remote the war seemed then.": ibid., 177.

THE WIND

This incident is described in Hollister's *Journal* (LoC), August 26, 1930.

"flared up with glorious intense rose . . . the wet, dripping wind.": ibid.

"on the breast of the breeze.": ibid.

DR. BARRY

Mary Hunter's story of her grandfather is from a typed page inserted in Beebe's *Journal* (WB), inserted after August 19, 1931.

Article in *The Lancet*: Beebe's note estimates the article must have been from "1900 or thereabouts" (typed page, ibid.). Hunter was most likely referring to George A. Bright, MD. "A Female Member of the Army Medical Staff."

On Dr. Barry: see Ann Heilmann, *Neo-/Victorian Biographilia and James Miranda Barry: A Study in Transgender and Transgenre*, esp: 29–37; and Michael du Preez and Jeremy Dronfield, *Dr James Barry: A Woman Ahead of Her Time*.

On pronoun use (which I have adopted), see Heilmann, 62.

Nightingale's description: *Letter from Nightingale to Frances Parthenope Verney*, quoted in du Preez.

"uncontrollable temperament," Heilman, 31.

"perfect female": ibid., 35.

CRADLE OF THE DEEP

Hollister describes Beebe reading to her in her *Journal* (LoC), June 29, 1932.

"goddamned wind": Jean Lowell, *Cradle of the Deep*, 37.

"blackbirdin": ibid., 165.

On the scandal, see: Anne Colby, "Meet the Grandmother of Memoir Fabricators."

"excessive sobriety": William W. White "A Backlands Road to Home."

KONG

Review: see Mordaunt Hall, "A Fantastic Film in Which a Monstrous Ape Uses Automobiles for Missiles and Climbs a Skyscraper."

"Some big hard-boiled . . .": James A Creelman and Ruth Rose, *King Kong*.

On Rose modeling characters after Shoedsack, see: Helmut Färber, "King Kong: One More Interpretation, Or, What Cinema Tells About Itself," 123; and Ron Haver, "Merian C. Cooper: First King of Kong."

"the golden woman": Creelman and Rose, *King Kong*.

"Blondes are scarce around here": ibid.

DeMille's Temple of Jerusalem, See: Roger Ebert, "King Kong."

"He was a king and a god . . .": Creelman and Rose, *King Kong*.

TO MONA WILLIAMS

"monument to luxe . . .": Gold and Fizdale, "Swan Song in Capri."

On Edmona Travis Strader Schlesinger Bush Williams von Bismarck-Shönhausen de Martini, see: Vicente Benavent, *"Mona von Bismarck, la gran dama de la elegancia."*

"the color of sea water . . . no matter how 'brio' the melody.": Gold and Fizdale.

"dried frizz . . . lashes coated with turquoise.": ibid.

"a rock crystal goddess . . .": Hattie Crissel, "Meet the Woman Coco Chanel Voted the Best-dressed in the World."

"One of the few . . . bring to flower.": ibid.

Guests: Gold and Fizdale.

Balenciaga: Crissel.

Early life: Benavent.

Cole Porter song: "Ridin' High," 1936.

Dalí painting: Salvador Dalí, *The Portrait of Mrs. Harrison Williams* (1943).

Meeting with Von Bismarck: Described by Cecilia Sternberg in *The Journey*, 102.

Martini on the Rocks: Gold and Fizdale.

"small and oblong and pink": *Letter from Beebe to Harrison Williams, April 14, 1935.* Harrison Williams Collection (Misc.).

Invisibilities

PASSING OF THE *GLADISFEN*

This event, along with the story of the ship, is described in Beebe's *Journal*, July 3, 1937, (WB), and in "The Passing of the *Gladisfen*," a typed manuscript with accompanying photographs in *General Records 1900–1961* (WCS).

On Sylvester's role, see: *Gould*, 278, 282, 326.

"a heavy, dead feeling": from the MS in "The Passing of the *Gladisfen*."

"but never before have I seen . . .": ibid.

HALF-LIGHT

Jalousie slats: Beebe, *Nonsuch: Land of Water*, 161.

elemental abacus: ibid.

Regressive fantasy: ibid., 206–207.

Periwinkle snail: ibid., 205.

Seahorse v mermaid: ibid., 224–225.

Seahorses calling to each other: ibid., 231.

The blue shark: ibid., 174–5.

INVISIBILITIES

Beebe's observation of the cedars is described in: "The Cedars of Nonsuch," in Beebe, *Nonsuch: Land of Water*, 17–32.

Sleep of plants: Beebe, *Nonsuch: Land of Water*, 18.

"the moulding power of the invisible,": ibid., 19.

"Cradles, wedding-chests . . . stools and gallows": ibid., 21.

"blue-green, close-scaled": ibid., 25.

Common names of plants: ibid., 29–30.

Describing the sunset: ibid., 156.

Oneness: ibid., 159.

halicystis . . . *green like emeralds*: ibid., 32.

MARBLE

Longing to feel the instinct for flight: Beebe, *Nonsuch: Land of Water*, 110.

Memory of piloting over Europe: ibid., 110–111.

Babbitts or John Smiths vs. *the gloriously discontented*: ibid., 88.

Roosevelt's saber-toothed tiger and the thing more important than comfort: ibid., 93. One might have also asked Ota Benga his estimation of comfort and contentment, safety and sanity. But Beebe did not think of Ota Benga.

Lucifer as a "monophyletic, mammalian . . .": ibid., 95.

Baby birds about to issue forth, and love: ibid., 154.

Ink Spills Everywhere

FEEDBACK FROM READERS

Jean Healey: Letter found in one of Beebe's books, in *DTR Additions* (WCS).

Jean Coleman: Letter found in one of Beebe's books, in ibid.

Upton Sinclair: Letter from Sinclair to Beebe, *Correspondence S* (WB).

Dr. Pilászy György: Another letter found in one of Beebe's books, *DTR Additions* (WCS).

Dr. Geza Entz: ibid.

Man from East Orange: Letter from Shelton Bissell to Beebe, December 13, 1939. *Correspondence B* (WB).

HOLLISTER'S HONORS

Hollister longing to live in the wilderness: "Birthday in the Ocean Depth," (WCS).

Girl Scouts: reported in *American Magazine*, 1935 (WCS).

Sir Thomas Shirley: From a leaflet by Mianus River Gorge Conservation Committee included in *Gloria Hollister Anable Papers* (WCS).

Modern Mechanix & Hobbies: "Women Win Honors in Science," *Modern Mechanix and Hobbies*, found in *Records by and about Gloria Hollister* (WCS).

Flag of the Society of Women Geographers: "Birthday in the Ocean Depth" (WCS).

Earhart's "no faith we'll meet anywhere again.": Judith Thurman, "Amelia Earhart's Last Flight." The letter continues: "though I hope we might."

ODDS AND ENDS

See: *Odds and Ends Left at Nonsuch* (WCS).

WINTER OF 1934

Details of Beebe's tour are from his "Daily Diary, USA, 1934" in *Journal* (WB).

"no hospitality": ibid.

"Bully": ibid.

cocktails: ibid.

On set in *Stanley and Livingstone*: Described in Beebe's *Journal* (WB), August 5, 1936.

Reading *Gaudy Night*: Beebe, *Journal* (WB), April 6, 1936.

Visiting Mary Hood: ibid., November 14, 1939.

Lunch at MGM studios: ibid., November 15, 1939.

"the only man . . . Clark Gable to his knees.": ibid.

The astrologer, "a continent would rise . . .": ibid.

THE OTHER BEEBE

This episode is described in Beebe's *Journal* (WB), November 27, 1937.

THE SUNSET OF LUISA VELASCO

This episode is described in *Adventuring with Beebe*, 134–137.

"wholly undisturbed by her audience of desperados . . .": ibid., 136.

"deftly dropped her handkerchief . . .": ibid., 136-7.

"the enveloping sleeves": ibid., 137.

"otro!": ibid.

"The sunset of such an actress . . .": ibid.

THE NAMES OF THINGS

On the ocean's surface: *Journal* (WB), May 8, 1936.

"a few particles of material substance . . .": ibid.

"a vibrating sheet of pure gold": ibid.

copyist's mistake: ibid.

"we can add little . . .": ibid.

The uncertain conchologist in San Francisco: ibid., May 25, 1936.

LAST VISIT

The oil spill: *Journal* (WB), May 19, 1941.

Scottish soldiers: ibid., August 28, 1940.

The "'alf-crown solicitor" joke: ibid., May 31, 1941.

"flat as paper, ruled with near rectangles . . .": *High Jungle*, 9.

"So tame and humdrum . . .": Beebe, *Journal*, June 7, 1941.

An old fashioned with the Yugoslav ambassador: ibid.

Ink spills everywhere: ibid.

TITANS OF THE DEEP

Barton's letter, "utterly absurd": Letter from Barton to Beebe, August 30, 1938. *Correspondence B* (WB).

Beebe's response: Letter from Beebe to Barton: ibid.

"Together with my staff . . .": Clipping enclosed in a letter from Fairfield Osborn, September 16, 1938. *Correspondence O* (WB).

Silence and Solitude

WORLD'S FAIR

On the bathysphere outliving humankind, see: *Half Mile Down*, 181.

Plans for the 1939 fair: see: "Proposal of the New York Zoological Society to Place on Exhibition at the 1939 Exposition Collections of Living and Dead Deep Sea Fish." In *Bathysphere, New York World's Fair Exhibition, 1939–1940* (WB).

"amazing creatures living . . .": ibid.

On Bernays and "engineering of consent," see: Edward Bernays, *The Engineering of Consent*.

A brochure for the fair, "Science in the Exhibit Area," can be found in *Bathysphere, New York World's Fair Exhibition, 1939–1940* (WB).

"scientific dairying . . . Rotolactor": ibid.

General Motors' history of the world: ibid.

Barton's "Bottom Gazer": described in "Conquest of the Deep."

RANCHO GRANDE

On Rancho Grande: Beebe, *High Jungle*, 60–65.

"the last great South American dictator": ibid., 60.

"auricula purple, rainnette green . . .": ibid., 65.

"protozoa, colenterata . . .": ibid.

"Even today there are one-celled lives . . .": ibid., 145.

"At times, when there develops . . .": ibid., 66.

SHORTER WORKS

These segments are taken from: A typed page titled "What Happens after Warmth in the North and Moisture in the Tropics," found in *Trinidad (Simla) Expeditions, Miscellaneous, 1950–1961* (WB).

MOTH WINGS

This section is based on: George Swanson, "Jungle Studio."

On *Pelléas*, see: Metropolitan Opera Archives, 1939–1940 (Misc.).

"the innately disconsolate . . .": Swanson, "Jungle Studio," 170.

"floating ladies aloft . . .": ibid., 171.

"carnivorous grasshoppers . . .": ibid.

"before death made everything . . .": ibid.

"Enterolobium seedpods . . .": ibid., 172.

"orchids bloom themselves to death . . .": ibid.

"Bakst's design of the chief eunuch . . .": ibid., 173.

"smoldering gems and minerals . . .":ibid., 174.

"broad-leaved heliconias . . . Mr. Paraiso.": ibid., 175

"A song like some latin chèvre . . .": ibid.

On Swanson's "sensuous and lustful" paintings of the Ballet Russe: Ali Baldenebro, "George A. Swanson (American 1908–1968)."

THINGS WE DO IN MOMENTS OF PENSIVENESS

This text is found among typed pages in Beebe's *Journal, 1939–1941* (WB).

ANIMALS AND MEN

This is based on the text "Animals and Men" found in the *DTR General Records 1900–1961* (WCS).

"Whenever a horse . . . than most men": ibid., 3.

"should end all human attempts at swing.": ibid., 27.

"needle's eyes": ibid., 25.

SOLITUDE

On Carson: William Souder, *On a Farther Shore: The Life and Legacy of Rachel Carson.*

Carson's correspondence with Beebe is found in the Rachel Carson Papers (Misc.).

Carson in Biscayne Bay: Souder, 136.

"a tidal wave of earthly substance": Carson, *The Sea Around Us*, 5.

"steady, unremitting, downward drift": ibid., 97.

"violent, explosive, earth-shaking . . .": ibid., 110.

"As with all that is earthly . . .": ibid., 192.

SILENCE

Strontium 90: Rachel Carson, *The Silent Spring*, 234.

Nerve gas sprayed over fields of alfalfa: ibid., 22

Dieldren and aldrin: ibid., 25–26.

Parathion: ibid., 29–30.

"Chemicals kill every insect . . .": ibid., 7.

"this ever-widening wave . . .": ibid., 127.

Lake Tule: ibid., 45.

"Spring now comes unheralded . . .": ibid., 103.

FINAL EXCHANGE

Both letters contained in *Memories of Beebe upon his 50th anniversary w. NYZS* (WCS).

TRINIDAD

"the minister who couldn't remember . . .": on typed note by Jocelyn Crane *PLEASE PUT IN THE BOOK*, found in *Trinidad (Simla) Expeditions, Report Data and Notes, 1950–1961* (WB).

"How a Beetle Laid Waste . . . to a Great City.": on a typed page titled "Time and Tide," found in ibid.

Cricket team: *Journal* (WB), January 25, 1950.

Girls with binoculars: ibid., April 3, 1950.

Aboard the *Sea Gypsy*: ibid., November 18, 1950.

Newspaper clippings: Found tucked into Beebe's *Journal* in *Trinidad, 57th Expedition, 1956* (WB).

"if you know how, you can pick up a scorpion": *Journal, Trinidad, 59th Expedition, 1957–1958* (WB).

"A bat falcon, crying 'ke-ke-ke-ke' . . .": ibid.

"gets mad at it": from "Symptons, etc., of Wm Beebe, June 1, 1958." Found in ibid.

"passes as his brain . . .": ibid.

"a multitude of . . . violet specks.": ibid.

"the Wedding of the Snows . . . the wide spreading repercussions": *Journal* (WB), June 7, 1958.

BETWEEN DAY AND NIGHT

"There is a certain hour . . .": "Between Day and Night," found in *Trinidad (Simla) Expeditions, Miscellaneous, 1950–1961* (WB).

"when sick men mostly die . . .": Plunkett, *Book of Wonder*, 50.

"Day is hope and light and life . . .": "Between Day and Night" (WB).

"tooth and fang . . . the death hour is past.": ibid.

"transparent luminosity . . .": ibid.

"the mobile mirrors of the mangroves changed": ibid.

"hot strong breath": ibid.

IF I COME UP

As reported in an untitled, unattributed note: *New York Times* April 25, 1934. Found among Gloria Hollister's papers in *Gloria Hollister Anable Papers* (WCS).

NEW SPECIES OF DEEP-SEA FISH

Linophryne arborifer: language extracted from description in Beebe, "Nineteen New Species and Four Post-larval Deep Sea Fish," 90.

Melanocetus murrayi: extracted from ibid., 99.

Aceratias edentula: extracted from ibid., 102.

Leaving the Body Behind

THE HOSPITAL CEILING

On Wegener, see: Mott Green, *Alfred Wegener: Science, Exploration, and the Theory of Continental Drift*.

REIMAGINING

On Tharp, see her autobiographical essay "Connect the Dots: Mapping the Seafloor and Discovering the Mid-ocean Ridge" and Hali Felt, *Soundings: The Story of the Remarkable Woman Who Mapped the Ocean Floor*.

"read nature": Felt, 27.

Details of Tharp's youth, see: Felt.

Kelvin, piano wire: Rachel Carson, *The Sea Around Us*, 78.

"I've been looking at your maps . . .": Tharp, "Connect the Dots."

THE BIG DIVE

On Piccard and Walsh's dive, see: Jacques Piccard, "Man's Deepest Dive."

VENTS AND CHIMNEYS

On Ballard's discovery of the hydrothermal vents and chimneys, see: Ballard and Hively, *Eternal Darkness: A Personal History of Deep-Sea Exploration*, 157–216.

"connected to hell itself": ibid., 202.

Tube-worms in the Arabian desert: ibid., 207.

BLACK BOTTOM

Rate of Atlantic and Pacific spreading: Marcia Bjornerud, *Timefulness*, 69.

On the Boxing Day earthquake of 2004, see: Sid Perkins, "Tsunami Disaster: Scientists Model the Big Quake and Its Consequences."

On the Cape Verde tsunami: Bjornerud, 88.

On the rock in Wyoming: ibid., 89.

Fossilized reefs below Bermuda: author's interview with Dr. Robbie Smith, marine biologist from the Bermuda Aquarium who had descended with the Nekton Project in 2016. See nektonmission.org.

On the anoxic pool in the Black Sea, see: Charles King, *The Black Sea*, 14–18.

On Ballard's trip to the Titanic, see: Ballard, *Eternal Darkness* (2017): 217–254.

On the sleeping dolphin, see: Ira Flatow, "Robert Ballard: 50 Years Exploring Deep Waters."

Later, spurred on by a blurry photograph of a small Pacific island, in which he thought he saw evidence of Amelia Earhart's wrecked plane, Ballard led a multi-million effort to locate its remains, but found nothing.

LEAVING THE BODY BEHIND

This chapter is based on the final chapter in the first edition of Ballard and Hively, *Eternal Darkness* (2000).

On Victor Vescovo, see: Josh Young, *Expedition Deep Ocean: The First Descent to the Bottom of All Five Oceans*.

"We can cut the ultimate tether . . .": Ballard, 311.

"The time will come when we will . . .": Letter from Kipling to Beebe, *Correspondence K* (WB).

"Nothing can math one's first mind-boggling . . .": Ballard, 300.

Recent Sightings

THE DESTINY OF SHIPS

This chapter is based on an undated, typed manuscript "The Destiny of Ships," found in *Writings, 1852–1961* (WB).

On marine drones passing the Titanic, see: Hannah Devlin, "Titanic Explorers' Dive Reveals 'Shocking' State of Wreck."

"wholly inhuman": "The Destiny of Ships" (WB).

"permanent animal blossoms . . . inorganic everlastings": ibid.

"the intaglio of the Brooklyn Belle": ibid.

"Soon . . . clouds of sheer luminescence": ibid.

"Of course of what we call time . . .": ibid.

"not even a mound": ibid.

"Everything that fell from the world . . .": ibid.

"scattered over the face": ibid.

KING NEPTUNE'S WHISKERS

This chapter is based on an undated, typed manuscript "Superstitions of the Sea," found in *Writings, 1852–1961* (WB).

"they have gone into . . .": ibid.

RECENT SIGHTINGS

This chapter is based on my observations while diving and listening to sound files from the Gray's Reef Foundation and Dr. Rodney Rountree (see: Sound Files).

On giant larvaceans, see: Yasemin Saplakoglu, "These Gorgeous, Intricate Sea Creatures Are Actually Giant Blobs of Snot."

List of Images

Bibliography

Archival Material

WILDLIFE CONSERVATION SOCIETY ARCHIVES (WCS)

All records: *Wildlife Conservation Society Archives,* New York Zoological Society. All images © Wildlife Conservation Society. Reproduced by permission of the WCS Archives.

American Magazine, 1935, Records by and about Gloria Hollister, 1935. Department of Tropical Research Additional Records (1016).

"Animals and Men" *DTR General Records 1900–1961.* Box 2, DTR History.

Bathysphere, circa 1929–1949. Bermuda records (1005J). Department of Tropical Research. Oceanographic expeditions.

Bathysphere log recorded by Gloria Hollister, 1930, 1932, and 1934; Department of Tropical Research. Oceanographic expeditions. Bermuda records (1005J). Box 10.

"Birthday in the Ocean Depth," 1958. *Gloria Hollister Anable papers,* 1914–2005 (bulk 1926–1947). Collection 1006. Box: 3, Folder: 1.

Color Notes, circa 1929–1949. Bermuda records (1005J). Department of Tropical Research. Oceanographic expeditions.

General Records, 1878–1962, bulk: 1920–1939. Department of Tropical Research additional records (1016).

Gloria Hollister Anable Correspondence. Bulk, 1934–1935, 1932–1935. Box: 2, Folder: 1.

Gloria Hollister Anable Papers, 1914–2005, bulk 1926–1947. Collection 1006.

Materials Related to Ota Benga, 1906–1924. 1001–01; 1012–01; 1012–02.

Memories of Beebe upon His 50th Anniversary w. NYZS. 1016 DTR Additions Box 1/f3. DTR General by or about Beebe.

"Odds and Ends Left at Nonsuch," *Bermuda Subject Files, 1935–1937.* DTR Additions (1016). Box 9, folder 17.

"The Passing of the *Gladisfen*," *DTR General Records* 1900–1961. Box 1, DTR History.

"St Francis of the Plaster Cast." *Variety of Typed Drafts, Especially Migration, Circa 1942–1949*. Box: 1.

"There Were Giants on the Earth in Those Days," *Typescript Writings, with Accompanying Photographs, circa 1900–1971*. Box 2.

William Beebe Vermix, 1950. Box 1, Folder 4. Department of Tropical Research Additional Records (1016).

WILLIAM BEEBE PAPERS (WB)

All records: William Beebe Papers, Special Collections, Princeton University Library.

Bathysphere Correspondence, 1926–1939. Box 17, Folder 1.

Bathysphere, New York World's Fair Exhibition, 1939–1940. Box 12, Folder 9.

Bathysphere, Records and Reports, Fish and Animal Data, 1930–1934. Box 12, Folder 7.

Bathysphere Records and Reports, 1930–1934, Box 12, Folder 1.

Bermuda Diary, 1928–1932, Box 7, Folder 4.

Bermuda Reports, 1929–1931, Box 7, Folder 5.

"Between Day and Night," *Trinidad (Simla) Expeditions, Miscellaneous, 1950–1961*. Box 13, Folder 11.

Correspondence 1856–1981. Box 15–22.

"The Destiny of Ships," *Writings, 1852–1961*. Box 14, Folder 11.

Journals, 1890–1961. Boxes 1–10.

Mid-Ocean, Manuscript Material for A Proposed Book, 1881–1939. Box 12, Folder 10.

Photographs 1929–1953. Box 18, Folder 4.

"Superstitions of the Sea," *Writings, 1852–1961*. Box 14, Folder 27.

Trinidad (Simla) Expeditions, Report Data and Notes, 1950–1961. Box 13, Folders 5–7.

"What Happens after Warmth in the North and Moisture in the Tropics," *Trinidad (Simla) Expeditions, Miscellaneous, 1950–1961*. Box 13, Folder 11.

GLORIA HOLLISTER ANABLE PAPERS (LoC)

Journal, Gloria Hollister Anable Papers. Box 2, Library of Congress.

MISC. ARCHIVAL MATERIAL (MISC.)

Biography at James B. Pond Papers. Clements Library, University of Michigan.

"Extract from a Book Concerning Eugenics," *Harvard Law School Library–Nuremberg Trials Project NMT 1* (Case Files/English, Exhibit Code: Brandt, K. 57, HLSL Item No.: 2703).

Leonardo de Vinci Codex Hammer f. 36 r (I B).

Letters from Beebe to Harrison Williams. Harrison Williams Collection on Expeditions of William Beebe and George Putnam. Box 1, Folder 14. University of California at San Diego.

Pelléas, 1940. Metropolitan Opera Archives, 1939–1940. Met Performance, CID:128290.

Rachel Carson Papers. Yale Collection of American Literature, Beinecke Rare Book and Manuscript Library, Yale University.

Edited Material

EDITED MATERIAL BY BEEBE AND EXPEDITION STAFF

Barton, Otis. *The World Beneath the Sea.* New York: Thomas Crowell, 1953.

Beebe, William. *Adventuring with Beebe.* New York: Dull, Sloan and Pearce, 1967.

——. "Animal Life at the Front," *Zoological Society Bulletin* 21, 1918: 1614–1616.

——. *The Arcturus Adventure.* New York: G.P. Putnam's Sons, 1926.

——. *Beneath Tropic Seas.* New York: G.P. Putnam's Sons, 1928.

——. "Bermuda Oceanographic Expeditions 1929–1930," *New York Zoological Society Bulletin* 13 (1), 1930.

——. "Birds of Northeastern Venezuela," *New York Zoological Society Bulletin* 1 (3), 1909.

——. "A Chain of Jungle Life," *Atlantic Monthly* 1923, 132 (4): 492–500.

——. *Edge of the Jungle.* Garden City, NY: Garden City Publishing Co., 1921.

——. "Exploring a Tree and a Yard of Jungle," *Zoological Society Bulletin*, July 1915.

——. *Galapagos: World's End.* New York: G.P. Putnam's Sons, 1924.

——. *Half Mile Down.* New York: Harcourt, Brace, 1934.

——. *Jungle Days.* New York: G.P. Putnam's Sons, 1924.

——. *Jungle Nights.* New York: Atlantic Monthly Press, 1918.

——. *Jungle Peace.* New York: Henry Holt, 1918.

——. "Nineteen New Species and Four Post-larval Deep Sea Fish," *Zoologica* 13 (4), 1932.

——. *Nonsuch: Land of Water.* New York: New York Zoological Society, 1932.

——. "On the Keeping of Ducks for Pleasure," *New York Zoological Society Bulletin* 10, 1903.

——. "Ontological Notes on *Remora remora,*" *New York Zoological Society Bulletin* 13 (6), 1932.

——. "Pagan Personalities," *Harpers* (May 1916. 132): 938–947.

——. "Patten Jackson," *New York Zoological Society Bulletin* 33 (6) 1930: 248.

——. "A Red Indian Day," *Atlantic Monthly* 122 (1) 1918: 23–31.

——. "Savages and Children," *New York Tribune*, June 25, 1905.

——. "Servants and Super-Servants," *Atlantic Monthly* 116 (5) 1915: 638–647.

——. "Three Hundred Fathoms beneath the Sea," *Popular Mechanics*, October 1930: 582–584.

——. "The Three-toed Sloth," in *Zoologica* 7 (1): 13.

——. *Two Bird-Lovers in Mexico.* Boston and New York: Houghton Mifflin and Company, 1905.

———. *The Unseen Life of New York*. New York: Dull, Sloan and Pearce, 1953.

Bostelmann, Else. "Notes from an Undersea Studio off Bermuda," *Country Life* February 1939: 67– 68, 102.

Cooper, Isabel, "Artist at Large," *The Atlantic Monthly*, July 1926: 85–93.

———. "Wild-Animal Painting in the Jungle," *The Atlantic Monthly*, June 1924: 732–743.

Rose, Ruth. "Cocos Treasure Again Exerts Its Lure," *New York Times*, November 29, 1925. Swanson, George. "Jungle Studio," *Animal Kingdom* 48 (6) 1945: 170–175.

OTHER REFERENCES

Alexander, Charles C. "Prophet of American Racism: Madison Grant and the Nordic Myth," *Phylon* 23 (1), 1960: 73–90.

Baldenebro, Ali. "George A. Swanson (American 1908–1968)," *Shannon's Fine Art Auctioneer—www.shannons.com/george-swanson-biography*, accessed February 24, 2021.

Ballard, Robert D. and Will Hively, *Eternal Darkness: A Personal History of Deep-Sea Exploration*. Princeton: Princeton University Press, 2000.

Bell, David. *Marxian Socialism in the United States*. Ithaca: Cornell University Press, 1996.

Bell, Janis. "Leonardo and Alhazen: Cloth on the Mountaintop." *Achademica Leonardi Vinchi* 6: 108–111.

Bellamy, Edward. *Looking Backward*. Bellamy, Edward. *Looking Backward*. Boston and New York: Houghton Mifflin Company, 1926.

Benavent, Vicente. "*Mona von Bismarck la gran dama de la elegancia*," *Harpers Bazaar España*, June 3, 2018.

Berann, Heinrick, with Marie Tharp and Bruce Heezen. "A Map of the Atlantic Ocean Floor." Washington, DC: The National Geographic Society, 1968.

Bernays, Edward. *The Engineering of Consent*. Norman: University of Oklahoma Press, 1969. Bjornerud, Marcia. *Timefulness*. Princeton: Princeton University Press, 2018.

Boas, Franz. "An Anthropologist's Credo," *The Nation* 147 (1938): 201–4.

———. *Beitrage zur Erkenntnis der Farbe des Wassers*. Kiel, Germany: University of Kiel, 1881.

Boyd-Jones, Edward and Owen Hall. *Florodora*. London: Francis, Day & Hunter, 1899.

Bright, George A. "A Female Member of the Army Medical Staff" (letter to the editor), *The Lancet*, October 12, 1895.

Britannica, Editors of Encyclopedia. "Miguel Primo de Rivera," *Encyclopedia Britannica*, 2021.

Broad, William J. "An Ocean Mystery in the Trillions." *New York Times*, June 30, 2015, D-1.

Brown, Thomas. *Pseudodoxia Epidemica: Or, Enquiries Into Very Many Received Tenents, and Commonly Presumed Truths*. London: E. Dod, 1658.

Butler, Rex. "Re-reading 'Kafka and His Precursors.'" *Variaciones Borges* 29 (2010): 93–106.

Carson, Rachel. *The Sea Around Us*. New York: Oxford University Press, 2003.

———. *The Silent Spring*. New York: Houghton Mifflin Harcourt, 2002.

Carton, Benedict. "From Hampton '[I]nto the Heart of Africa': How Faith in God and Folklore Turned Congo Missionary William Sheppard into a Pioneering Ethnologist," *History in Africa*, 36, 2009: 53–86.

Chirimuuta, M. *Outside Color: Perceptual Science and the Puzzle of Color*. Cambridge, MA: MIT Press, 2015: 19–22.

Coad, Brian W. *Marine Fishes of Arctic Canada*. Toronto, Can.: University of Toronto Press, 2018.

Colby, Anne. "Meet the Grandmother of Memoir Fabricators," *Los Angeles Times*, March 14, 2008.

Corby, Jane. "Life below the Ocean's Wave Provides this Woman Artist with Many-Hued, Fantastic Models," *The Brooklyn Daily Eagle*, February 13, 1930: 16.

Creelman, James A. and Ruth Rose, *King Kong*. RKO Radio Pictures, 1933.

Crissel, Hattie. "Meet the Woman Coco Chanel Voted the Best-dressed in the World," *Vogue*, July 4, 2018.

Davis, Jr., Donald G. "The Ionaco of Gaylord Wilshire," *Southern California Quarterly* 49 (4), 1967: 425–453.

Devlin, Hannah. "Titanic Explorers' Dive Reveals 'Shocking' State of Wreck," *The Guardian*, August 21, 2019.

Dolan, John R. "The Neglected Contributions of William Beebe to the Natural History of the Deep-Sea." *ICES Journal of Marine Science* 77(5), 2020: 1617–1628.

Drexciya, *The Quest* (liner notes). Submerge, 1997.

Dueden, Colin. *Bloodwater*. Moonshine Cove, 2016.

du Preez, Michael and Jeremy Dronfield. *Dr James Barry: A Woman Ahead of Her Time*. New York: Simon and Schuster, 2016.

Eastlake, Charles, trans. *Goethe's Theory of Colors*. London: John Murray, 1840.

Ebert, Roger. "King Kong." *RogerEbert.com*, February 2, 2002—www.rogerebert.com/reviews/great- movie-king-kong-1933, accessed February 22, 2021.

Eshun, Kodwo. *More Brilliant Than the Sun: Adventures in Sonic Fiction*. London: Quartet Books, 1998.

Etherington, Norman. *Theories of Imperialism: War, Conquest and Capital*. London: Routledge, 2014.

Färber, Helmut. "King Kong: One More Interpretation, Or, What Cinema Tells about Itself," *Discourse* 22 (2) 2000: 104–126.

Felt, Hali. *Soundings: The Story of the Remarkable Woman Who Mapped the Ocean Floor*. New York: Henry Holt and Company, 2013.

Fiorani, Francesco and Allesandro Nova. "Leonardo da Vinci and Optics: Theory and Pictorial Practice." *Studi e Ricerche* 2013: 9–27.

Flatow, Ira. "Robert Ballard: 50 Years Exploring Deep Waters." *National Public Radio*, July 3, 2009.

Geisel, Theodor Seuss. "The Beginnings of Dr. Seuss—An Informal Reminiscence," *Dartmouth Alumni Magazine*, April 1976.

Gold, Arthur and Robert Fizdale. "Swan Song in Capri," *Vanity Fair*, August 1987.

Gould, Carol Grant. *The Remarkable Life of William Beebe*. Washington, DC: Shearwater, 2004.

Graham, Stephen. *New York Nights*. New York: George H. Doran, 1927.

Green, Mott. *Alfred Wegener: Science, Exploration, and the Theory of Continental Drift*. Baltimore, MD: JHU Press, 2015.

Guerlac, Henry. "Can there Be Colors in the Dark? Physical Color Theory before Newton," *Journal of the History of Ideas* 47 (1) 1986: 3–20.

Guicciardini, Niccolò. "The Role of Musical Analogies in Newton's Optical and Cosmological Work," *Journal of the History of Ideas*, 74 (1) 2013: 45–67.

Hagedorn, Hermann. *Roosevelt in the Badlands, Vol 1*. New York: Houghton Mifflin, 1921.

Hall, Mordaunt. "A Fantastic Film in Which a Monstrous Ape Uses Automobiles for Missiles and Climbs a Skyscraper," *New York Times*, March 3, 1933.

Harper, Kenn. *Give Me My Father's Body: The Life of Minik, the New York Eskimo*. South Royalton, VT: Steerforth Press, 1986.

Haver, Ron. "Merian C. Cooper: First King of Kong," *American Film* 2 (3) 1977: 14–23.

Heilmann, Ann. *Neo-/Victorian Biographilia and James Miranda Barry: A Study in Transgender and Transgenre*. London: Palgrave MacMillan, 2018.

Hornaday, William. *Our Vanishing Wildlife: Its Extermination and Preservation*. New York: Scribner, 1913.

Hulbert, E.O. "The Transparency of Ocean Water and the Visibility Curve of the Eye," *Journal of the Optical Society of America and Review of Scientific Instruments* 5 (13) 1926.

Huyghe, P. "Incident at Curuça," *The Sciences*, March–April 1996: 14–17.

Johnson, Frank H. *Edmund Harvey Newton, 1887-1959: A Biographical Memoir*. Washington, DC: National Academy of Sciences, 1967.

Johnson, James Weldon. *The Book of American Negro Poetry*. New York: Harcourt, Brace, 1922.

Keynes, Milo. "The Personality of Isaac Newton," *Notes and Records of the Royal Society of London* 49 (1) 1995: 1–56.

King, Charles. *The Black Sea*. Oxford: Oxford University Press, 2005.

King, Charles. *Gods of the Upper Air: How a Circle of Renegade Anthropologists Reinvented Race, Sex, and Gender in the Twentieth Century*. New York: Knopf, 2019.

Kremer-Marietti, Angèle. "Schopenhauer, Goethe et la théorie des couleurs," *Revue Internationale de Philosophie*, 63 (249) (3) 2009: 279–294.

Lawson, Ellen NicKenzie. *Smugglers, Bootleggers, and Scofflaws: Prohibition and New York City*. New York: SUNY Press, 2013.

Lévy-Zumwalt, Rosemary. *Franz Boas: The Emergence of the Anthropologist*. Lincoln, NE: University of Nebraska Press, 2019.

Lowell, Jean. *Cradle of the Deep*. New York: Simon and Schuster, 1929.

Lowell, Thomas. *Count Luckner, The Sea Devil*. Garden City, N.Y.: Doubleday, Page & Company, 1927.

Lunde, Darrin. *The Naturalist: Theodore Roosevelt, A Lifetime of Exploration, and the Triumph of American Natural History*. New York: Crown, 2016.

Matsen, Brad. *Descent*. New York: Knopf, 2007.

McLeod, Katherine. "Beyond the Biological: William Beebe, the Bronx Zoo, and U.S. Biological Field Stations in British Guiana." New York: CUNY Graduate Center. Unpublished dissertation. 2016.

McLeod, Katherine, Mark Dion, and Madeleine Thompson. *Exploratory Works: Drawings from the Department of Tropical Research Field Expeditions*. New York: The Drawing Center, 2017.

Miller, Laura. "Minor Magus," *The New Yorker*, November 29, 2004.

Mills, A. A. "Newton's Prisms and His Experiments on the Spectrum," *Notes and Records of the Royal Society of London* 36 (1) 1981: 13–36.

Montefiore, Simon Sebag. *Stalin: The Court of the Red Tsar*. London: Weidenfeld & Nicolson, 2014. Murray, John and Johann Hjort, *The Depths of the Ocean*. London: MacMillan and Co., 1912.

National Ocean Service (NOAA), "What Is the Bloop?"—oceanservice.noaa.gov/facts /bloop.html, accessed February 21, 2021.

Nelson, Mark W. "Henry Gaylord Wilshire," *Southern California Quarterly* 96 (1): 41–85.

Newkirk, Pamela. *Spectacle: The Astonishing Life of Ota Benga*. New York: Harper Collins, 2015.

Newton, E. Harvey. *A History of Luminescence from the Earliest Times to 1900*. Philadelphia: American Philosophical Society, 1957.

Newton, Isaac. *Of Colours*. MS Add. 3975, Cambridge University Library, Cambridge, UK: 21.

Perkins, Sid. "Tsunami Disaster: Scientists Model the Big Quake and Its Consequences," *Science News*, January 8, 2005.

Peterich, George. "Mrs. B Paints for Beebe," in *Bostelmann Paints for Beebe* (exhibition catalog). Hamilton, Bermuda: The Bermuda National Gallery, 1997: 4–8.

Piccard, Jacques. "Man's Deepest Dive." *National Geographic*, August 1960.

Plunkett, Edward J. M. D. (Lord Dunsany). The *Book of Wonder*. Boston: John Luce, 1912.

Prout, Jerry. *Coxey's Crusade for Jobs: Unemployment in the Golden Age*. Ithaca: Cornell University Press, 2016.

al-Qazwini, Zakariya. *Marvels of Creatures and the Strange Things Existing*. Baltimore: Walters Art Museum: manuscript W.659.155B.

Ridgway, Robert. *Color Standards and Color Nomenclature*. Self-published, 1912. Reprint by Port Chester, NY: Adegi Graphics LLC, 1999.

Sabath, Adolph J. "Statement by Outstanding Authors and Scientists." *Congressional Record: Proceedings and Debates of the . . . Congress*. U.S. Government Printing Office, 1941.

Sabra, A.I., ed. *The Optics of Ibn al-Haytham: Books I–III, On Direct Vision*. London: Studies of the Warburg Institute, 1989.

Saplakoglu, Yasemin. "These Gorgeous, Intricate Sea Creatures Are Actually Giant Blobs of Snot," *LiveScience*, June 5, 2020—www.livescience.com/giant-larvacean -mucus-houses-3d-imaging.html, accessed February 24, 2021.

Sepper, Dennis L. "Goethe, Newton, and the Imagination of Modern Science," *Revue Internationale de Philosophie*, 63 (249) (3) 2009: 261–277.

Souder, William. *On a Farther Shore: The Life and Legacy of Rachel Carson*. New York: Crown, 2012.

Spiro, Jonathan. *Defending the Master Race*: *Conservation, Eugenics, and the Legacy of Madison Grant*. Burlington, VT: University of Vermont Press, 2009.

Sternberg, Cecilia. *The Journey*. New York: Dial Press, 1977.

Thane, Elswyth. *Riders on the Wind*. New York: Frederick A. Stokes Company, 1926.

———. *Tryst*. New York: Grosset and Dunlap, 1939.

Tharp, Marie. "Connect the Dots: Mapping the Seafloor and Discovering the Mid-ocean Ridge," in: Laurence Lippsett, ed., *Lamont-Doherty Earth Observatory of Columbia Twelve Perspectives on the First Fifty Years 1949–1999*. Palisades, NY: Lamont-Doherty Earth Observatory, 1999.

Thurman, Judith. "Amelia Earhart's Last Flight," *The New Yorker*, September 14, 2009.

Vendler, Zeno. "Goethe, Wittgenstein, and the Essence of Color," *The Monist* 78 (4), 1995: 391–410.

Westfall, Richard S. *Never at Rest: A Biography of Isaac Newton*. Cambridge, UK: Cambridge University Press, 1983.

Whitaker, Jan. "Anatomy of a Restauranteur: Don Dickerman," *Restauranting Through History*—restaurant-ingthroughhistory.com/2008/12/09/anatomy-of-a-restaurateur -don-dickerman, accessed February 19, 2021.

White, William W. "A Backlands Road to Home," *New York Times*, May 4, 1952.

Wilshire, H.G. *Fabian Essays in Socialism*. New York: The Humboldt Publishing Co., 1891.

Wittgenstein, Ludwig. *Logisch-Philosophische Abhandlung.* W. Ostwald's *Annalen der Naturphilosophie*, 1921.

Young, Josh. *Expedition Deep Ocean: The First Descent to the Bottom of All Five Oceans.* New York: Simon and Schuster, 2020.

UNATTRIBUTED MAGAZINE AND NEWSPAPER CLIPPINGS

"Beebe Betters Own Mark in 3,028-ft Dive," *New York Herald Tribune*, August 16, 1934.

"Canada's First Kidnapping," *The Royal Gazette and Colonist Daily* (Hamilton, Bermuda), August 17, 1934.

"Conquest of the Deep," *Science Illustrated*, January 1947: 39–40.

"Else Bostelmann, Artist, Dies at 79," *New York Times*, December 29, 1961. "Fire in Pirate's Den Ruins Relics of the Sea," *New York Times*, April 24, 1929.

"Girl Explorer Extends Women's World to Ocean Bottom and Jungle Depths," *The Tribune* (Scranton, PA), July 15, 1936.

"Girl Fleeing Gay White Way Finds It at Sea Bottom," *New York Evening Journal.* November 26, 1932.

"Gloria Hollister Anable, 87, Dies; An Explorer and Conservationist," *New York Times*, February 24, 1988.

"Human Oddity Photos," *Billboard Magazine*, June 24, 1950.

"Unashamed Romance in Vigorous New Novel," *New York Times*, February 7, 1926.

"Undersea Paintings Go on Exhibit Here," *The Brooklyn Daily Eagle*, May 8, 1938.

SOUND FILES

"Information Please with William Beebe." July 18, 1939. Archived at: www.myoldradio .com/old- radio-episodes/information-please-william-beebe/12, accessed July 1, 2017.

Gray's Reef Foundation, soundcloud.com/graysreef, accessed February 24, 2021.

Rodney Rountree, soundcloud.com/rodney-rountree, accessed February 24, 2021.

Acknowledgments

I'm endlessly grateful for the network of friends and family and colleagues who I've been able to keep close. May those relationships deepen!

Many thanks to Akin Akinwumi for taking on this book and so miraculously landing it in the hands of Ben Schrank and Signe Swanson and the excellent people at Astra. Thanks to Robin Myers for putting in a good word at the right time.

The Graduate Center, CUNY, provided both financial and intellectual support, and it's impossible to express my sense of good fortune for the chance to work with Ammiel Alcalay, Wayne Koestenbaum, and Joan Richardson.

Enormous thanks to Katherine McLeod, my guide and collaborator through early stages of research. "A Siphonophore Manifesto" is a response to a prompt from her, and the entire book owes a tremendous debt to her. Thanks to Ala Tannir, who included that piece in *Broken Nature*, and to Nadja Spiegelman, who ran "Notes from the Bathysphere" in *The Paris Review Daily*.

Thanks to Madeleine Thompson at the Wildlife Conservation Society Archives for facilitating my research and granting permission to include so many amazing WCS images and excerpts from the logbooks; to Gene Shannon for permission to reproduce George Swanson's painting of the Ballet Russes; to Cole at Condé Nast for permission to reproduce Cecil Beaton's photo of Mona

Williams, and to Loretta Deaver at the Library of Congress for help with the Hollister papers.

Joyful gratitude to Christine Burgin for supporting the project and opening the door for me in Bermuda. And in Bermuda, huge thanks to Julie Sylvester, Samia Sarkis, Richard Winchell, Ian Walker, Karla Ingemann, Robbie Smith, and Joanna Pitts.

In Peru, where I was quarantined while writing most of this, boundless thanks to Miguel Tapullima, Luis, and Jonathan. And to Domjan, longtime family. Akos Papp, Szilvia Gagolczi, Nafis Sabir, and Jean-Paul Dubois were invaluable comrades during that strange adventure.

Thanks to the Art Foundation La Napoule and my fellow residents for a wonderful season in the chateau. Thanks to Claire Messud for sending me there (and for so much). A bottomless champagne chalice for Erin LeAnn Mitchell.

Many thanks to Khaled Malas for sending me back to grad school, and to Martina and Walid. Raphael Aladdin Cohen was my sheikh. Ayana V. Jackson created new deep-water encounters. Jace Clayton encouraged me to "embrace the non-self." China Miéville offered mutual aid. Frances Hall brought natural life. D. Graham Burnett and LaTasha Diggs introduced me to the wonders of birding. Translator Nico Groen's students provided last minute copy edits. MacDowell provided a lovely place to finish the book.

To Drew, Lucy, Monique, Madhu, Farrah, Nkomo, Starlee, Ricardo, and Darius. To Yasmine and Edward, Hector, Carlos, Veronica, Clare, Cynthia, Mert, Ceren, Antonnis, and Raluca. To 409 and the ICC. To the Bradys. To Hilary Plum and the Rescuers. To Ana, Sean and Shelley, Lili and Aron, Marco and Daff, Andy and Borduska, Nikola and Zsofi, Sadia and Andreas, Carl and Claire, Yasmin and Omar and the kids. And as ever to Jack and Jeanne, Sarah, Ayla, and Mete.

ABOUT THE AUTHOR

Brad Fox is a writer living in New York. His novel, *To Remain Nameless*, was published by Rescue Press in 2020. His stories, articles, and translations have appeared in *The New Yorker, Guernica, Public Domain Review,* and the Whitney Biennial. He has worked as a researcher and story consultant for novelists and filmmakers, and he had an earlier career as a journalist and relief worker in the Balkans, Mexico, the Arab world, and Turkey.